Embracing
the Infidel

Embracing the Infidel

*Stories of Muslim Migrants
on the Journey West*

Behzad Yaghmaian

DELACORTE PRESS

EMBRACING THE INFIDEL
A Delacorte Book / December 2005

Published by Bantam Dell
A Division of Random House, Inc.
New York, New York

All rights reserved
Copyright © 2005 by Behzad Yaghmaian
Maps by George Ward
Photo on page 312 by Bahman Akhbari
All other photos by the author

Book design by Virginia Norey

Poems on pages 164–165 and 175 used by permission of their author.

Delacorte Press is a registered trademark of Random House, Inc.,
and the colophon is a trademark of Random House, Inc.

LIBRARY OF CONGRESS CATALOGING IN PUBLICATION DATA
Yaghmaian, Behzad, 1953–
Embracing the infidel : stories of Muslim migrants on the journey
west / Behzad Yaghmaian
p. cm.
ISBN-10: 0-553-80393-X
ISBN-13: 978-0-553-80393-8
1. Refugees—Abuse of—Europe. 2. Muslims—Travel—Europe.
3. Refugees—Crimes against—Europe. I. Title.
HV640 .Y34 2005   2005049701
305.6/97/086914 22

Printed in the United States of America
Published simultaneously in Canada

www.bantamdell.com

BVG   10 9 8 7 6 5 4 3 2 1

Contents

Author's Note

All the characters, places, and events described in this book are real. To protect their identities, I have changed the names of most of the migrants whose stories appear in the book.

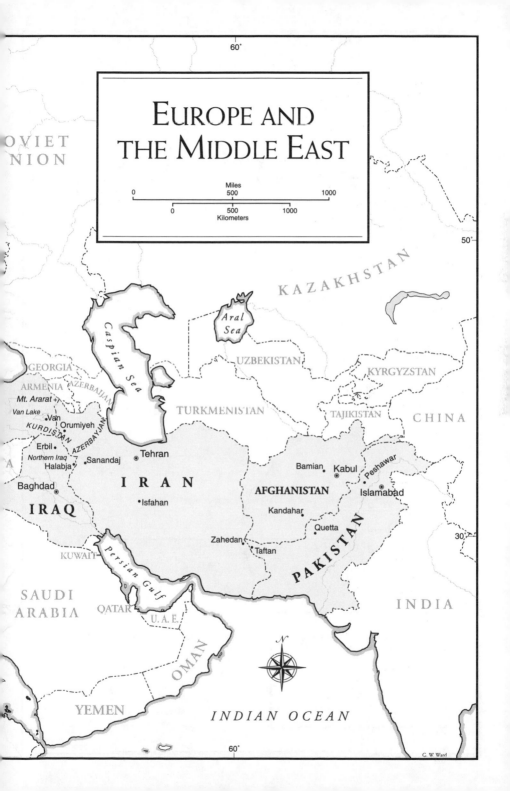

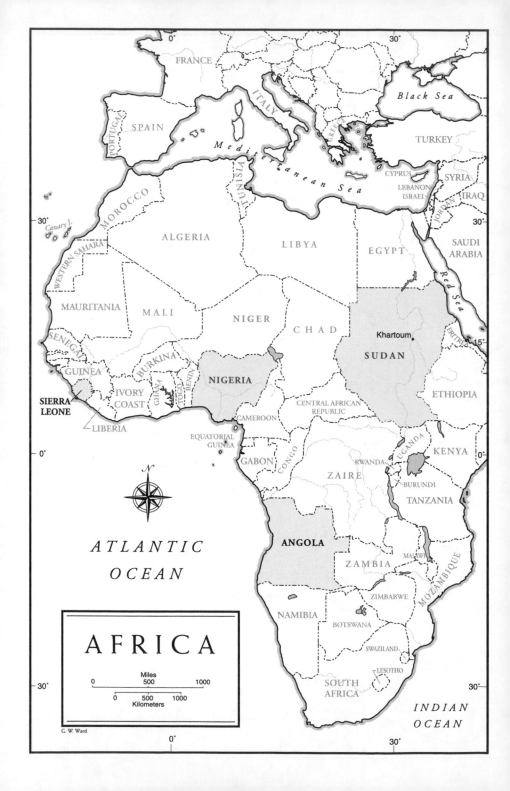

Embracing
the Infidel

Prologue

July 20, 1989, 4:00 a.m.

The border guard at the train station knew just enough English to demand a bribe. If I wanted to get back on the train and cross the border from Turkey into Greece, it was going to cost me.

I could not believe what I was hearing. "Five hundred dollars!"

The man at the desk didn't take his eyes off the book he was reading. "Five hundred dollars," he repeated. I could hear the train, just outside the guardhouse, as its engine started up. Its loud whistle pounded in my ears. I was going to be left behind.

"Why do I have to pay this?"

Finally he looked me in the eye.

"Iran passport."

"I don't have that much money!"

He said a word or two in Turkish to a gendarme. They laughed. The man repeated the price.

I rushed to the train to rescue my bag, then stepped back onto the platform and watched as the doors closed. The train slowly pulled out, leaving me alone in the middle of nowhere.

The place was unlit, deserted, and deadly quiet except for the barking of stray dogs. Two gendarmes held their rifles upright and marched back and forth in front of the guardhouse.

I was getting nervous. My Iranian passport might have been worthless for getting me across the border, but I was also a legal resident of the United States. Turkish border guards were notoriously corrupt and underpaid, and my green card was worth almost $10,000 on the black market.

I spent the next few hours sitting on the ground, my back against the wall of the guardhouse—the best position, I thought, to defend myself if I had to.

Later my friends in the United States were puzzled at my description of this situation, the hostility of the guards, the threatening atmosphere. They seemed to think my respectability—my doctorate, my good job at an American university—should have been some kind of protection. After all, they reasoned, I wasn't a criminal. I wasn't trying to sneak across a border. I was doing what other people on that train were doing, those with German and U.S. and British passports: traveling. I was in Turkey to see family members who had come from Iran to meet me in Istanbul. I had decided to take a brief side trip to Greece, a few days to see yet another country before returning home.

None of that would have mattered to those guards. What they saw when they looked at me was a tall, heavily bearded man with an Iranian passport. And that turned the border into a line I couldn't cross. The law said that nationals of Iran were only allowed to leave Turkey the same way they had entered the country, the man at the desk told me. A train ride to Greece was out of the question. I had flown to Istanbul from New York. I could fly out of Istanbul, or I could pay an exorbitant bribe.

The Islamic Republic and Turkey had made an agreement aimed at stopping Iranians—political activists, war deserters, and others—from escaping to Europe. Many Iranians entered Turkey illegally in those days, fleeing the repressive regime of Ayatollah Ruhollah Khomeini. The lucky ones contacted human smugglers, forged European visas in their passports, and succeeded in gaining asylum in Europe. The unlucky ones were arrested in Turkey and returned to Iran. Many were jailed. Some were executed. To the border guards, the agreement between Iran and Turkey was a way to make fast money from desperate Iranians who would pay any price for their freedom.

The hours passed. As the sun slowly rose, I could see signs of life that had been buried in the darkness: a humble food kiosk, hot tea from an old samovar, a few villagers, more dogs and cats. Moving away from the shelter of the wall, I took a deep breath, smiled at the man in the kiosk, and bought a cup of tea.

The train to Istanbul finally arrived at ten in the morning. I chose an empty compartment and sat down next to the window. After a few minutes, an old village woman entered the compartment with two small children. Sitting down across from me, the three nodded in acknowledgment of my presence. The woman smiled, said a few words in Turkish. I replied in English. My foreign words amused the children. They laughed. Our reciprocal smiles continued for nearly an hour. I was slowly dozing off. The children were more active now, trying to engage me in their games, staring at me, making faces, and talking to me.

It was noon, time to eat. The old woman reached for a small, neatly wrapped cloth bundle, which she gently untied and opened on her lap. A few pieces of thin village bread and a number of hard-boiled eggs were to be their lunch. I looked the other way, trying to give them privacy to eat their humble meal, and then I noticed the old woman's arm stretched forward. She was holding a hard-boiled egg, offering it to me. I declined. She continued to hold the egg in her outstretched hand. The children watched me anxiously. They would not be fed until I accepted. Thanking the old woman with body language, I took the egg from her hand, gently touching her wrinkled and rough skin.

The old woman and her grandchildren left the train at a small town long before Istanbul. Others entered and left the compartment. Nearly twenty-four hours after leaving Istanbul, I was back at Sirkeci Station. Wishing to continue the trip that had been aborted at the border, I flew to Athens. A week later, I returned to the United States.

I became a U.S. citizen in 1994. Hoping to make the most of the privileges that came with a U.S. passport, I frequently traveled to Canada and Europe, visiting places I had always dreamed of seeing. I moved from one airport to another without being questioned. "Have a nice visit," I would often be told after flashing my blue passport. Though there were exceptions, respectful treatment remained.

Returning home was always a different story. Unusual and, at times, strange questions were asked of me by immigration and customs officers. As I traveled more, the questioning became more frequent. By now, it was clear to me that this was not routine. I was different from others returning home. Having been born in Iran was a liability I could not escape. It was the 1990s, and to the customs officials my U.S. citizenship was secondary. I was reminded of that each time I entered the country.

"What do you do for a living?" they would ask.

"I am a professor of economics."

"A professor of economics! Do you know Keynes? What was his theory?" they asked suspiciously, referring to the famous British economist whose theory is taught in every introductory course in economics.

"Do *you* know Keynes?" I would ask with surprise.

"Answer the questions," they would snap. Then they went on to ask, "What countries did you visit, sir?" while staring at a customs form where I had listed the places I visited during my trip. "Did you visit Iran?"

I had not been to Iran for years. The last time had been in July 1979, the summer after the revolution that brought Khomeini and the other clerics to power. I would answer calmly, pointing to the customs form. Iran was not listed on the form.

"Did you visit Iran, sir?" they would ask again, seconds later.

As the questioning continued, sometimes other travelers would pass me, having already been cleared; at other times, a long line of tired travelers anxious to get home would form behind me, and, feeling embarrassed, I would quickly answer the questions asked of me, hoping to become invisible. As time passed, returning home caused me anxiety. Anticipating the harassment, I would be defensive and at times nervous.

In April 1995, sixteen years after my last visit to Iran, I returned to lecture at a university in Tehran through a special United Nations program. The city bore no resemblance to what had been my home during the formative years of my life. Bearded men in slippers stared at frightened travelers. The city walls were covered by oversized murals of religious leaders and the martyrs of the Iran-Iraq War, paintings of dead men flying to heaven, angels, blood, red tulips, and political slogans.

My childhood house was gone, replaced by a wide boulevard that also ran through the grocery store I had shopped at as a child. Three houses at the end of the alley remained. The alley now had a different name, carved on a bent plate nailed to a wall: "Martyr Ali Sharbatoughlou." Ali was my playmate while growing up. I left to study in America. He stayed behind and was killed in the Iran-Iraq War; he became a martyr with an alley named after him.

Nearly every day in Tehran someone would ask me, "How can we go to the United States? Can you help me?" Some who asked were young, others older. Some were educated, with university degrees. There were women tired of living under the scrutiny of the Islamic state, and young men weary of their idleness. "What do you know about Europe? Is it easier to get a visa there?" many would ask. A twenty-year-old once told me with disappointment, "I need twelve thousand dollars. This is what the lawyer is charging for a visa to Canada. It is a sure deal. But where can I get the money?"

One day I met an old friend in an outdoor café at the foot of the Alborz Mountains, which surround Tehran. We were drinking tea, smoking a *nargile* (a traditional water pipe), and enjoying our time away from the traffic jams and pollution of Tehran. We began reading poems, a common pastime among many Iranians. One poem caught the attention of the young man sitting on the bench next to ours.

"Forgive me for intruding. I overheard your conversation. I too have an urge to fly away. I cannot stay here, but I have nowhere to go. Who is that poet? Can you read that again?" he asked. I complied.

> *I must leave tonight*
> *pack a suitcase the size of my loneliness*
> *I must leave tonight*

Intrigued by what I had seen in my place of birth, for the next three summers I returned to Tehran. As on my earlier visits, each summer I met men and women who dreamed of leaving for a new home elsewhere in the world. Their stories captivated me. Slowly I began to read about migration and refugee issues in my free time. I would go through academic journals concerned with migration and read the scattered accounts of the journey: stories of death in the Strait of Gibraltar, accounts of the drowning asylum seekers who had been jammed into small boats in the Mediterranean Sea, and other tales of men and women who, facing strict visa policies in the West, chose to cross borders clandestinely. For the vast majority of those wishing to enter the European Union, there was no legal migratory option available.

Inside Iran, historic changes were occurring. A new youth movement was sweeping across the country. The election of Mohammad Khatami as president created new prospects for reform. A reborn sense of activism and hope was evident everywhere. Young and old Iranians took part in national and local elections. New magazines and newspapers emerged. Old taboos were questioned. Tehran had become an exciting city again, and I wished to witness this new Iran.

In July 1998 I left the United States for a yearlong visit to Iran. Energized and excited by the general mood in the country, I gave lec-

tures at universities, wrote weekly columns for the newly emerged re-
formist papers and magazines, and participated in street protests for
change. Once more Tehran felt like home. Walking on its streets
brought a smile to my face. The mountains blew life into my body.
The teahouses eased my soul. I felt alive.

I had been in the country for a year when, on July 9, 1999, tens of
thousands of youths poured onto the streets of Tehran and twenty
other cities to protest the violation of human rights in Iran. The
protests began as a response to an unprovoked raid in the housing
compound of Tehran University on July 8. Soon the situation was
out of control. The streets around the dormitories were barricaded
by the students. Youths ruled the universities and their surrounding
streets. The Islamic Republic's most sacred institution, the rule of the
supreme religious leader, was challenged and discredited as the students shouted, "Death to the dictator." The Islamic Republic responded by brutally suppressing the student uprising. More than
two thousand students were jailed; some received long prison sentences, and three were sentenced to death.

On July 17, I received a call from a friend: "Do you have an exit
visa on your passport? Leave Iran quietly, and soon." It seemed that a
cell within the Ministry of Intelligence had compiled a thick file
about my activities during the year. The government was looking for
scapegoats, and I was an American citizen who traveled in and out of
Iran, gave lectures on political economy, and had close ties with some
students. So on July 19, I boarded a flight leaving Tehran for Dubai.
I left without saying farewell to my family and friends. Only a few
knew of my plans.

There was a sense of finality in my last departure, as I knew that
returning to Iran would not be possible, at least for a number of
years. I was in exile, and that reawakened in me the yearning for
home. I was both angered and saddened by my new predicament.
Driven from my place of birth, I felt estranged in America. The past
treatment by U.S. customs officials troubled me more as I recalled it.
I felt caught between two unwelcoming worlds.

As time passed, I became more attracted to stories of migrants in search of a new home, those who could not return to their place of birth. Their stories resonated deep inside me. Although I had a secure and comfortable life in America, I identified with them and their journey. I wanted to know about the people who risked their lives hoping for the day when they might hold a European or U.S. passport in their hands. I wished to see the faces of the migrants when they told their stories, be with them in their living spaces, and feel what they feel. I wanted to be on the road with them. Library research was no longer sufficient.

On September 1, 2002, I boarded a plane to Istanbul, beginning a journey that took me along the route used by many migrants from the Middle East and Africa. The people I met there were also trying to cross borders, but not for the pleasure of traveling, nor to engage in some criminal enterprise. Shadi and Nima from Iran, Shahrokh Khan from Afghanistan, Roberto from Angola, Nur from the Sudan—all were fleeing for their lives. Bombs had landed on their villages, armed strangers had burst into their homes, soldiers had executed their loved ones. In the course of their escape, they had been preyed on by criminals, weakened by disease. They wanted only a safe place where they could live in peace and work quietly, put their lives back together. But in their flight they hit borders, lines they couldn't cross. This is their story.

PART ONE

Istanbul

Shadi and Nima

Shadi had been a schoolteacher in Iran before the government banned her from teaching in 1981. Now it was September 2002, and she and her son, Nima, were seeking permission to enter Europe. In the meantime, they lived at the end of an unpaved alley in Aksaray, a poor but developing neighborhood in Istanbul.

Most Iranians—migrants and tourists—knew of Aksaray before arriving in Istanbul. There are Iranian travel agencies, restaurants and cabarets, and real estate agents along its main streets, and it is famous for its bargain shopping. It is also home to many other migrants, including Bangladeshis, Afghans, and Africans. In some ways, Aksaray was a migrant city within the larger metropolis of Istanbul. For Shadi, its attraction was the relatively cheap rents.

When Shadi arrived in Istanbul, Aksaray was going through many changes. Two separate worlds were emerging. In the trendy part of the neighborhood, billboards advertised new fashions in clothing and displayed oversized photos of glamorous models. In renovated buildings, storefront boutiques sold popular Turkish and foreign clothing—Mavı and Levi's jeans, Nike sneakers. Other shops specialized in textile products and leather for markets in Russia, Bulgaria, Romania, and other countries in Eastern Europe. Their names resonated with imitations of famous brands from New York City: Proud Sportswear, Juris Collection, Murat Collection, Ronaldo Sport Collection, Lisa Collection, Joan Jeans, Premier Life, Bonny Jeans. Merchandise was priced in both dollars and euros.

This was the facade of Aksaray. Away from the main road, the boutiques were replaced by auto repair shops, small corner stores, men selling fresh produce from horse-drawn carts. This was the old Aksaray: run-down buildings with narrow dark stairways, back alleys, abandoned building lots. It was home to Roma, Kurds, and poor Turks living on the margins of society: street vendors, manual laborers working at incomes below a living wage, and those who hustled many long hours and dwelled in overcrowded tenements.

Aksaray had an unusually high number of hotels and hostels. In the 1980s, many migrants and their smugglers used such hotels for negotiations and deal making. Crossing the borders in the Turkish southeast, the migrants came straight to Aksaray. They checked into already designated hotels, sat in the lobby, and sipped tea with other hotel guests. In less than a few days, they found a smuggler, made the deal, and left Istanbul for their destination in Europe. Traveling was easier in those days. Border control was less strict. Europe was more receptive to migrants and asylum seekers.

"The job was easy," an Iranian-born British citizen told me. "You didn't have to do any searching. Everything was ready. Most people in the lobby were migrants themselves. They knew the routes and their prices, reliable smugglers, everything you needed to know." He spent one week in Aksaray in 1986. Soon he was on the road to Britain. In fall 2002 he returned to Turkey for a short visit. "Everything started here for me. I owe a lot to Aksaray."

All that changed in the 1990s. Trying to win the support of the European Union in its bid for EU membership and hoping to stop the influx of migrants through its eastern borders, Turkey imposed stricter border controls. Making travel plans became more difficult. Migrants and the smugglers were more secretive. The Aksaray hotels lost their old role. Then a new population of migrants arrived, with less money and different travel networks and arrangements. Aksaray became flooded with poor working men and women, unemployed urban youth, and villagers from the Middle East and North Africa.

Leaving Aksaray now took longer. Some migrants succeeded.

They reached Greece and moved forward. For others, Aksaray became a morass of prostitution, drugs, and human trafficking. "Aksaray is like a swamp: once in it, you cannot escape it," an Iranian smuggler once told me.

On my first visit to Aksaray, I walked aimlessly, watched the passersby, and tried my best to avoid hustlers of all types. *"Salam, agha,"* a Turkish man greeted me in Persian. He stood in front of a restaurant, and his job was to get people inside. "Hello, sir. Come in for a good meal. We have kebabs and soup." A block or two away, a young man dressed in a blue polyester suit walked behind me. *"Khanoom-haye ziba,* beautiful women," he said in bad Persian. I turned a corner to escape him. Walking toward the McDonald's on the main street of Aksaray, I noticed a tall, skinny African bouncing around like a star soccer player, kicking an imaginary ball in the air. He bought a pack of cigarettes from a corner store, turned into an alley, and disappeared from sight.

I stood by the McDonald's and stared at a police wagon parked by a police station only a few feet from the fast-food place. The van was packed with young men; some looked Pakistani or Bangladeshi, others Iranian. Earlier in the week I had read about the arrest of clandestine migrants in Istanbul. The men in the station wagon were perhaps the latest catch in that operation.

Busy restaurants, hotels, and confectionaries surrounded the McDonald's and the police station. From early morning until late at night, men and women crowded the street and the shops, which provided a feeling of security to the migrants living in the safe houses of Aksaray. The McDonald's was used as a meeting place by migrants and their contacts. In a strange way, its proximity to the police station protected it from the police. This arrangement was a common practice throughout Europe. Smugglers set up meetings between clients and their hired hands in McDonald's restaurants in London, Rome, and other capitals. Istanbul followed the rule. The fast-food chain, especially in crowded neighborhoods, seemed immune to police raid.

Arrests in Aksaray were common, however, and quiet back streets were the usual sites. Often the police had no real interest in detaining the arrested migrants; rather, they were out in the streets in search of extra income. Fifty million Turkish liras (TL) was the price they demanded. Those without money were robbed of their mobile phone, watch, or other valuables. Occasionally some were taken into custody.

I first met Shadi and Nima in the office of the Istanbul Interparish Migrants Program (IIMP). Helen Bartlett, the organization's director, had asked me to help with Persian interpretation every Wednesday.

It was minutes past noon, and I was translating a testimony written in Persian when I heard a knock. Opening the door, I saw Shadi and Nima, smiling, looking excited. They were clean and nicely dressed. Nima wore a blue shirt and a pair of trendy jeans. He looked like a shy teenager. Shadi had a motherly face. *"Salam,"* they greeted me in Persian. I replied in Persian and introduced myself.

I invited Shadi and Nima into the office, thinking they wished to see the director. They declined. "We heard about you from other Iranians, *agha* Behzad, and came here to welcome you," Shadi said. Word was out that an Iranian writer from America was working for the IIMP, and the Iranian migrants were intrigued. Some saw in me their only chance to leave Turkey and find their way to America. I could get them a visa to America, they thought. Others were comforted by having someone who understood their language and patiently listened to their stories.

"Will you give us the honor of visiting our *kolbeh,* our humble home?" Nima asked. I accepted without hesitating, and we exchanged phone numbers.

I had to climb three flights of narrow stairs to reach the rooftop where they lived in a rickety shack. I looked up and saw her waiting to greet me, a lit candle in her hand. "Welcome to our home," she said.

The main room of Shadi's apartment was devoid of furniture. She had spread old blankets on the floor for people to sit on. A few other folded blankets and bedsheets, along with two pillows, were piled neatly in a corner, and a pair of blue jeans, a shirt, and two towels hung on the wall by the door. The room's blue walls were streaked with yellowish water stains. Layers of plastic covered a hole in the ceiling. A piece of thick blue cloth separated the room from a four-foot-long space that Shadi called her kitchen, though it had no stove, sink, or refrigerator. She cooked her meals on a single gas burner in the living room. The kitchen space was used as a closet and a place to change in privacy.

At the other end of the kitchen was a room with broken pipes, a broken toilet, a sink with a hole not connected to a pipe, and a large container of water. There was an electric immersion heater inside the container, which they used to heat water for showering. This was considered the bathroom. Electricity was free; the owner illegally brought it to the building. "We're lucky, we don't have to pay."

Shadi was neatly dressed in brown corduroys and a striped shirt over a white turtleneck. A middle-aged woman with short graying hair, she set about boiling water for tea in a cooking pot on the gas burner. "We've just moved here," she said. "This is really not the way we usually live."

The next time I phoned Shadi and Nima, we agreed to meet in the evening at the McDonald's on Aksaray Avenue and then walk together to their apartment. I showed up at the McDonald's at seven but had to wait nearly fifteen minutes until I saw Shadi and Nima running toward me, waving to get my attention.

"Sorry we're late," Shadi said, catching her breath. "We're coming from work. We walked for one hour, all the way from Taksim Square." The last time we'd met, both Shadi and Nima had been unemployed. I congratulated them on the job.

They had found work at a candle-making factory. This was their second day. They started work at half past eight in the morning and finished at half past six in the evening. To save money, they left home early to walk to work. "We work together. That's the best part," Shadi said. She decided to go on ahead, walking fast to reach home and start preparing the dinner, while Nima and I followed more leisurely. "I hope you aren't too hungry," she told me. "I'll make you a nice dinner, Nima's favorite."

Strolling with Nima, I asked about his new job. "It's good," he said casually. "It's a job."

A long street connected Aksaray Avenue to the alley where Nima and Shadi lived. A block past the police station, we turned right at the corner. We passed a restaurant or two, a corner store, and an Iranian nightclub in the basement of a hotel, with large pictures of belly dancers in the lobby windows. Then came garages and one auto parts shop after another. Halfway to Nima's home, a square of some sort—a space filled with waist-high grass—stood in the middle of the street. Across from the square, piles of trash surrounded an overflowing garbage bin. Cats jumped in and out of the bin.

Hurrying to escape the smell of garbage and auto grease, we passed a bus station, a large open space with buses destined for Bucharest and other cities in Romania. Men carried large bundles to the station. Blond men and women queued to board. Traders and store owners back in Romania, many came to Aksaray to buy leather jackets, blue jeans, and other textile products. A number were there for pleasure. Some came for work. Joining the Russians, Moldovans, Bulgarians, and others, they made up the sex workers of Istanbul's transnational sex industry.

Past the bus station, the street became quieter. The auto repair shops gave way to barbershops and more corner stores. At the store closest to their home, I bought yogurt, pickles, black olives, and bread. "Shadi loves these olives," Nima said. Finally we turned onto a half-dirt, half-paved alley full of foot-wide potholes. A crane stood in the middle of a construction site to our right. There were a dozen or so one-story houses and *gecekondu*—homes erected illegally overnight. Three women dressed in traditional Kurdish clothes— long swinging skirts and white head scarves with colorful flowers embroidered on their edges—sat on the steps of their home. Children played in the dirt of an abandoned building site on our left. Next door, a lone woman sat behind a closed window in her street-level room.

The building's front door was wide open. We walked up the narrow stairs in darkness, since the lightbulb had burned out. Our path was lit only by a dim ray coming out of the apartment on the second floor. The metal railing rattled when I grabbed it to walk up the stairs.

Night had fallen on Aksaray. I stood on the roof looking at the surrounding streets and alleys. There was no sign of the auto repair shops and boutiques. All I could see were half-finished *gecekondu* and decaying rooftops, tin roofing and clay shingles covered with blue and black plastic to prevent water leaks from the rain.

By the time we got there, Shadi had already begun her preparations. Sitting in a corner in front of the gas burner, cutting potatoes and adding them to the pot of frying onions, she asked about my work with the migrants. "I have a lot of stories to tell you myself," she said.

The fragrance of the frying onions and potatoes filled the small room. Sensing my hunger—my eyes were fixed on the pot—Shadi laid old newspapers on the floor; Nima placed the olives, bread, and the rest of the food we'd bought on the newspapers. Two plates were brought out from the space behind the blue curtain. A family-size bottle of Pepsi and two small glasses were added to the collection.

"You start with this now. I know you're hungry. The food will be ready soon." Shadi added rice and water to the pot, covered it and lowered the fire, and joined her boy and me. The rice was soon ready, and tasted as good as it had smelled. Shadi kept placing more rice on my plate the minute she saw it empty. For more than two hours, we sat around the newspapers, ate, and told stories.

Shadi talked about Van, a city near Turkey's southeastern border, where she had lived for four years after leaving Iran. "Please forgive us for hosting you in this inadequate way. We are new here," she said. "In Van, I had a humble home with most of the things one needs." That night, Shadi and Nima told me about the journey that had brought them to Van.

Van is an impoverished city surrounded by barren hills, the snow-covered Taurus Mountains, the beautiful Van Lake, valleys, and farmland. Not long ago, at the turn of the nineteenth century, Van and many other towns and villages in southeastern Turkey were predominantly Armenian. In 1915 a large-scale organized effort was made to uproot the Armenians and drive them away from Turkey. Among other cities, Van was the site of what became known as the Armenian genocide. The city was depopulated. By the early 1920s Van and other towns and villages in the southeast had become home to the ethnic Kurds.

There are twenty-five million Kurds living in a two-hundred-thousand-square-mile area divided between Iran, Iraq, Turkey, and Syria. In Turkey, the Kurds have been called "mountain Turks." Only in Iran have they been able to maintain their national identity, where the label Kurdistan names their ancestral land. In Turkey, however, the use of the name Kurdistan to identify the southeastern part of the country resulted in imprisonment. The Kurds lacked the right to speak their language, attend Kurdish-language schools, or give their children Kurdish names.

The Kurds of Turkey rebelled many times in the past—eight

times in the fifteen years following the creation of the Turkish Republic in 1923. Each time, the Turkish government responded with force. The last rebellion began with a guerrilla war waged by the Kurdistan Workers Party (PKK) in 1984. The war ended in 1999 with the arrest of the PKK leader Abdullah Öcalan. By then, government forces had partially or fully depopulated more than 2,000 villages. A million and a half Kurds became displaced. Some left the southeast. Others relocated to towns such as Van. The population of Van nearly doubled during the years of the civil war, increasing to 284,500 in 2000 from 155,600 in 1990.

Nima arrived in Van clandestinely in 1988, when he reached eighteen. Having reached the age of military service, he was not allowed to leave Iran unless he served two years in the army. The government refused him a passport. Shadi was able to emigrate legally, and she had no choice but to leave her son in the hands of human smugglers. She flew to Istanbul from Tehran, took a bus to Van, and waited for the arrival of Nima.

"I did not want him to serve in the army," Shadi said.

"Is that why you left Iran?" I asked. She nodded.

Nima remained silent, staring at the plate in front of him, until she urged gently, "Will you tell *agha* Behzad about how you came to Van?" That animated and excited Nima. Looking like a boy describing one of his mischievous acts to a friend, he told me about his clandestine crossing to Turkey.

Helped by a human smuggler, Nima left his home in Sanandaj, a town in Iran's province of Kurdistan, near the border with Iraq. They crossed the Zagros Mountains, separating Iran from Turkey. "My smuggler was very knowledgeable. He knew the way very well. We used a donkey for part of the way and walked the rest," Nima told me. In less than ten hours, Nima was in Turkey. The smuggler left him in a Kurdish village near the border with Iran. Because he knew Kurdish, Nima was able to mingle with the villagers, and he pretended to be a PKK activist. He was soon their friend, a guest to the Kurds of Turkey.

"I told them that I was on my way to Europe to study medicine. I was doing this to help the struggle," he said, laughing. Shadi had a big smile on her face.

To many Kurds, the PKK was the only hope for gaining their rights. Nima's claim of affiliation with the party gained him respect. Young and charming, he stole the villagers' hearts. "They offered me a wife," a young girl from the village, he told me, laughing. He joked with the villagers, rested, got rid of his mountain-crossing fatigue. A week passed. Shadi was awaiting her boy in Van and Nima had to move on, so he asked for help. A villager drove him to Van, and Nima and Shadi reunited.

With the support of her father, Shadi stayed in Van for nearly four years. Nima made new friends, became fluent in Turkish, and found a Kurdish girlfriend, a university student in Van. He spent his days playing pool, going to Internet cafés, and staying home with Shadi. "My girlfriend's family liked me a lot. They wanted me to marry her."

Nima removed the newspapers from the floor and the empty dishes, then began to play a game on his cell phone. Sitting opposite me, Shadi was leaning against the wall near the pot of boiling water she used for making tea. "Why did you leave Van?" I asked. Leaning forward, she poured me another cup and said, "The UN rejected me."

Arriving in Van, Shadi had applied for asylum with the Office of the United Nations High Commissioner for Refugees (UNHCR), hoping to be granted asylum, accepted as a refugee, and resettled somewhere in the West. Shadi had to convince the UNHCR staff that her migration was political in nature and was based on "a reasonable fear of persecution" by the government of Iran "for reasons of race, religion, nationality, membership of a particular social group, or political opinion." This was a universal criterion used by the UNHCR and member states and had been established by the 1951 Convention Relating to the Status of Refugees.

Although it ratified the convention, Turkey took advantage of an option that allowed it to offer protection only to refugees from Europe, and to this day it categorically refuses asylum to non-Europeans. Those wishing to apply for asylum must register with the police and the UNHCR within ten days of their arrival. The UNHCR reviews the application of Iranian, Afghan, and other asylum seekers, and upon acceptance finds them a country of resettlement in the West.

Registering with the UNHCR, Shadi presented a case that was based on her being banned from teaching by the Islamic Republic. Weeks and months passed while she waited for a response. The decision came after two years: Shadi's case did not fit the criteria.

"Did you have documents to show the UNHCR?"

"I showed them the order from the Ministry of Education. I told them everything."

Bringing a plate of apples and oranges, Shadi told me the story she gave the UNHCR.

She was born to a financially comfortable family in Sanandaj. The owner of one of the largest grocery stores in town, her father was a man known and respected by other Kurds. Two years after finishing high school, at age twenty, Shadi took a job teaching elementary school in her hometown. In those days in Sanandaj, teaching was the only job available to women. There were no government offices or a developed private sector to hire women. Most women with education (a high school degree or more) and the desire to work found their place in the school system.

"Teaching was my love," she said, falling into momentary silence.

For Shadi, teaching was a way to escape a loving but controlling father and older brother. In a small town such as Sanandaj, young women were confined to their homes. There were no outings for women, no socializing, no life as an independent person. Teaching changed all that for Shadi. Above all, it gave her financial independence. "I would travel to Tehran to visit my older sister," a doctor practicing in the capital. "I would buy clothes and everything that I couldn't find in Sanandaj." Shadi told me about the parks, the department stores, and other places she frequented in Tehran. She spoke with excitement, and the melancholy temporarily disappeared from her voice. These obviously were fond memories. But her independent, happy life came to an end with the victory of the Islamic Republic and the war in Kurdistan in 1979.

Although they enjoyed more rights than Kurds in Iraq and Turkey, for many decades the Kurds of Iran aspired to autonomy. Iran experienced a short period of political opening immediately after the fall of the shah in February 1979, and during that time the Kurdish demand for autonomy gained new momentum. The central government responded with full force. Ayatollah Khomeini declared a holy war against the Kurds: Sanandaj and other Kurdish towns and villages were attacked, homes were searched, and men and women were executed in public.

The Kurdish movement for autonomy was crushed, and Kurdistan fell under military occupation by the central government's forces. Kurdish political parties were banned, and many party members were arrested, imprisoned, and executed before the war ended in 1983.

Like many Kurds, for a short period in her life Shadi was drawn to politics. Following a younger brother, she became a sympathizer of Komala, a Marxist-nationalist political party fighting for autonomy and workers' rights in Kurdistan. Soon after the 1979 revolution, the soldiers raided Shadi's family home. They searched the house, looking for the family's affiliation with Komala. Nothing was found connecting her with the party. She remained free, but her brother was taken away and executed. Shortly after, suspicious of her politics, the authorities fired Shadi from her job and banned her from teaching. Her professional career ended. No explanation was given.

"I wrote to them, visited the district office, pleaded with them," she said, her face showing her frustration and anger. Looking me in the eye, she said, "They destroyed my life."

In her request for asylum, Shadi explained her story in detail. However, the UNHCR focused on the fact that many years had passed since her activities in the Kurdish national liberation movement. She was banned from teaching, true, but she was free to leave the country, could return to it, and could engage in other activities. She would not be persecuted upon returning to her place of birth, they decided, and so Shadi was not considered a refugee by the UNHCR.

Hoping for a new vote, Shadi appealed the decision. Many months of waiting followed before a decision rejecting the appeal came in the mail.

In the world of migration, those who fail to prove a reasonable fear of persecution are labeled "bogus refugees," "economic migrants," "illegal migrants," or "irregular migrants." Men and women escaping poverty, even when poverty is caused by political violence or war, do not qualify for international protection. The UNHCR did not regard Shadi's inability to work as a reason to grant her international protection. With that refusal, she became an "economic migrant," and legal ways for access to the West were exhausted. However, she could not bear the thought of returning home, and Van could not become the last stop on her journey.

Shadi had come to Van legally. Leaving Van for Europe required illegal border crossing. She contacted other rejected asylum seekers. A family of four from Sanandaj had made preliminary plans to leave for Istanbul. Shadi and Nima joined the family. Soon they were ten in total, all Iranian Kurds. "We arrived in Istanbul. I had never been in Istanbul, did not know anything. We were asked to go to the McDonald's, the same McDonald's here. An Iraqi smuggler was waiting for us. He bought us ice cream and took us to a hotel," Shadi said. The hotel was located in the alley behind Shadi's home. An older man in the group was designated to search for a reliable smuggler for the group's transport to Greece. "We contacted a lot of smugglers, but they were all lying to us." Shadi and the group were told they would be taken to a refugee camp upon arriving in Greece. From there a contact person would be able to send them to Athens. "They would give us a phone number and say, 'Call this number when you get to the camp. He will take care of the rest.' But that was a lie. Nobody can have a cell phone in the camp."

Finally a deal was made with a smuggler. The fee was low, $200 per person; the service was limited. Two weeks after arriving in Istanbul, they left for the border in "two fancy Turkish cars," Shadi said. Passing the border town of Edirne, they were taken to a watermelon field. "He gave us lunch, but we had no other food with us. We broke open a couple of watermelons and ate them." When the sun set, the group began walking toward the border. They walked for three hours. "Once again, the smuggler asked us to wait until the evening *ezan*, the call to prayer. We sat on the wet ground. Nobody made any sound. It was dark," Shadi said with the voice and tone of a mother telling an exciting story to her children. She would pause between her sentences, look at me, and continue. "We began to walk again and soon reached a scary *jangal*, woods. The ground was slippery. My shoes would come off all the time. Holding on to each other, we walked in a line. We were afraid of getting lost. We were not allowed to make any sound, even the sound of our feet on the ground." After two hours of walking, they reached the Meriç River—a natural border separating Turkey from Greece. "Three men were waiting for us. One of them was holding a very big bag." The bag contained a float, the boat that was to take them across the narrow stretch of water. "I panicked. 'What is this? Is this the boat you promised us?' " Shadi asked the smuggler. After minutes of arguing, the smuggler asked Nima and the other young men in our group to blow air in the float with their mouth.

Hearing the story of the border crossing, Nima put away his cell phone, looked at me, and said, "We blew air in the float. The float was small and scary." The migrants were divided into two groups of five. Shadi waited for the safe delivery of the first group before she boarded the float. Nima said, "They took us to the other side and returned to Turkey. 'You are in Greece now,' they told us."

"We walked through cornfields. It was dark and we did not know where to go. We could hear the morning *ezan* behind us; we knew we were still very close to the border." Shadi paused, and I could sense the fear and anxiety she had felt that night. "A young man among us said he could find the way by following the stars." They followed the stars, walking through a vast field in the early hours of the morning.

They were now in Greece. The smuggler had advised them to seek the police and request asylum. No one was deported from Europe without due process and a fair consideration of their applications, he told the migrants. Greece is a member of the European Union and has ratified the 1951 refugee convention. By international agreement, the police are mandated to give migrants a chance to apply for asylum and ask for protection. The right to apply for asylum and receive full consideration and due process without facing discrimination for illegal entry into the country is guaranteed by the refugee convention.

Having left the field, Shadi and others walked along a road, hoping to be spotted by the police. "Our clothes were muddy and wet. Everything was wet. The dampness had made our bags heavier. We were tired."

In a few hours they found themselves in a small village, where they approached a passerby and asked for the police. The police arrived in a car followed by a van. All were put in the van and taken away. "The van was very hot. We were all sweating. Breathing was very difficult," Nima said. An older man suffering from chronic asthma passed out.

"We had to sit so close to each other, like animals loaded in trucks. There was no window, no air," Shadi added.

The convoy was taken to a detention center where they joined other men and women arrested after illegally crossing the border to Greece. The rooms were filthy. "The smell was nauseating," Shadi said, making a face that showed her disgust. She might be living a life of poverty in Istanbul, but her rooftop home was clean and tidy. Filth was unacceptable to her. Once again, she made a face, laughed, and shook her head.

Still hopeful, they waited to be interviewed for asylum by the Greek authorities. No one arrived. No interviews were conducted. A night passed in confusion. The second day of custody was tiring. Then came the second night. The doors opened. Men in uniform arrived. The men and women were herded into a van and taken away. Not long after, the driver stopped the vehicle. They were asked to leave the van. Surrounded by men with guns, they were walked to the Meriç River and put in small boats. Greek soldiers rowed them across. Minutes later, the boats stopped. Shadi and others were asked to walk away. The boats disappeared. They were back in Turkey.

That night a group of thirty migrants was deported to Turkey. Accompanying Shadi and the other Iranians were five Africans and eight Iraqis, she recalled. Once on Turkish soil, most dispersed and proceeded in smaller groups. Four Africans and eight Iranians remained with Shadi and Nima. Disappointed and tired, they began walking in the woods, not knowing where to go. Not long after, they found themselves standing before a swamp—"a pool of human waste," said Nima. "It smelled horrible." With care and caution, the migrants walked through the swamp.

Nima continued the story of his deportation to Turkey, acting out the walk through the woods to the first village in Turkey. Miming carrying a big bag on his head, he bent down and pretended to walk with difficulty. "I had to carry my mother's and my own bag at the same time. She had *so* many clothes in the bag," he said, and both he and Shadi broke into laughter. "We did not think we were returning to Turkey. I did not want to buy anything in Greece."

Coming to the end of the woods, he separated from the group and walked along a road leading to a village. In wet clothes, smelling bad, he walked around the village looking for someone to help them return to Istanbul. "We had money, but we didn't know what to do," he said. It was early morning, and the streets were empty. The shops were just opening. Standing near a street corner, Nima noticed a man leaving a car. He ran toward the man, asking him about the bus to Istanbul. "All of a sudden, he pulled out a gun, pointed the gun at me, and began yelling, 'On the ground! On the ground!' " Nima posed like the man with the gun. Then he dropped down on the floor near the newspapers. Shadi could not stop laughing.

The man with the gun turned out to be an undercover police officer. On the ground, prone, Nima pleaded for mercy and begged for help. The man continued to hold the gun to Nima's head but slowly pulled away. Nima stood up, and negotiations began. Finally a price was set for his release, and Nima paid the bribe. Then the man arranged for two taxis to take the migrants to Edirne, the town nearest the border with Greece. Later that evening, Nima and others were back in Aksaray. "The police helped us come back to Istanbul," he boasted.

Unlike other migrants I met in Turkey and elsewhere, Shadi lost her courage and refused to try another illegal border crossing after the first failed attempt. But then she thought of a new possibility for gaining legal entry to Europe.

Before leaving for Istanbul in the summer of 2002, when she was still living in Van, Shadi heard from many asylum seekers that in return for converting to Christianity, a church in Laleli, a neighborhood close to Aksaray, would help the migrants gain refugee status from the UNHCR by reasons of religious persecution in Iran. Conversion from Islam to any religion, including Christianity, was a sin punishable by death in the Islamic Republic. It helped migrants meet one of the criteria of the 1951 refugee convention, and made them eligible for international protection.

I had met many converts in Istanbul, men and women waiting for a miracle from the church. All wore crosses around their necks. They visited the church in Laleli every Sunday, sang religious songs, moved their heads and bodies in harmony, closed their eyes, and repeated after the preacher "Amen" and "Praise the Lord." Some succeeded in their quest and were resettled in the West. Most were still waiting in Istanbul.

Shadi began attending the Iranian church in Laleli. She participated in religious classes during the week and the mass every Sunday.

Nima was skeptical; he laughed at how churchgoers addressed each other as "brother" and "sister" and said "amen" at the end of every sentence. "Thieves" and "Christian mullahs," he called the preachers in the church.

With time, Shadi became more committed. Now a convert, she sent a new letter to the UNHCR, asking for the reopening of her case for asylum. Weeks passed. She faithfully attended the church meetings. No new decision came from the UNHCR.

Meanwhile, I continued my regular visits to their home in Aksaray. Nima would meet me by McDonald's and we would walk home, buying food and drinks. At times we wandered around for some time before going home. We would joke and laugh. Soon the way Nima addressed me changed, and I was no longer *agha* Behzad; instead, I became *dadash* Behzad, a traditional way of calling someone a brother in Persian.

At the beginning, Nima was jubilant and full of life. Working with Shadi at the candle-making factory, he was kept busy for most of the day. But the job didn't last long. After ten days of hard work, the owner of the factory refused to pay their salaries. Being illegal in Turkey, they couldn't complain to the police. They left the factory and began searching for a new job. Soon after, Nima found employment at a bag-making sweatshop within walking distance of his rooftop home. Shadi was happy. "At least we can pay the rent."

The happiness came to an abrupt end when Nima was injured in a job-related accident. A sharp cutter nearly took off one of his fingers. The cut was deep and bled heavily. He was fired from the job the same day, with no compensation paid. Nima returned home with a bloodstained shirt and five stitches. Two weeks after his accident, Shadi found a job as a cook in an Aksaray office.

The cold weather soon arrived, and Nima remained unemployed. For the first time in my visits, he showed clear signs of journey fatigue. "I am tired of being homeless," he said. Nima longed to be back with his friends in a place where everyone knew and loved him. He was frustrated and confused.

One cold evening in November 2002, strolling in the back streets of Aksaray, Nima told me about his life in Sanandaj, about his grandfather and his uncle. "They're loaded," he said. His grandfather had given Nima all a teenager could ask for: a motorbike, money, freedom, ample love. The boy had left behind a comfortable life when he moved with his mother to Turkey.

When he was only sixteen, under supervision, he had managed his grandfather's grocery store in Sanandaj. "I had many men working for me in Sanandaj. Look at my life now," he said sadly. In Istanbul, Nima was a manual laborer, moving from one job to another, never having a steady income. Leaving his place of birth had not been his decision, and Nima had never understood the reasons for being on the road. Puffing on a cigarette, he said, "I'm tired of this. Nowhere is like Iran. I'll go back to Iran if things don't work out."

As time passed he became quiet and withdrawn. He rarely smiled.

"I'm tired, *dadash* Behzad, tired of life away from home. I'm tired of carrying a passport with me all the time. I won't have to do that in Iran. That's my home. No one can ask me for identification."

Slowly the journey separated mother and son. Nima was angry. His sympathy for his mother was disappearing. He wanted me to convince Shadi of the insanity of still waiting for a decision by the UNHCR. He stopped attending Sunday mass and ridiculed his mother and other converts, but Shadi remained hopeful. "This is our last chance," she told Nima. "We'll go back if we get rejected. I promise."

Our walks home from McDonald's gave Nima a chance to share with me stories and secrets he could not reveal to his mother. Shadi too had stories she did not wish to tell before her son. "I have a lot to tell you, Behzad," Shadi told me one day on the phone. "You know, Nima is young. There are things I don't want him to hear."

One Sunday afternoon in early December, when Nima was out with friends visiting from Van, I took the opportunity to hear Shadi's story.

Tea was already brewing in the pot when I arrived. It was an unseasonably warm day; Shadi placed a small rock in the doorway to keep the door ajar and allow fresh air into the apartment. I sat on the corner leaning against the pile of blankets and bedsheets. She offered me tea, sat beside me, and smiled. "I want to talk about Nima's father," she said.

We had known each other for nearly three months now, but never in our conversations had she mentioned Nima's father, and that had puzzled me. An important part of the mother and son's past was missing, and Shadi knew it. That December evening was her chosen time to tell me her story.

She lifted her cup of tea, took a sip, and then took me back to 1981, the year the government banned her from teaching. She was then twenty-seven years old, unmarried, and unemployed.

Weeks and months passed. Grieving for the senseless killing of her brother, frustrated by unemployment and boredom, she lived under the scrutiny of a traditional father and older brother. "All my moves were watched." Young and full of energy, she wished to go out, be active, and live like an independent woman, but that was not possible. The daughter of a traditional man, a man well respected in town, she had to abide by her family's rules.

Shadi's father constantly worried about her "inability to find a husband." The neighbors talked behind her back. To the townspeople, a single woman in her late twenties was *torshideh*—"rotten" or "spoiled." Shadi said with a bitter smile on her face, "As far as the backward people were concerned, my time was past." There were endless rumors. "People talked. They had nothing better to do. Sanandaj is a small town." The pressure mounted, and the family's reputation was at stake. She had to be taken by a husband, any husband.

A husband was found at last. A man approached Shadi's father, asking permission to marry his daughter. He agreed. Terms of the marriage were negotiated, and Shadi conceded. The father was relieved. Finally his daughter was worthy of a husband and a family. A big party in her father's home—food, music, and dance— announced the wedding to all concerned.

As mandated by tradition, Shadi remained in her father's house while preparations were underway for the bride and groom to move into their new home. A number of meetings occurred between the newlyweds. "Many times, we had to have a chaperone with us." At other times, they were allowed limited privacy.

The meetings were revealing for Shadi. Weeks after the wedding, she was becoming acquainted with the stranger with whom she was to share the rest of her life. But what she found out horrified her: "He was a heroin addict."

Shadi approached her father and pleaded for permission to divorce her husband before moving into their common space. That was not possible, he told her. A divorce before even forming a household would have brought disgrace on her family. It would have been proof of all the rumors that forced Shadi to marry. Above all, though she had not yet moved to their new home, Shadi would have become a "touched woman." "What would people think?" her father said. "Who would want to marry such a woman?" In Iran's traditional communities, including Sanandaj, a divorced woman was stigmatized and considered "used merchandise." She had to wait in agony until another man—often in these cases a much older widower with children—accepted her. Shadi succumbed to her father's wishes.

Pouring me another cup of tea, she leaned back and said, "My father destroyed my life." With horror and pain, she allowed herself into the arms of an addict, but her family's reputation remained intact. A year later, Nima was born. "I don't forgive my father," she said, staring away, remembering. The memories dampened her mood. Her usual warm smile disappeared from her face. Then, controlling her emotions, she smiled again and continued her story.

Shadi's husband was abusive and a drain on her energy and the family's resources. "I didn't love him to begin with. Now, with all these problems, I could not bear him." Once more she pleaded for help, asking for permission to divorce. Her father again resisted, but one day, seeing the pain in his daughter's eyes, he finally acquiesced to her wishes. Shadi took her boy and returned to her family home. The divorce was finalized.

"I was very happy. I kissed my father's hands."

A new life had begun for Shadi, and she did all that was possible to raise Nima and live as an independent woman. To earn money, she traveled to Kish Island, an Iranian free-trade zone in the Persian Gulf, where she bought juicers, mixers, and other household appliances, and returned to Sanandaj to sell them at a profit. She was also a good tailor, and so she began sewing custom-made dresses and shirts. When she left Sanandaj on business, her family took care of Nima. In her free time, she visited her sister in Tehran, bought presents for her boy, and once again enjoyed her financial independence. "I felt alive again."

But this too did not last long, as the old pressures returned. "Think about your loneliness in the future," her father would say. "Who will take care of you in your old age? How long can you go on without a husband?" Her family's tactics were demoralizing. The frequency of her business trips to Kish declined. There were no more visits to Tehran. She was free from her addicted husband, but she felt trapped in her family home. She gave in again and this time agreed to marry a divorced man with three children.

Not long after moving into his house, Shadi was told troubling news about her husband's last marriage. His first wife had set herself on fire in a moment of insanity in reaction to his abusive behavior. "He was not a bad man, but, without any reason, for days and weeks, he would not talk to me. He would return home from work, eat, and retreat to a room for the rest of the day." As time passed, the periods of isolation became longer. "He was not violent. But this was intolerable for me." At times he would return from his solitude and enjoy life with the rest of the family. But soon he would be back in the room, alone. "I couldn't tolerate this," Shadi said, "and I had no intention of burning myself."

After two years of married life, Shadi left her husband and returned to her father's home. Once again the old social pressures surfaced. Limitations were many. People—family and strangers—continued to interfere in her life. Rumors continued. The prospect of a third marriage repulsed her: "I preferred to die." Wishing to teach again, she pleaded with government authorities to be allowed to return to the classroom. The ban remained.

By now Nima was sixteen, a teenager. He had money and many friends. Shadi was worried about Nima's future. The Islamic Republic's ban on alcohol and music and its attempt to create a society of virtuous Muslims had pushed many young people into despair. They were unemployed, had no entertainment, and lacked hope for a better future. Drugs were the only escape from the boredom of everyday life. Herion or opium addiction was rampant throughout Iran, but in Kurdistan, drugs were epidemic.

The defeat of the earlier nationalist movement by the Islamic Republic had demoralized many. The war was over, but Kurdistan's problems remained. The central government's soldiers were everywhere, and many in high government positions benefited from the drug epidemic. It was a lucrative trade. Many were convinced that the top commanders of the Revolutionary Guards—the force responsible for stopping the drug trafficking in Iran—were in on the drug business. A *peshmergeh* (Kurdish liberation fighter) once told me, "The government brought heroin to our cities." It was a new way of disarming the Kurdish movement for autonomy, he said.

Was Nima destined to fall victim to drugs? Shadi couldn't bear the thought. Images of her first husband returned to haunt her. Day and night, she lived in fear of losing her boy to the epidemic. Meanwhile, family pressures and the limitations of a traditional community made life unbearable for her. Months passed. Her fears increased. One day in mid-1998 she decided to take her boy and leave. Escaping military service was the excuse she gave her son.

Shadi took her boy away from Sanandaj to save him from drugs, but drugs followed him to Van. One rainy day in December, as Nima and I walked through the narrow streets and alleys of Aksaray, dodging potholes and cars splashing dirty water, Nima confessed that his life in Van had been an odyssey of drugs and madness. Keeping his head down, ashamed, he kept taking long drags from his cigarette while he told me of his heroin addiction.

Soon after arriving in Van, Nima became hooked. Many of his friends used drugs. He started with hashish. They spent many nights smoking and laughing. Smoking hashish made the boys happy. Then came harder drugs. Heroin changed everything. "The fun was gone. We weren't laughing." His addiction increased with time. "I became a skeleton," he said, still ashamed even now, as he told me about it.

Money was not a problem. One of Nima's friends, Ali, once a *peshmergeh* fighting for the Kurdish Democratic Party of Iran (KDPI), had found a lucrative hustle in Van. Pretending to know witchcraft, he emptied the pockets of poor townspeople who visited him for advice and help with their problems. I met Ali in Istanbul. Tall and slim, he was a handsome young man with dark hair, thick eyebrows, and penetrating black eyes. Ali had charisma. Like Nima, he was in Van waiting for a decision on his asylum case. His case rejected, he came to Istanbul looking for a way out. Not long after, he became a human smuggler.

In Van, Shadi watched her son melt away before her eyes. Determined to save her boy, she forbade him to leave the house, and painfully, patiently helped him defeat his addiction. He was bedridden for three months, but Nima succeeded in kicking the habit.

Once again unemployed and idle, in Aksaray Nima was surrounded by men using drugs, human smugglers, and those making quick money through illegal activities. While Shadi worked five days a week, Nima escaped the boredom of the rooftop apartment by roaming with friends from Van who were in Istanbul on business. He returned home in the early hours of the morning.

Among the visiting friends were human smugglers, those with years of experience on the route between Iran and Turkey. Some had large operations, made a good living, and boasted to Nima about their easy life in Turkey. They wore expensive watches and jewelry, and frequently changed their cell phones. Nima was impressed. Expensive cell phones intrigued him. He took good care of his phone, bought it a case.

When we first met in September 2002, he had no interest in making fast money. "I want a quiet life in my own country, where people understand my language," he said. With time, however, his interest in money changed. The men from Van told him tales of making a fortune in a short time. "I have to make a lot of money and leave this hell for Iran," he told me in late December.

In Istanbul, Nima's visiting friends spent their time in Iranian restaurants in Aksaray. At night, they frequented nightclubs with Iranian dancers and music. Nima accompanied them. A time or two he did not return home at night. Shadi stood on the roof waiting for her boy. "Please talk to him," Shadi said. "Ask him to at least let me know when he stays out all night."

When I told him of Shadi's concern, he replied, "I go to these people's homes, stay till late at night, watch them sleep, and ask myself: 'Why am I here?' "

There were all types of Iranians in Aksaray: the good and the bad, the innocent and the outlaw. There were many Iranian hangouts: restaurants, discotheques, and cabarets. The Iranian outlaws of all types crowded the discotheques, made deals, found customers, and planned for action.

After weeks of waiting, Nima found employment at one such discotheque. He became a bouncer. It was December 24, 2002. A day later, we met in front of McDonald's. For the first time in our meetings, we didn't walk home to meet Shadi. The young man had left work to greet me. He had put on a pair of black trousers, a white shirt, and a black V-neck sweater. His black shoes were newly polished. "You look very handsome, Nima," I told him. Like a shy boy, he laughed and said, "It's for the job, *dadash* Behzad." He wanted to show me his place of work.

Walking away from McDonald's, passing Aksaray Bridge, Nima stopped in front of a small Iranian restaurant. There were cheap polyester curtains on the windows, two rows of tables, and a small bar at the end of the restaurant. A few men had gathered around a table to drink tea and smoke cigarettes. A metal door and a narrow stairway connected the street-floor restaurant to the basement, the discotheque where Nima worked at night. There were no fire exits, no way to escape to the outside world in case of emergency. It was early evening, three or four hours before the customers would arrive for a night of drinking, and Nima treated me to tea. Lighting a cigarette, he said, "I have a lot to tell you, *dadash*. I want to return home. I have lost four years of my life. Look at me now. I have nothing. I work all night, sleep till noon, and repeat the same thing over and over. I'm tired, *dadash* Behzad."

The basement air was heavy. The smell of beer mixed with cigarette smoke made it unbearable. Seedy-looking men entered and left. Nima greeted them all, introduced me to some, and told me their secrets. A man played with the microphone and the wires on what was to be the stage for the night. I felt nauseated.

"My job starts a lot later. But the boss wants me to be here early in the evening. He likes me," he said in a somber voice. He looked pale and had rings under his eyes.

"This is not a place for you, Nima."

"I need a job, *dadash*," he said.

Four hours after I left, a fight broke out in the discotheque. A drunken customer attacked the dancer on the stage, grabbed her by the hair, and forced her to sit on his lap. A second drunk angrily rose to defend the dancer. In a minute or two all the men in the smoky dungeon were on their feet. Blades flashed through the air, slashing expensive jackets. Chairs and beer bottles broke on men's heads.

Since he was the bouncer, Nima had to intervene. "I didn't want to get killed for these animals," he told me. Grabbing the dancer, he escaped the fight and took refuge in the streets, and waited for the police to haul the warring drunks away. He never returned to the job.

I saw Nima in January, a week after he quit his job. He was restless and depressed. A few days later came a call from Shadi. She wanted to meet me that afternoon.

Busy with my work, I suggested we meet for lunch the next day. I wanted to take her out of Aksaray, so I asked to meet her somewhere on Istiklal Street instead of visiting her in the small room on the rooftop. Shadi never dined in restaurants. She didn't visit famous mosques such as the Aya Sofia or the Suleymaniye. I wanted to stroll with her on Istiklal Street, take her to a nice restaurant, give her a temporary break from Aksaray.

The next day, a beautiful, warm Saturday, I walked to our meeting place at noon. Shadi had arrived early. I suggested a nearby restaurant for lunch. "Can we just go somewhere for tea? I have to tell you something," she said. I chose a calm, quiet café off Istiklal Street. Shadi hardly touched her tea. Minutes passed in silence. "How is Nima?" I asked.

"Well, this is what I wanted to talk to you about. Nima was arrested. He's in custody in the Yabanci Şube," the Foreigners Branch of the Ministry of Internal Affairs.

A day earlier, a man introducing himself as a friend of Nima had visited Shadi. Her son was in police custody, he told her. She was given a phone number to call.

"Did you know the friend? Do you know his name or phone number?" I asked. But Shadi had never seen the man before, and he hadn't left a name or number.

"Can you help me? You met some of Nima's friends. I don't know where to find them."

I paid for the tea and left the café with Shadi, heading for Aksaray. My earlier plans had changed. Instead of strolling on Istiklal Street and having lunch in a restaurant, Shadi and I were returning to Aksaray in search of news about her boy.

We visited Iranian restaurants, hotels where Iranians spent time, and the discotheque where Nima had worked last. No one had any news. We walked around the neighborhood, stood by the police station and McDonald's. There were no familiar faces, no word about Nima. I suggested that Shadi go home and rest. "I'll keep asking around," I told her. After I walked her home I decided to go back to Nima's place of work and wait. Perhaps someone with news would stop by. My instincts were right. I had just passed the bridge when someone called my name. I turned around and saw two men I had earlier met through Nima.

"Do you know what happened to Nima? Did they find anything on him? Do you know why he was arrested?" I asked many questions without waiting for the men to respond. "Was he clean?"

Nima was clean, the men assured me. The boy was not involved in smuggling or drugs. His arrest was the result of a random raid by the police. Along with four others, Nima was arrested in an Iranian restaurant in Aksaray. "They found a fraudulent passport on him. He may stay there for a while."

Nima had left Iran without a passport. Like most other migrants, he was often stopped and harassed by the police. "They aren't human," he had told me one day. "I wish I had a gun to kill them. They treat you like animals, insult you, throw you out of the car like garbage." To escape the harassment, he pressured Shadi to buy him a passport. For $200, a smuggler sold him a stolen Iranian passport, replacing the original picture with Nima's. An Afghan smuggler placed an entry stamp on the passport for $75. "I can now show them the passport if they stop me in the streets," he had said. But the passport didn't save him. For nearly ten days Shadi fought the Turkish police for the release of her son. Her efforts failed.

After the police roughed him up a bit, Nima confessed to having purchased a stolen passport in Aksaray. Soon he revealed his real identity and story to the police. A hearing was held the next day, and the verdict was deportation. Nima was kept in custody to await transfer to Van and deportation to Iran.

The day before he was sent to the border, Shadi visited her boy.

"He looked so beautiful," she said. Nima was clean-shaven, she said, and "smelled like roses. His face was shining."

I remembered my own visit to Nima in detention. With the help of a Turkish friend, I had succeeded in getting the approval of the police to visit him. We had embraced, and I tried hard to control my tears. He'd looked pale, not bathed, not smelling like roses. He had pretended to be happy, and I tried to hide my sadness at seeing him behind bars.

"This will be the last time I see you, *dadash*," Nima had said.

I hadn't wanted to respond. All I had been able to manage was an unconvincing smile as I told him, "I'm sure we'll meet again someday."

On the afternoon of January 25, 2003, Shadi arrived late for our meeting. Waiting at McDonald's, I paced nervously, fearing that she too had been arrested on her way from home. Seeing Shadi walking toward me was an enormous relief. For the last time, we walked together to her home.

This was Shadi's last day in Istanbul. Arrangements had been made between the Turkish police and the Iranian border authorities to facilitate her return to her place of birth. Earlier that day, Nima had been put on a bus carrying thirty other illegal Iranians to Van. Shadi was to join her boy on the other side of the border.

She had packed her meager belongings. A day earlier, she had donated her old pots and pans to IIMP for use by other migrants. She put together a large plastic container, the old immersion heater, and a pan or two for a poor Turkish woman, a neighbor who had given her a blanket and mattress when she first moved to her rooftop home. "She was very kind to me," Shadi said.

Following her old routine, Shadi prepared a meal. For the last time, we ate together her tasty dish of rice and potatoes. She told me about her fears of returning to Iran and her determination to stand up to all those who would question her choice to go to Turkey.

"I'll tell them nothing," she said, trying to convince herself of her ability to withstand the criticism and intervention in her life by others that were awaiting her in Iran. Shadi expected to be scorned by her brother, ridiculed by neighbors and other relatives, and forced to abide by the rules set for her by the male members of her extended family, even though she was fifty years old, "a grown woman," she said.

She had no money, nothing to her name. Back in Sanandaj, she was going to move to the second floor of her father's three-story building. In the latest version of his will, her father had put the building and everything else he owned under his only surviving son's name. "I am going back to where I left more than four years ago, but even poorer." Her lack of financial independence worried her the most. She had to live with the family and tolerate their harsh words. "I have to go back to that hell. I am tired of having to explain to people what I do and whom I meet," she said. "I'm going to tell them off." After a minute or two she turned to me, looking determined.

"It's my life and my decision," she said. "At least I experienced something different. I saw a new place. What have *they* done?"

It was early evening. The time had come to say farewell. "I'll never forget you," she said.

That night, Shadi boarded a bus to Van.

Shahrokh Khan

I stanbul is a city of mosques, large and small. You'll see them in every neighborhood, domes and minarets glowing under colorful lights after dark. They give the city a sense of the past gracefully making its way into the present. Five times a day, the call to prayer, *ezan*, is heard from loudspeakers across the city, in rich and poor neighborhoods, in Turkish and immigrant quarters.

If you walk around the Old City, you'll see the world of imperial rivalry captured in architecture: mosques, churches, and palaces. On the top of a hill facing the Bosphorus stands the Topkapı Museum, an impressive complex of Ottoman palaces and gardens. It contains some of the best examples of Ottoman art and architecture, a reminder of Istanbul's imperial past. A short walk away is Aya Sofia. Originally built as a church during the Byzantine Empire in the sixth century, this was once the grandest of all buildings in the world. With the Ottoman conquest of Istanbul (then Constantinople) came the transformation of Aya Sofia into a mosque. The Ottomans built new rooms, a dome, and a minaret, and used this as a symbol of their dominance. Across from Aya Sofia, they built the Blue Mosque, with six minarets and a dome larger than any other in its time. Constructed nearly a millennium apart, and standing opposite each other, the two buildings and their surroundings became living symbols of two of the greatest world empires that ruled this ancient city.

Divan Yolu—a narrow, curving street full of restaurants, old religious schools, cemeteries, *nargile* cafés, shoe stores, and kilim shops—leads away from Aya Sofia and the Blue Mosque to the fascinating world of Beyazit Square and Kapalı Çarsısı, the Grand Bazaar. Built by the Ottomans, the bazaar became a center of commerce for more than half a millennium. Its collection of old and new shops, mosques, restaurants, and teahouses —more than four thousand in total—witnessed the glory of the Ottoman Empire, its demise, and the creation of modern Turkey in 1923.

Stretched above the Golden Horn estuary stands the Galata Bridge with its colorful assortment of fish restaurants and teahouses. Under the bridge, men and women crowd the cafés, sip tea, smoke apple-scented tobacco, and forget the city traffic and its noise. Above, street vendors and petty traders lay out their meager merchandise on the bridge, hoping to sell an item or two before returning home. A Gambian migrant sells smuggled Chinese watches to low-income Turks. A retired Turk sells batteries; another sells key chains and beads. A vendor sells cooked rice mixed with chickpeas. Hoping to attract customers, two old women hold up a few cheap skirts and scarves in their wrinkled hands and call out their prices at the passersby. Some sell cheap plastic Chinese toys: tanks, Robocop, and Rambo. Others sell alarm clocks for less than a dollar. And amid all this chaos, some come with their fishing poles, throw their hooks into the dirty waters of the bay, and wait patiently for a catch of anchovies and other small fish.

Facing the bridge stands the historic Eminönü, a sixteenth-century Ottoman mosque, and a myriad of old and new shops and trading centers built around it. In the historic Egyptian Spice Bazaar (Mısır Çarsısı), the magnificent colors of the spices—blue, red, yellow, green, purple, white—resonate with the beauty of the grand paintings of Van Gogh and other masters. Outside the bazaar is a mosaic of sights and smells and sounds: the rising smoke and the inexpensive barbecued fish sandwiches sold on small boats, men selling pickled cucumbers and cabbage, countless vendors selling all types of dried fruits and nuts, the loud voices of merchants crying the price of their merchandise, men and women bargaining for better deals for jeans, shirts, and scarves. An old Roma sells birdseed to tourists. Flying low in the open market in front of the mosque's entrance, hundreds of pigeons rush after the seeds tossed on the ground.

One day I was negotiating my way through the crowded sidewalks of the Old City when I noticed a solemn old man sitting next to a scale—his sole source of income, perhaps—hoping for a passerby to take him out of the boredom of his solitude. I walked toward the man without thinking. When he saw me approaching, the old man's face brightened up, pulling me toward the scale with magnetic strength.

I stepped on the scale, took note of the reading, and gave the old man a 1-million-lira note—a bit more than 50 cents at the exchange rate then. His body and hands bent and moved in every form and direction to show me his gratitude. So much joy for only 50 cents. I wanted to embrace his shrunken body, touch his wrinkled face, apologize for being more fortunate than he and for spending many more million liras every day. Showing him my camera, I asked if he would allow me to photograph him. He put his hands together, rested them on his chest, and bowed to me in a kind gesture of acceptance. With a big smile, he turned toward me. I locked his unshaven face inside my lens and released the shutter.

Moving back to his side, I sat next to the old man on the ground. Trying to show him my appreciation for his kindness, I took words out of my limited Turkish vocabulary: *merhaba, maşallah, teşekkür.* Holding my hands, he taught me new words. Like a student following his master, I repeated after him, one word at a time, carefully and accurately. Then, using both words and body language, the old man asked for my nationality. That is how I understood his words.

"Iran," I replied.

"Iran," he repeated with excitement, immediately continuing with "Reza Shah."

I repeated, "Reza Shah!" As if testing the old man's knowledge of Iran, I cried, "Khomeini."

He repeated, "Khomeini," and laughed, overjoyed at having found a way to connect with my history and me.

I packed my camera, shook the old man's hand, and continued on my way. Still glowing with happiness, he said to me as I left, *"Iranlı, Türk, arkadaş"*—Iranians and Turks are friends.

The Suleymaniye Mosque is another magnificent structure in the Old City. Standing after sunset in the mosque's hilltop courtyard, hearing the echo of the *ezan* from the near and distant mosques, is an escape from the madness of everyday life in this bustling transnational city. From the courtyard you have a view of Eminönü with its illuminated domes and minarets, the bridges across the Bosphorus and the Golden Horn, the small boats and large ships dancing in the strait—a view right out of fairy tales and old paintings.

Shahrokh Khan, a teenager from Afghanistan, told me that the Suleymaniye Mosque was one of his favorite places in Istanbul. He often went there for solace for hours on end.

When I first met Shahrokh Khan, in the office of the International Catholic Migration Commission (ICMC), he alternated between smiling and looking petrified. He stared at the floor, rubbed his hands together, looked up, said a word or two in English with a Pakistani accent, and lapsed into silence again. Sara Akkaya, a psychologist at ICMC, had asked me to help Shahrokh Khan audit classes at Boğaziçi University, an English-language university where I was guest-lecturing. He was waiting for a decision on his asylum case with the UNHCR and wanted to use his time constructively.

A week after our first meeting, we took a taxi to the campus. Located on the top of a cliff by the Bosphorus, Boğaziçi University has vast green areas, trees and beautiful flowers, and well-kept old buildings. I took Shahrokh Khan for a tour of the campus, introducing him to my students and some of the faculty. I don't know if it was the lovely natural surroundings or his feeling of trust in me that made Shahrokh Khan more relaxed and talkative, but he smiled frequently, and as we walked around the campus he told me of his dream of studying at a university somewhere in the West. At times he admired the scenery. "I've never seen anything so beautiful," he said.

Since it was a sunny day, we decided to go for a stroll by the Bosphorus. Leaving the campus, we passed Rumeli Hisarı, an impressive half-century-old Ottoman fort, and walked down the hill, a large cemetery on the left and beautiful villas on the right. The Bosphorus stood at the foot of the hill. Small fishing boats crowded the strait. There were no clouds in the blue sky. The flying seagulls, the men fishing in the strait, and the sun reflecting on the water had widened the smile on Shahrokh Khan's face. An old man nearby sold egg sandwiches. A woman sold hot tea. I shared an egg sandwich with Shahrokh.

Sitting on a bench, watching the boats and the passersby, I noticed Shahrokh's worn-out shoes: the holes on the sides, the gaps between the top and the sole. It was late January 2003, and they clearly were inadequate for this time of year in Istanbul. He laughed when he noticed what I was looking at. "They've traveled a very long distance from Afghanistan to here."

Shahrokh Khan shared a room with a Russian and two Turkish men near Aksaray and spent his time sleeping, visiting his favorite house of worship, and studying Turkish. A fourteen-year-old Iraqi refugee was one of his two friends in Istanbul. Orphaned when bombs destroyed his home, the boy left Iraq for Iran, lived there for two years, and entered Turkey illegally in search of asylum. I asked Shahrokh Khan how often he saw his Iraqi friend. He told me they had met only once, on a trip to Ankara for their asylum interviews with the UNHCR. Accompanied by an ICMC staff member, they spent a day together and got to know each other's stories. They maintained their friendship through occasional phone conversations but never met in person again.

Yussuf, a twenty-year-old Turkish manual laborer from Adana, was his other friend. They had met the day he arrived in Istanbul. The Turkish man helped Shahrokh Khan find a hostel and showed him the city: "He was very kind." But not long after they met, Yussuf left Istanbul to get married in his hometown.

I thought of introducing Shahrokh Khan to Nima and Shadi, but Nima's arrest and deportation changed that plan.

Soon after meeting, Shahrokh and I became friends. I was a stranger he could trust. We spoke on the phone often, and spent time strolling the streets of Istanbul away from Aksaray. Neslişah Café, a teahouse and *nargile* café off Istiklal Street near Taksim Square, was where we frequently met. There one afternoon I told Shahrokh of my life in Iran and the United States, and he told me the story of his journey.

In a small village near Kandahar, Shahrokh Khan was born to a family of farmers. "My father was an agricultural man, growing crops and selling them in the market. We had a normal family," Shahrokh Khan told me.

In December 1979, a few years before his birth, the Russians invaded Afghanistan. Soon the country was the scene of a holy war against the communists. The Russian army left Afghanistan in 1989. A civil war followed. Shahrokh Khan did not have much recollection of the war. "I stayed on the farm most of the time," he said. "Sometimes I went with my father on business trips to the city. We did not do much. We were a simple family."

Shahrokh Khan's father wished his son to grow up away from the violence of the civil war and become an educated man. So after the boy finished third grade, his father sent him to Peshawar, a city in neighboring Pakistan where many Afghan refugees were given shelter. "My father wanted me to be unlike the others in Afghanistan," Shahrokh Khan said.

"In the beginning I was very depressed. Integration was so very difficult. I would cry all the time." These were the formative years of his life. Living in hostels with Pakistanis and other Afghans, Shahrokh Khan continued his studies in Peshawar, learned English, and developed a love for schooling. Slowly he became accustomed to a life away from home. He had many friends, other boys from his school and the hostel. Salim, a Pakistani youth who was a classmate in Peshawar for six years, was his closest companion. They spent their free time playing cricket, watching Bollywood movies, and dancing in their rooms to Bollywood music. An Indian actor, also called Shahrokh Khan, was his idol. Like many boys his age, he wanted to grow up and be a movie star.

From time to time, during school holidays, Shahrokh Khan returned to the village to visit his family. "In Pakistan, I used to wear trousers and dress like people in other parts of the world. I didn't wear the *shalvar* [the baggy pants worn by men in Afghanistan]. When I came to visit my family in Afghanistan, people looked at me in a strange way, as if I had come from another world. They wanted me to be like them. My father was a simple man. He was tolerant. My mother wore the *chador* [a long garment covering the head and the rest of the body except for the face] when she visited places outside our home. Inside, she didn't wear the *hijab* [veil]."

After finishing the tenth grade, Shahrokh moved to Abbottabad, a city near Islamabad. Enrolling in a new high school "with very high educational standards," Shahrokh Khan continued his studies until one day, not long after his last visit to Afghanistan in the summer of 2001, a message in his hostel room informed him of a call by the principal, Mr. Javeed, who wanted to see him right away. He rushed to the principal's office, where Mr. Javeed told him, "Sit down. You need to be strong. Promise me you won't fall apart."

The principal had received a phone call from Shahrokh Khan's mother. "She called to tell me about the death of my father," he told me, then sank into a long silence. Staring at the coffee cup on the table before us, he finally said, "I felt the ground was shifting from under my feet. This was not easy news for me. Not at all. Tears started coming down my face." The principal took Shahrokh Khan back to his hostel. "The next day, I took a bus to Kandahar. In situations like this, you remember the past. I could not believe this. He was okay the last time I saw him. But he wasn't there anymore." A long pause followed again. Biting his fingernail and trying to control his emotions, he said at last, "I went back home. Everyone was crying. My mother was crying. I saw his dead body. They were just waiting for me to see the dead face of my father. Together, we buried him. We did not know how the funeral was arranged. Some neighbors took care of everything. They cooked food for everyone."

After the funeral, Shahrokh Khan returned to Pakistan. His father had wished him to become a learned man, and Shahrokh Khan had vowed to remain committed to his studies; staying in Afghanistan was of no use. "I wanted my mother to come with me. But we didn't know how to support ourselves if all of us moved to Pakistan. These were days of war. The Pakistanis wouldn't have issued a visa to my mother and brother and sister. We didn't have any money and couldn't pay for smugglers."

Days passed. Focusing on his schoolwork, Shahrokh Khan hoped to distract himself from his father's death and the predicament of his family. Then came another call from Afghanistan, less than a month after the death of Shahrokh's father: a neighbor, calling Shahrokh Khan to inform him that his home had been destroyed in an American aerial attack against the Taliban. He had lost his mother and his siblings. "I could not believe the news. I had just seen all of them." Tears filled his eyes, and he was silent for a while.

"Shall we stop, Shahrokh?" I asked.

"No, I want to talk," he said, biting his lip and giving me a warm smile.

Once again, Shahrokh Khan boarded the first bus to Kandahar. He recalled his feelings during the bus ride home.

"I was blaming myself. I could have saved my family. If I had money, I would have taken my family with me, even though they did not have Pakistani visas. We would have paid money to a smuggler. My mother would have lived in a hostel. She would have still been alive today. I asked myself, 'Why did I leave them alone? Why was I not with them?' They are dead now. That is what happened. A bomb fell on our house. Everyone was sleeping. And they kept on sleeping forever."

Shahrokh Khan returned to his village and his family farm. The house he had grown up in had been utterly demolished. "There was no shape to my home. No roof. All the walls were destroyed. Every thing was burnt. When I saw their bodies, they were totally burnt. In these situations, you don't feel anything. You have lost something that you know you can't have again. You remember your life from the past.

"There were burnt bodies of many people who I knew, people who I saw growing up. It was terrible. The whole surroundings were ruined, and I could see lots of crying faces around me, mourning and hugging each other and hitting their own faces. That was the worst moment of my life, when I looked at the faces of my family who weren't alive anymore."

Unable to cope with his new predicament, he wanted to end his life. "I took poison to kill myself. But I wasn't lucky enough to die with them. My neighbor took me to the hospital."

For nearly a month, he stayed at the neighbor's house recovering. "To recover yourself in this situation isn't easy at all. It's true that time is a cure for every kind of pain. But to pass that time isn't easy. Every single second is like a year." After a month, Shahrokh Khan "felt alive again."

Many things had changed now. Staying in Afghanistan was too painful, but Shahrokh Khan didn't feel like returning to his school in Pakistan. Following the advice of a kind neighbor and family friend, Muhammad Fida, he decided to leave for a faraway land in the West, to continue his studies and fulfill the vow he had made to his father.

Muhammad Fida helped him find a buyer for the family land. A man living in Kabul offered $1,000 for a piece of land that "was worth thirty thousand in normal times." Having no other option, Shahrokh Khan accepted the offer. The land was sold. Early one morning, with $1,000 in his pocket and a small backpack full of clothes, he left the village and headed for Pakistan.

Unlike previous times, Peshawar was not his destination. He took a bus to Quetta and continued to Taftan, the last town near the border with Iran. A map in his hand, he walked parallel to the border for three hours until there were no checkpoints in sight. Feeling safe, he crossed the border and walked through the endless barren and dusty land to Zahedan in Baluchistan province.

Shahrokh Khan was now in one of the most desolate and impoverished towns of Iran, a center of drug trafficking, and a place of occasional armed battles between smugglers and Revolutionary Guards of the Islamic Republic. The landscape, language, currency, and people were all unfamiliar. "I was scared. Everything was strange for me there. Also, I was barely able to communicate in Farsi. I had learned some basic sentences for buying tickets and food. I did not know anything about the *toman* [Iranian money], with the picture of Khomeini on every bill," he told me, now laughing.

In Zahedan, Shahrokh Khan cleaned himself up in a mosque, dusted off his clothes, and inquired about the main bus station. His next stop was to be Tehran. "You can go to Tehran directly, but I took the wrong bus, to Isfahan."

By now, the Taliban's government had collapsed. Many Taliban warriors and supporters were on the run. Some hoped to reach Iran and disappear there among the large Afghan refugee community. Many were arrested and returned to Pakistan. "I didn't dress like the other Afghans. I had regular clothes on." That proved important for not being spotted and arrested by the soldiers at the many different checkpoints on the way to Isfahan. Buses and cars were checked for carrying drugs and illegal immigrants. Even Iranians who did not carry an identification card were removed from the bus and put under arrest. "I was so afraid of the controls. The bus was stopped every few kilometers. The first control was very terrible for me. I began losing my confidence. I was praying that the soldier wouldn't come to me. I was lucky; I looked like the other Iranians. So they didn't ask me anything. At every checkpoint, a soldier came to the bus. He walked to the end of the bus and asked some people for their papers. I got lucky at every stop."

After many hours of fear, the bus pulled into the main *garadj* (bus station) in Isfahan. With a few hours to pass before the next bus to

Tehran, Shahrokh Khan left the station, strolling along the nearby streets. "It was early morning when we reached Isfahan. There were flowers everywhere. I had never seen such a beautiful city." Isfahan remained like a vivid picture in his memory. "That is the most beautiful city," he told me another time.

"Did you see the mosques or other important sites of Isfahan?" I asked him, but he hadn't; he'd stayed around the bus terminal. What he saw were clean streets and flowers.

The long ride through a dusty and dry landscape was now over. He walked around, enjoyed the fresh early morning air and the flowers, and thought about Tehran. Resting by a flower bed, he imagined Tehran, its people, its police, its streets. Unlike Zahedan, Tehran was a big city, with twelve million people. Where would he find a place to stay? How would he find the next town and the stop after Tehran, the next border crossing?

Shahrokh Khan returned to the bus station, bought a ticket, and boarded the first bus to Tehran. Eight hours later, he stood in the middle of a crowded and large terminal outside Tehran. Following other migrants, he took a city bus to Toopkhaneh, a busy neighborhood in the center of old Tehran, a place known for its traffic jams, noise, and the suffocating fumes of old cars. Its surrounding area is full of cheap, dirty hostels and hotels. Manual laborers who come to Tehran from other cities, poor Afghan refugees, and outlaws of all types crowd the hotels. Here, all sorts of trading take place in the streets.

Within walking distance from Toopkhaneh Square is Naser Khosro Street, a busy center of trading for inexpensive clothes, electronics, and furniture. Shahrokh Khan took a room in a dirty hostel near Naser Khosro. For three months, he stayed in old Tehran, spent most of his time in the hostel, and planned his next steps. There were other Afghans in the hostel. Many had traveled between Iran and Turkey in the past and knew of all possible exit routes, the borders, and the most secure ways to reach Turkey. After studying a map of Iran and talking to others, Shahrokh Khan chose a route. He selected Orumiyeh, a town in Iran's northwestern province of West Azerbaijan, as the best crossing.

"Tehran is a nice city," Shahrokh Khan said. "It has a new part that is beautiful. But I didn't see much of the new Tehran. I liked the public phones the most. You just put a coin in the slot and talk forever—of course, inside Tehran. That was the best."

Saying goodbye to his Afghan friends, Shahrokh Khan left Tehran for Orumiyeh. "I had learned a good deal of Persian in the three months of staying in Tehran. But people spoke a different language in Orumiyeh," Azeri. He was disappointed. With much difficulty, he found a taxi to take him to the border with Turkey. The fare was less than $10, he recalled. "He [the cabdriver] took me very close to the immigration section of the border. He thought I was someone traveling legally."

Shahrokh Khan spoke casually about the borders, the police, and a journey that seemed to me formidable, unimaginable, in some ways epic. At times I doubted his tale. But here he was, sitting in front of me in a café in Istanbul. Small and childlike, he knew many details, correct details, about the lands and the borders he claimed to have crossed. I tried to picture him standing alone before the immigration booths.

The immigration control was at the foot of the Zagros Mountains. "This was the border with Turkey. When I saw the border, perhaps only five hundred meters ahead of the taxi, I asked the driver to stop. I told him to turn left and not to go directly. I left the taxi and walked toward Serou village before the border. I walked to the village and sat on a corner, waiting, making plans.

"A man was passing by. I approached him and asked if there was a way to cross the border." The man offered to take Shahrokh Khan to Turkey for a hundred dollars.

"He took me to his home and told me we would leave the village at night. I rested a while." When dark came, Shahrokh Khan and the villager started their hike.

"I threw away most of my clothes and made my bag lighter. The mountain was steep. It was very cold. The bushes were terrible on the way up. You know these bushes get stuck to your legs. They were terrible. We walked all night. I threw away more things. I even threw away my bottled water.

"We walked the whole night and stayed somewhere up on the mountains during the daytime. There were mountains after mountains. At the end, at around five the next morning, we reached a Turkish village. The man had a friend in the village. He took me to the friend's house. We ate and rested."

The Iranian villager brought Shahrokh Khan to Turkey and left him in the hands of a Turkish friend who would take him to Van. Shahrokh Khan paid the $100 he had agreed to, but the man demanded more. "He grabbed my money and took another three hundred by force. I was obliged to give him the money. I had no other way. I was in their home. They could have done anything they wanted. I was scared. I didn't know Turkish. I guess he really needed the money. That is perhaps why he agreed to take me for only a hundred dollars. Or maybe he knew he could take my money after reaching Turkey. That's what he did, anyway."

From Van, Shahrokh Khan proceeded to Istanbul, bought a map of Europe, made his exit plans, and boarded a bus to Edirne, near the border with Bulgaria and Greece. Bulgaria was his destination. A train connected Edirne to Bulgaria. He found the track on the map, went to the last train station in Turkey, and waited until dark. This was the seventeenth of Ramadan in 2002, the month of fasting for Muslims. "I broke my fast when it got dark and followed the tracks toward Bulgaria. There was fog everywhere. I hid under a bridge. It was dark. I took advantage of the dark and the fog. Nobody could see me."

"Were you scared?" I asked him.

"I had no option. I could only go forward. You know that there is no right, no left, no going back. Everybody does the same thing. I didn't want to give up. I had a strange courage in my heart.

"I followed the railroad tracks and walked for hours. I don't know how many kilometers I covered in those hours. It was very cold that night. The tracks continued on a bridge. There were cars passing under the bridge. I saw a dim light in the fog. I walked toward the light."

Thinking these were lights from a home, Shahrokh proceeded with a feeling of relief, but stopped when he saw soldiers with rifles standing before him. "Now I wished I had not gone in that direction."

Shahrokh Khan was arrested. The border police kept asking him questions about other migrants accompanying him on the journey. They shouted at him, questioned him over and over, until they saw the map in his backpack. It was only then that they realized that they had a lone migrant before them. "He [a border police officer] hit me on the head with my map."

Shahrokh was taken to a prison where he spent two days and nights. The Bulgarians took his small backpack and all his belongings, along with the rest of his money.

"This was a terrible prison. There were three mattresses, pieces of foam, something like mattresses on the floor. They were dirty. They had many big stains. Some had missing parts.

"The prison was a long hall with an entrance. You had to find your own place. There was an Afghan and an Iranian man in the prison. The Iranian spoke very good English. He was an educated man. I told him my story. The Iranian told me that I was going to be deported to Turkey. He told me to look for the UNHCR and apply for asylum once I reached Istanbul.

"They did not give us anything to eat. The Iranian man had brought some food. He shared his food with me. The Bulgarians treated us like animals. The room was so cold. There was a wood burner in the room. We asked the guards if we could make a fire. They brought us three pieces of wood. We made a fire. But the fire didn't last long. We were shivering. So we cut pieces of the foam from the mattresses and put them in the burner. This was so funny. We finished the foams that night. There was no other way."

After two days of custody, Shahrokh Khan was handed over to the soldiers at two o'clock in the morning. The soldiers took him to the border, circled him, kicked him, and set their dogs on him.

"The dogs bit me. My leg was bleeding hard. I could barely walk."

The soldiers showed him a mud field separating Bulgaria from Turkey, ordered him to cross the field, and shot in the air to scare him.

"I was not scared of their gun or dying," Shahrokh Khan said. "There was mud up to my knees. I was bleeding from the dog bite. I put mud on the wound to stop the bleeding."

Shahrokh walked across the field and reached the Turkish side of the border. Exhausted from the walk in the mud, he rested till sunrise, then walked for hours till he heard the call for prayer. He was in Turkey indeed.

Shahrokh found his way to Edirne and took a bus to Istanbul. There, helped by ICMC, he applied for asylum with the UNHCR. Not long after, we met in Sara Akkaya's office.

One afternoon I found I had six missed calls from Shahrokh Khan. Unable to reach me, he had tried again and again. I had discovered that a call of this nature from a migrant was always followed by news of arrest, financial crisis, or other problems beyond their capacity to resolve. I rang him quickly.

"Can we meet today?" There was something urgent he had to tell me, he said. I rushed to meet him in Aksaray. This was February 2, 2003.

At five-thirty in the afternoon we met outside the McDonald's. But, defying my expectations, Shahrokh Khan was relaxed; he greeted me with a smile. Hungry after a day of work, I suggested getting a quick bite at a restaurant across from the McDonald's. While we waited for the food, he asked, "Will you photograph me?"

I had told Shahrokh Khan that I had been taking photographs of migrants for my book. Now I asked if he wanted his picture to be included among the others. No, he told me, still smiling. That wasn't the reason for the urgent calls. He had a different audience in mind.

Shahrokh Khan shared with me the story of a meeting in his favorite house of worship. He told me about a "French girl" he had met a week or two earlier in the magnificent Suleymaniye mosque.

"A very strange thing attracts me to this mosque. When I hear the *ezan,* I rush there. I want to come for the prayers. My soul feels basic happiness after saying the prayer in this mosque. There's something in the Suleymaniye mosque that is different from other places of worship. There's something inside there. When you're there, you feel you're doing the best meditation anyone can do. Your mind gets washed out. You feel comfortable. Once you feel comfortable, you forget everything. You forget your real life."

Many things in Aksaray—its shops and its people—had been unfamiliar and, in the beginning, alienating to Shahrokh Khan. "When I first came to Aksaray, I remember, I was scared of the women I saw in the streets," he told me the first time we walked through the neighborhood together. "I had never experienced that environment in my life. Women were always covered. Here I came to Istanbul, and everything was open."

In the uninviting room in his hostel, he felt lonely and bored, but the mosque reconnected him with a familiar world he had lost touch with since he began his journey to the West. It brought him peace. "I wanted to talk to God. I wanted to complain to him, ask him questions. Why did these things happen to me? I would go two times a day." The Suleymaniye mosque took Shahrokh Khan away from the life he wished to forget. "I could communicate with God. I would feel far from all those problems that I was suffering from at that time."

It was in the courtyard of the Suleymaniye mosque that one afternoon Shahrokh Khan noticed a beautiful young girl, alone, staring at the low domes surrounding the mosque and making sketches on a drawing pad. An unknown feeling came upon him. Without thinking or planning, he found himself standing next to the girl, smiling, looking at the domes with her. "Something made me go close to her. Maybe it was her nice smile. Maybe her beautiful face. This was the first time I talked to a girl with those feelings. In times like this, you feel something in your heart. Something touches the bottom of your heart." For the first time in his many visits to the mosque, he had now found an attraction other than his prayers.

In all his adolescent years, Shahrokh Khan's contact with women had been minimal. In Pakistan, his friends were boys his age. Living in a strictly Muslim society, he rarely spoke to women. If he did, they were older women, classmates' mothers and relatives. At times he said a word or two to female students in his coed school. "You know, girls are very shy in these societies," he said. But here in the courtyard of his favorite mosque, he was standing close to an uncovered woman, one whose beauty was not disguised by a tentlike *burqa*. Since she seemed friendly, he found the unimagined courage to say "Beautiful drawings." She took a quick glance at Shahrokh Khan and asked if he knew the name of the building. "I don't know. I'm also a tourist," Shahrokh Khan replied.

In an unexpected instant, Shahrokh Khan was taken out of his refugee life in Aksaray. He introduced himself as an Indian tourist, a description made credible by his Pakistani-English accent. He didn't want to be an Afghan.

"I lied to her. I was afraid she wouldn't talk to me. Everyone thinks of Afghans as terrorists."

Continuing with her sketches, "with a nice French accent," the girl told Shahrokh Khan about her studies in an architecture school in Hungary. Soon she put the pad away and sat with him on a stone bench by the wall facing the water and Galata Bridge. They talked about Istanbul's beautiful old buildings and the joy of traveling and seeing the world. They sat close to each other. At times they innocently touched, momentarily held hands. Later in the afternoon, they walked side by side through the back streets surrounding the mosque. He impressed her by showing her the streets and places he knew by heart. Never in the past had he impressed a girl. Never had he walked so close to a girl.

Later that day, the French girl left Istanbul to return to her studies in Budapest. Shahrokh Khan walked her to Sirkeci Station, said farewell, and returned to Aksaray. He cherished the memory. "Unfortunately too short," he told me.

The reason for his urgent calls to me, it turned out, was that the girl had e-mailed Shahrokh Khan from Budapest the day before, asking for pictures, images that would bring to life her last day in Istanbul.

As if seeking a witness to the time he spent with the French girl, Shahrokh Khan took me to the Suleymaniye mosque and showed me the place of their accidental meeting. The mosque was nearly empty. We walked quietly between the tall columns in the big hall, stared at the wall paintings, and whispered about the architectural magnificence of the place.

"Strange silence," Shahrokh Khan said. Sitting next to me in the middle of the prayer hall, he closed his eyes. I too felt taken by the "strange silence" of the mosque. It was time for the evening prayer. Leaving him in the prayer hall, I returned to the courtyard.

The *ezan* heard from loudspeakers in mosques across the city created a musical effect appealing to the ears of Muslims and non-Muslims alike. The tourists had left the site. Only the worshipers and I were there to take in the scene: the occasional singing of birds flying low in the mosque's courtyard, the sound of the *ezan,* the echo of the footsteps of solitary worshipers walking in the courtyard, the breathtaking sunset on the hilltop where the mosque showed off its graceful beauty. I watched the worshipers zealously perform their pre-prayer ritual of washing their faces and hands in the courtyard.

The night had fallen on the city; colorful lights brightened its domes and minarets. Shahrokh Khan emerged from his prayers, calm, at peace, and ready to show me the spot in the courtyard where he met the French girl.

The third week of February was the start of the spring semester at Boğaziçi University. With the consent of the faculty, Shahrokh Khan sat in on mathematics, physics, and computer science classes. I left Istanbul for Athens. Some time after, an e-mail arrived from Shahrokh Khan. "I had a very bad experience this week. Please come back soon." Three human smugglers, a Bangladeshi and two Turkish men, had assaulted him in his hostel. Entering his room at night, the Bangladeshi demanded that he meet them outside the building. He refused. The men circled him, pushed him to the floor, assaulted him, and took his cell phone.

Shahrokh Khan complained to the police, hoping to get back his phone. The men were arrested and, in turn, beaten by the police. The Bangladeshi was deported to Iran. The Turks were released. Shahrokh did not see his cell phone again. He left the hostel and took shelter with a kind Turk who allowed him to spend nights in his Aksaray residence. A few days later, Ma'sumeh, a friend of the kind Turk, a mother of two, and a migrant from Iran, accepted Shahrokh as a son. Spending many hours with the woman and her two children in their basement room in Aksaray, he waited for news from the UNHCR.

"I'm very worried," he wrote in his last e-mail before I returned to Istanbul. "There's been no news from the UN. Why is my case taking so long?"

Returning to Istanbul at the end of March, I immediately contacted Shahrokh Khan. We were to meet at Taksim Square.

Arriving on time, I waited for him. Ten minutes passed. I waited, looked around, returned to our meeting spot, but he was not there. Half an hour later, I returned to my flat, phoned Ma'sumeh, and inquired about Shahrokh Khan's whereabouts. It turned out that he had never left her home for Taksim Square.

"Will you please come here to see him? He took a handful of pills to kill himself yesterday. I don't know what to do. Please come and help."

On the day before his attempted suicide, Shahrokh Khan's asylum case had been rejected by the UNHCR. He did not qualify for refugee status under the 1951 refugee convention. The Taliban was gone, a new government existed in Kabul, and the Afghan war was declared over, so the UNHCR decided that Shahrokh Khan would not face persecution upon returning to Afghanistan.

Not long after, he appealed the decision. Now aware of the criteria of the 1951 convention, Shahrokh Khan added new information to his appeal letter, hoping to convince the UNHCR of his fear of returning to Afghanistan. He told the UNHCR that his father was killed by distant relatives over a land dispute and old animosity, and that he too was afraid for his life.

The appeal letter was sloppy, the new information unconvincing, and his appeal was rejected in less than a few weeks. Poor and illegal and trapped in Istanbul, slowly Shahrokh Khan began to turn into a bitter and angry young man.

An article I published about his story brought some attention to his case. Men and women from the United States and Britain contacted us, expressing their sympathy and their willingness to help. A woman in Austin, Texas, embraced Shahrokh Khan as a son—she wrote to him, consoled him, contacted lawyers to see if she could bring him to the United States, offered money, and did all one can do to help from afar. But not much could be done, and his status remained unchanged.

Worried about his psychological condition and his helpless situation in Istanbul, Sara Akkaya suggested he return to Afghanistan, go to a university, and try his chances for doing graduate studies in the West. That outraged Shahrokh Khan. He had no one in Afghanistan. The Taliban were gone. The allied forces had not done much to improve the Afghan economy. Unemployment, poverty, idleness, and violence persisted. Bands of armed men still fought for control of different parts of the country. The central government exerted power only in Kabul. Afghanistan remained in a de facto civil war. "How can I go back? What is there for me in Afghanistan? Nobody understands that," he told me.

Shahrokh Khan had no money, no loving family and friends, and no future in his country of birth. When Akkaya repeated her suggestion, Shahrokh Khan's rage escalated. He refused to see her. "They don't do anything for me anyway," he told me.

This was the beginning of a new Shahrokh Khan: a desperate young migrant demanding help from the world and regarding people as instruments for escaping his miseries. He dismissed people who were unable to help him and questioned the humanity of those who did not offer assistance. He spoke angrily about those who showed no interest in his case. "These people only care about superficial things."

I introduced Shahrokh Khan to my friends and connected him with a network of sympathetic people in Istanbul. In May 2003 he lost his living space in Aksaray. With the help of friends, he moved to Tünel, an up-and-coming alternative neighborhood in Istanbul, home to artists, musicians, painters, and many foreigners. No longer isolated and living in loneliness in Aksaray, Shahrokh met new friends: young and old, Turkish, French, American, German, and others.

Though penniless, he spent time in sleek cafés and restaurants, always cared for by his new friends. The first time Shahrokh Khan entered a bar became a memorable incident. He ordered a soft drink. We clinked our glasses and drank to his health. He had the biggest smile on his face I'd ever seen. "Look at me, in a bar," he repeated. Shahrokh Khan did not drink alcohol. He did not smoke. Bars were simply places to socialize with the new friends he was meeting in Istanbul. Soon he was a popular person in the Tünel area. Many knew about his situation. Many empathized with him, helped him, took pleasure in spending time with him, and invited him to their parties and gatherings. An article in *Cumhuriyet*, a daily paper, brought further attention to him. Gone were the days of living with other migrants and marginal people in Aksaray. Gone were the long hours of meditating and praying in the Suleymaniye mosque.

Shahrokh remained faithful to his religion, but, as time passed, a different sense of religiosity emerged in him. In Pakistan and Afghanistan, he was a Muslim by default, religious by custom. In Istanbul, his religiosity became conscious, chosen by will. "I don't go to the mosque anymore, but I am still a Muslim. My religion is in my heart now." Shahrokh was a "spiritual Muslim" and believed in "humanity." "I think of Christians and everybody else as my equals."

As time passed, Shahrokh Khan developed new interests and fantasies. He came to believe in the possibility of becoming a famous movie star.

"Why don't *you* become an actor?" he asked me. When I laughed, he insisted, "You would be very good."

He believed in his chances. He raised his glass of Pepsi-Cola and drank to my health. "*I'll* be good," he said firmly.

A miracle occurred one day in early September 2003. He was given his first chance to act before the camera. Along with a number of foreigners, Africans and Asians, all illegal migrants in Istanbul, he was chosen to appear in a new international promotional commercial for DHL.

"This is my chance to become famous," he shouted with joy.

They spoke before the camera in their respective languages, introducing the carrier service to the world. Shahrokh Khan noted proudly, "I was better than all of them." He was paid $50 for his first acting role and hoped that more would follow.

But none did, and Shahrokh Khan became more desperate. Many tried to help him, but all attempts to change his illegal status failed. A brave young Turkish woman offered to marry Shahrokh Khan. But her family was both heartbroken and horrified, and she had to back down.

With each failure came more anger and frustration. He was in Istanbul wasting time. Seeing other migrants trapped in Turkey increased his sense of despair. Steve, a Somali living in Istanbul for thirteen years, was his nightmare.

"I don't want to become another Steve. At nights, I wake up seeing myself in his position."

Steve had arrived in Istanbul in 1990. He too had tried to leave for the West. Like Shahrokh Khan, he had tried asylum, sponsorship in other countries, a student visa, every possibility. All his efforts failed.

Shahrokh Khan eventually became more aggressive toward those giving him love and attention. Soon friends stopped returning his calls. His e-mails remained unanswered. That further frustrated him. He began manipulating people. Taking advantage of their compassion and paternal feelings, he tried to instill guilt in them. The result was further isolation.

The once likable and innocent young Afghan was becoming a seasoned survivor. An e-mail he sent to me by mistake was alarming:

> *To the Mothers' Union:*
> *I have no option except suicide. A young boy of eighteen years old from Afghanistan writing from Istanbul, Turkey . . . With love to all the mothers of the world!*

Shahrokh Khan's threat of suicide was a desperate attempt to buy the sympathy of compassionate strangers. He was consumed by the dream of escaping Turkey for the West.

"I want to be a normal person, get rid of the word *refugee* stamped on my forehead. I don't want to be seen as a refugee," he told me when I confronted him about his e-mail to the Mothers' Union.

Although away from his family, he had felt normal in Pakistan. Like boys his age, he studied, played cricket, and watched Indian movies. All of that had stopped when he arrived in Istanbul, and for a time he tried to re-create that environment, going to see Indian movies and busying himself with an ambitious project of forming a cricket team in Istanbul. He printed professional-looking flyers inviting those interested in the game to contact him, via e-mail, cell phone, or land line and put them up in Internet cafés, fancy coffee shops and restaurants, foreign cultural centers, and even consulates. Shahrokh Khan even contacted the British consulate and the Pakistani and Indian embassies to request their sponsorship. Weeks passed, and no one responded to Shahrokh. No help arrived from the embassies. He gave up the idea.

I left Istanbul for a two-week visit to New York City in May 2003. There I met Zahra, an Afghan refugee whose parents had been killed by the Taliban. Zahra agreed to speak to me and tell her story. The day before our meeting, I gave her my article about Shahrokh Khan. She stayed up the whole night reading the story, and wept. When we met, she told me with tears in her eyes, "There are thousands of other Afghans like Shahrokh Khan and me. No one knows their stories."

I asked Zahra's permission to give her e-mail address to Shahrokh Khan. She agreed. Not long after, the two Afghans were exchanging e-mails.

Hello Zahra. I am very sorry about what had happened to you in Afghanistan. I think both of us have the same stories. You should forget all of that like a bad dream and enjoy your present life. It is very nice to hear that you are also fond of studying like me.

Hello Shahrokh. I know about you and I am also very sorry about all those tragedies that happened to you in Afghanistan. You should be brave and ambitious.

Shahrokh Khan and Zahra quickly became friends. They communicated through e-mail, spoke on the phone, and chatted online. The frequency of their contacts increased, and soon they were speaking or e-mailing once a week. "Zahra called. We talked for a long time," he would say. Estranged from his surroundings, he sat before the computer screen and the Web cam for many long hours. Zahra sent Shahrokh pictures of herself. In Zahra, he found a new confidante. She was a symbol of everything he admired and longed for in a woman. She was "Muslim, an Afghan, and caring." Every week, he impatiently waited to hear her voice.

Weeks passed. In August, Shahrokh Khan lost his residence in Tünel. Penniless and unemployed, he looked for a new place. A nearby church sheltered him temporarily. September came. After months of waiting and relying on handouts from others for his everyday survival, Shahrokh Khan started paid employment at a Swiss clothing company in Istanbul. His boss trusted him and used his talents on computers and languages. A sense of usefulness slowly emerged in Shahrokh, and he worked with discipline and loyalty. "My company," he called the Swiss firm.

The job brought new energy to his life. The expensive outfits given to him by his new employer transformed his appearance. He felt normal. Once again he smiled frequently. Soon a talented young Turkish photographer working for a leading French news agency offered to share his apartment with him. Shahrokh Khan moved to a flat in Nişantaşi, one of the most expensive neighborhoods of the city, an exclusive area beyond the reach of most Turks.

He spent his days working at the Swiss company. In the evenings, he chatted online with Zahra or wrote to her. He asked Zahra to visit him in Istanbul, but she could not: still waiting for her green card, she could not travel outside the United States. "Have you talked to Zahra? Tell her to come here for a visit after she gets her green card," he told me a number of times.

Shahrokh Khan's insistence on getting Zahra to Istanbul began to concern me. Was he using Zahra? Was his love for Zahra a convenient way of reaching the United States? For a time I was full of doubt about his affection for her, but my worries disappeared when I saw the delight on his face at the mention of her name. And I became convinced of his love when, visiting his home on the anniversary of the death of his mother and siblings, I saw large prints of Zahra's photos hung on the wall of his room.

Fall 2003 was Shahrokh Khan's happiest time in Istanbul. He had found a student who wanted private lessons in English. Teaching twice a week and working at the Swiss company, he now earned enough money to buy new outfits, chat online more frequently, and even send a bouquet of red roses to Zahra on Valentine's Day.

"Love changes everything in life. No matter how much you suffer, when someone loves you—someone whom you have not even seen in person—everything changes," he told me.

In December, though, despite liking and trusting Shahrokh Khan, the Swiss company began to fear the repercussions of hiring illegal migrants, so they gave him a month's salary and dismissed him. Soon afterward, the student stopped calling for English lessons.

Since Shahrokh Khan had no job, the frequency of his visits to Internet cafés declined, and Zahra began to call less often.

"How is Zahra?" I would ask.

"She must be busy with her studies. We don't talk very often," he would reply. "Do you have any news from her?"

As the weeks passed, he began to realize that things were different between them. "People change in time," he mused. "We never met in person. Her interest may be changing. She's in New York City. Many exciting things happen there. Who knows?" he said sadly. He had not spoken to her for more than a month.

Shahrokh stopped smiling. The sad and frightened look I had seen in him during our first meeting returned. He asked me about Zahra anxiously: "Did she write to you? Did you call her lately? Did she mention me?"

In February, Shahrokh Khan's photographer friend and flatmate vacated the apartment and moved back to his family house.

Shahrokh was homeless again. Putting up ads at the university, he found a small place that he shared with three exchange students from the United States. Folding the pictures of Zahra, he moved to his new place and waited.

Months passed. Soon it was a year since Shahrokh Khan's friend-ship with Zahra had begun, but now there were no phone calls, and long gaps followed every e-mail exchange. One afternoon, meeting at the Neslişah Café, I asked him about the importance of Zahra in his life. "You never met Zahra. What made her so special to you?" I asked.

"That was a very good influence. Especially, sentimentally, you feel a little comfortable. You need to share your ideas with somebody. I used to talk a lot in my school [in Pakistan]. I used to talk a lot in my hostel. Since I came to Turkey, I think I haven't talked as much as what I said in one week in Pakistan. [There] I talked to my teachers, other students. I spoke to people around me. I would talk to every-body.

"Here, I didn't even have anybody to share my ideas with. So the world was very limited for me. I would have gone crazy if I did not recover myself. I would have gone. So I talked to Zahra about differ-ent things. That helped me a lot. You share your ideas with someone, even if she is not here. I felt comfortable talking to her. That is what happened.

"I would be happy all the time. It's like you have hope. You're waiting for someone. Waiting to talk to her. Waiting for something good. She always tried to encourage me to forget all those bad things that happened to me, forget them like a bad dream. She would say sometimes, 'I know it isn't easy to forget. But you can at least pretend to be forgetting that.' "

For many months, Shahrokh Khan forgot his past and status in the world. With the loss of his job and the decline in the frequency of contacts from Zahra, he once again remembered.

This was May 2004. Shahrokh Khan was still in Istanbul. Still illegal.

Roberto

In 2002, Turkey was at the peak of its worst economic crisis in years, following a massive capital flight and a drastic decline in the value of the Turkish lira. The sharp contrast between poverty and wealth in the country was vividly apparent in Istanbul. Many in the city's poorest and most overcrowded neighborhoods suffered from the steady decline in the value of the national currency, unemployment, and inflation. But in Istanbul there were also new and modern high-rises, fancy financial centers, and a burgeoning tourism industry.

Escaping poverty and economic crisis, many came to Istanbul from the Turkish heartland in the 1980s and after. Among those resettling in Istanbul were the Kurds, who were escaping a devastating war in southeastern Turkey. They left Van, Diyarbakır, and other towns and villages, moved to Istanbul, and settled in Tarlabaşı, Aksaray, and other ghettolike neighborhoods of the city.

"I'm a refugee too. They came to my village, burned my home, destroyed everything we had; I can't go back," Ahmed, a thirty-year-old Kurdish resident of Tarlabaşı, told me in a teahouse. Tears in his eyes, he told me about his village, located in the mountains. He remembered catching fish from the fresh waters of the lake nearby. That was before the war. Now the mountain is mined. The road to the village is a death trap.

Not long ago, Tarlabaşı was home to well-to-do Greeks who had settled in Istanbul. But by the 1970s, most Greeks had left the neighborhood, and with their departure, the neighborhood lost its vitality, and many homes were abandoned. Today, though neglected and run-down, the beautiful facades, high ceilings, and wide and artfully constructed stairways of some of Tarlabaşı's old buildings still testify to its affluent past.

Many Kurds arrived in Tarlabaşı in the 1980s. Some bought small homes. Others lived in tenements or squatted in abandoned homes. A few, those able to put together a little capital, started small businesses; they opened corner stores, electronics shops, bakeries, and teahouses. They brought to Tarlabaşı their old professions and their old ways of survival.

Living in a flat near Tarlabaşı, I often visited the neighborhood for its Kurdish bakeries. The smell of freshly baked bread wafting from the brick ovens reminded me of my childhood in Iran. Kurdish hospitality was an added delight. At each visit, the baker would treat me to tea, cheese, and bread. A conversation about Kurdish politics always followed. Nearly every week, I treated myself to a long stroll through Tarlabaşı's magnificent Sunday bazaar with its assortment of many colorful fruits and vegetables, cheeses, and olives of all kinds, artfully laid out on stands and carts. I enjoyed walking through the neighborhood's narrow alleys and hilly streets, taking pictures of children and spending time playing with them, and stopping by shops and greeting their owners.

On one such day in early fall 2002 I stopped by a shoe repair shop with my camera. In a space smaller than a hundred square feet, an old man had set up a home and a workshop. In a far corner of his small room, he sat behind a table with his tools and a few worn-out shoes scattered around him. Boxes of glue and shoe polish were laid open on the table. Shoestrings hung on the wall behind him.

Unshaven and with thinning gray hair, wearing thick glasses and a blue vest over a checkered shirt, the old man gently moved his hand, up and down, a calm and peaceful expression on his face. Under a dim lightbulb hanging from the low ceiling, he hammered a nail into a shoe, then picked up another nail, gently stroked it with the hammer, and tapped it into place. Seeing me at the entrance, he welcomed me into the shop.

Pushed against the wall to his left was a single bed covered with a dirty, colorless blanket. There were two pairs of shoes—his shoes, perhaps—a cardboard box, a glass jar, and a stack of old newspapers under the bed. An old mirror was propped inside a small space

Shoe repairman's home and workshop, Tarlabaşı, Istanbul

carved into the thick wall above the bed. On the sole coat hanger, an old gray jacket, a striped tie, and a white shirt were hung against two large pieces of wrapping paper nailed to the wall. A small red pin decorated the jacket. A silver-colored pen shone in the front pocket.

Not far from the old man's workshop was a sweatshop, a long, narrow, street-level building with two rows of sewing machines. A dozen men and two women (both wearing head scarves) labored in a narrow and crowded workplace. One woman ironed pieces of fabric; the other made hand stitches. At the table next to a sewing machine, a child—perhaps younger than five—played with his father's cell phone. His head down, the father continued to sew, finishing one piece, picking up the next.

In front of a tenement, next door to the sweatshop, an African man stood silently. At times he picked up his cell phone and checked for messages or missed calls. Many walked past him, but there were no greetings or conversation between them. He was young and dressed in light brown pants and a shirt made of the same material. When he was not busy staring at his cell phone, he put his hands in his pockets, occasionally shook his head, and looked indifferent to the movement around him. He was one among the many Africans who came to Istanbul after the 1990s.

Some found temporary homes in Tarlabaşı. The Africans and the Kurds lived in peace, but there was no interaction between them. The Africans stayed in their own overcrowded apartments. The Kurds, some nearly as impoverished as the Africans, lived alongside them, never visiting or engaging them.

Outside Tarlabaşı, the Africans faced a different world. They were noticed and whispered about. Their black skin stood out. Many Turks had seen blacks only in Hollywood movies and on American television shows. Seeing them in their own streets was unsettling.

"Seventy-five percent of them are drug dealers and pimps," a professor of economics in the most prestigious university in Turkey told me.

"They are mostly drug dealers," a student of political economy said.

"Petty drug dealers," a human rights activist declared.

"Africans have it worst. No state wants them," a friend working for a refugee NGO said. She told me that a European embassy employee had once said to her, "All Africans are liars."

At one end of Tarlabaşı stood the famous Taksim Square. This was the heart of Istanbul, home to the luxurious Marmara Hotel, Atatürk Cultural Center, and fancy cafés and bars. Thousands passed through the square every day.

Some forty feet away from Taksim Square, at the edge of the Tarlabaşı neighborhood, a large McDonald's—as in Aksaray—was a magnet for migrants. The place was always packed with customers: Turks, tourists, and the Africans of Tarlabaşı. The migrants met their friends, killed time, made contacts, and planned for their journey.

Most migrants in Istanbul feared the police. Many had seen their share of arrests and extortion. Even Shadi was stopped somewhere in Aksaray and asked to show her passport in an attempt to extort money from her. "I screamed at them, 'What do you want from me? I'm like your mother.' " Shadi looked Turkish, but the police had keen eyes.

The migrants learned to live with this, and avoided the police when they could. After all, this treatment was not official policy. Harassment of the migrants was done as random acts by individual officers. But sometime before my arrival in Istanbul, an abrupt policy shift focused attention on a particular group of migrants: Africans. The presence of illegal blacks on the streets of Istanbul was troubling to many Turks. Not only ordinary people—workers, shopkeepers, students— but also the Turkish establishment seemed to believe the stereotyped image of the African as drug dealer, pimp, and all the rest. Turkey did not know what to do with them. To deport them to Africa wasn't possible. The continent was too far away, deportation too costly.

In July 2001 the Turkish authorities found a solution to their African problem: they made them disappear. "During the first two weeks of July there was a sizeable roundup of foreigners in Istanbul, and possibly in Ankara. The group is said to include more than two hundred fifty Africans, of various nationalities. [They] were separated from other nationalities such as Afghans, Iranians and Iraqis," the UNHCR reported on July 27, 2001.[1]

The Africans were picked up in their homes or on the streets and transferred by buses to the border with Greece. Groups of men, women, and children were boarded onto small ten-person boats and sent off to the Greek side of the Meriç River. The Greek authorities arrested the Africans, detained them, and kept them in jail overnight. Next evening, they secretly took them to the border, placed them on small boats, and returned them to the Turkish side. Once in Turkey, the Turkish authorities arrested the Africans again. They spent nearly a week in prison near the border and were once more deported to

African migrant playing football with Turkish children in Istanbul

Greece. The Greek authorities sent the unwanted Africans back to Turkey a second time. The Turks returned them to Greece, the Greeks dropped them off in Turkey, and on it went. An Amnesty International report said the following:

> On 7 July 2001, approximately 200 people from Nigeria, Ethiopia, Eritrea, Tanzania, Ghana and Sudan were detained in Istanbul in a police "round up" which appears to have focused only on African nationals. . . . It is reported that the detainees were made to sign statements, in Turkish, that they had entered Turkey from Greece. . . . On 14 July 2001, Turkish gendarmes took the group to the border with Greece and reportedly left them there without food or water. They were apparently made to run to the Greek side, and warned by the gendarmes that they would be shot if they turned back.[2]

"Many people died. We were left with nothing, no food, nothing. We spent many nights in a police bus. We were not prepared for the journey," Donald, an African who was deported, told me. Among those deported, there were at least twenty people who had already filed an asylum case with the UNHCR in Turkey, and whose cases were under consideration by the agency. At the time of their deportation, they were under UN protection.

The Africans returned to Istanbul feeling more paranoid and isolated. Fearing harassment and deportation, many stayed in their homes and went out only when absolutely necessary.

Some found a new way out, becoming "Somalis." Somalia had no embassy in Turkey. Its citizens were poor, had no legal representation, and were a burden for the police and Turkish authorities if arrested, so they were often released after a short detention. Also, the police were often kinder to the Muslim Somalis. Consequently, upon arrest, Sudanese, Nigerians, Angolans, and other men and women from across Africa became "Somali." Soon, however, the police caught on to the scheme. They beat a few "Somalis" and threatened them with deportation, hoping to force them to confess to their real nationalities. Many continued to insist that they were Somalis, and eventually the police conceded.

I met one such "Somali" on October 8, 2002. His name was Roberto. He was an illegal migrant living in Tarlabaşı. An American artist living in Istanbul had told him about me. Looking for a way out of Turkey, Roberto agreed to talk to me. To him I was a possible key to the world outside. He made that clear in our first meeting.

I phoned Roberto and asked him to meet me in front of the Marmara Hotel at Taksim Square, but he declined. "No! I am scared of the police. I do not go to these places without a white guy," he said. For our meeting, he suggested the McDonald's off the square.

When I entered the fast-food restaurant I spotted an African sitting alone at a table on the far corner. Roberto looked up and smiled. He was skinny yet muscular, with a bony, intense-looking face and a shaved head. The place was crowded, not suitable for taking out a writing pad and conducting an interview, so I suggested leaving for a place nearby, the Neslişah Café. The café had recently opened and did not yet have a regular clientele, which made it a perfect place for our meeting.

The walk was short, but Roberto seemed troubled. He walked like a fugitive avoiding the authorities and looked visibly suspicious. "I only leave home for important meetings," he told me. His nervous walk affected me; perhaps, I thought, there was a real reason for his fear. I was new in Istanbul and didn't yet know the rules of the game. I became nervous, too, and like Roberto, I avoided eye contact with the police.

Arriving at the café, I chose a table by the window, but a police car parked on the street corner across from the café made Roberto uneasy. He couldn't focus.

"Why are they here?" he asked a number of times.

"This is Istanbul," I replied. "The police are everywhere. They aren't here for you." The streets of Istanbul were full of armed city police, armed traffic police, and armed riot police. The police could not be ignored. Some strolled with their guns in their hands. Others moved around in their cars, clustered in small or large groups.

Roberto remained anxious. My explanations didn't ease his fear. The police car moved from the corner. Others arrived. Hoping not to be noticed, he would slightly turn his head, look at the police through the window, and return to our conversation. I hid my camera to avoid unnecessary attention to our meeting, ordered tea and a *nargile,* and listened to Roberto's story.

Our first meeting was formal. Roberto spoke for nearly three hours; I took notes. No chatting about anything else, no jokes, no laughter. "Can I trust you?" he asked before telling me his life story. "Contact lawyers, or anyone who can help," he pleaded. I told him about my work and why I was interested in his story. Leaning back in his chair, holding his hands together on the table, he began.

Roberto was born in Angola in 1975, the year after Portugal ended its colonization of Angola. Once sold as slaves to Brazil and their other colonies by the Portuguese, the Angolans became victims of a civil war between local rebel leaders and profiteers, aggravated by intervention from the United States, South Africa, the Soviet Union, and Cuba. Two major rebel forces, the Popular Movement for the Liberation of Angola (MPLA) and the National Union for the Total Independence of Angola (UNITA), fought for the control of the ex-colony and its natural resources. On November 11, 1975, the MPLA formed a government and declared Angola an independent country, but soon afterward a civil war erupted that lasted nearly thirty years. Aided by Cuban fighters and Russian arms, the MPLA controlled most of Angola and its oil fields by the mid-1980s. Supported, armed, and financed by the CIA and the government of South Africa, UNITA gained control of Angola's diamond-rich regions.

War became an excuse for robbing the country of its resources. Millions of land mines were laid on farmlands. Violence reached unprecedented levels. In a bloody war that began when Roberto opened his eyes to this world and continued to the day we met in Istanbul, one in every four Angolans became displaced.

In 1984 Roberto became another faceless statistic. He recalled the night the UNITA rebels attacked his village and he became a refugee. He was nine years old.

"We were asleep in the house. All of a sudden the shooting started. There was noise everywhere. We all ran for our lives. Everyone was running. I left the house and followed a group of fleeing villagers. The armed men killed everyone. They killed children and women." In the chaos of running from the gunshots, Roberto was separated from his family. That was the last time he saw them.

"I know my father was killed in the war. My brother and sister disappeared," he said quietly. I asked about his mother. He didn't know what had happened to her. His one remaining family member was an older brother, who had made it to Germany and later to the United States.

Roberto had followed the other strangers running for their lives. They walked for days and nights, passed dead bodies along the way, swam across rivers, ate "raw wild animal meat," and finally reached Sierra Leone. He did not remember how long he was on the road.

In Sierra Leone, Roberto had met a "kind and wealthy Angolan" who took him under his wing and sent him to school. Helped by this man, he learned English in a school in Freetown.

"I learned English to be able to go to America someday," he said, smiling for the first time since we had left McDonald's for the café.

For six years Roberto had lived in relative peace in Sierra Leone. This was the longest time he lived in one country after fleeing Angola. In 1991, a devastating war broke out in Sierra Leone. Like the civil war in his place of birth, this too was a war for the control of the country's diamond reserves. The Liberian-backed rebel forces, the Revolutionary United Front (RUF), began a brutal war. Diamonds mined in the areas under their control financed the rebels' war against the government and their campaign of terror against civilians. Nothing was sacred in the bloody struggle for diamonds.

Under pressure by outside forces, the central government, the National Provisional Ruling Council (NPRC), agreed to hold general elections in 1996. To counter the NPRC's campaign slogan, "The future is in your hands," the rebels began cutting off people's hands, a practice that continued and became more frequent after the elections.

Roberto had to run again.

In 1996, for the second time in his life, he fled civil war and violence. Once again he was on the road. Aboard a Nigerian ship, Roberto and more than a thousand other Africans arrived at a UNHCR camp in Nigeria. A new life had now begun for Roberto—life in a refugee camp.

"They fed us well. The food was good," Roberto said, but he was idle and restless. Fed and sheltered, nonetheless he suffered from boredom. His days were long and uneventful. He was twenty-one years old, was willing to "work any hard job," and wanted to live like a "normal" person. Living in the camp, he didn't feel normal. He was wasting away.

Roberto and some Liberian and Angolan friends ventured into

the outside world, searching for work and the opportunity to be normal. A man named Dave, "a very good man," suggested that they leave the camp and move to Lagos in Nigeria. They agreed. In Lagos the African friends were introduced to a man who housed them for half a year and helped them find work off-loading cement from big trailers. This was now 1998.

Having been able to earn some money, Roberto and his friends sought to leave for the West. Three attempts to leave Africa on a ship to Europe failed, each time costing the men $200 apiece.

I heard Roberto repeat the story of his life with the same details on many occasions. Each time, he became emotional at certain parts: his voice changed, and his eyes became filled with tears. At other times in our meetings, he quietly withdrew from his surroundings, overwhelmed by memories of his past.

"Where are you, Roberto?" I would ask.

A sad smile on his face, he would say, "I was thinking about my friends who died on the journey."

He told me the story of two friends, Andrea and Elias. The three of them and some other friends had moved to a farm in Nigeria, where they grew watermelons, yams, and other cash crops. They labored hard for nearly two years and survived by selling their output at the market.

"We worked hard, hard, hard," he said, animated and excited. "They were good guys, very good guys," Roberto said about Andrea and Elias. With tears in his eyes, he told me about Andrea's sudden death in 1999 from an unknown infection. Less than a month later, Elias died of the same infection.

"They were humble boys. We played together," Roberto said, looking away to hide his emotions.

With the death of Andrea and Elias, the men decided to leave Nigeria for the West. There were many failed attempts. They were once stranded in the large and deadly desert in Libya. "Our Jeep broke down after only a short distance in the desert. We would have all died if we had gone further. God saved us."

By 2001, the war in Sierra Leone had ended, and the men returned to safety in Sierra Leone. Roberto took a job at a department store, saving money for his journey. In December of that year he and thirty-four other Africans paid a smuggler $200 each and boarded a ship headed for Europe.

"We were so happy that we had finally made it. We were all going to Europe."

The men were housed on the lowest deck of the ship. For many weeks, the ship traveled around Africa and Europe, loading and offloading cargo in many countries. Living in the dark, without seeing the light even once, the men lost all sense of time. "We didn't know that we had been there for months."

Throughout the journey, Africans in groups of three to five were taken out of the hold and dropped off on different shores in the dark of night. By May 2002, there were only a dozen Africans left on the ship. On May 22 they were put on a float and sent off to the shore. They had reached Greece, the captain told them. After long years of life in poverty and war, and many failed attempts to reach freedom, Europe was finally in sight. The float reached the shore. The Africans quietly cheered.

"We were so happy. We embraced each other. Our dream had come through."

Roberto and friends had planned to go to the UNHCR, register as refugees, get jobs, and start a normal life. They spent the night in the bush, waiting for the light of day. When the night ended, the highway signs and the language spoken by people betrayed the identity of the place the Africans so joyfully had embraced as Europe. They had been dropped off in Turkey.

Roberto and his friends were in Izmir, a town on the Aegean coast. Disoriented from months of isolation in darkness, and confused about where they had landed, the Africans wandered around. Soon they were picked up by the gendarmes and taken into custody.

"They were very kind. They took us to the hospital and fed us well," Roberto said. "Yes, they fed us well."

While in custody, the Africans met a group of Iranian, Iraqi, and Afghan refugees who had been arrested while trying to leave Turkey for Greece. They told the Africans of opportunities in Istanbul.

"We didn't know anything about Istanbul. They told us about other blacks in Istanbul. We were glad," Roberto said.

The Africans pleaded with the police to send them to Istanbul, where they could be with other men and women from their home continent.

On June 12, 2002, the men arrived in Tarlabaşı. A Nigerian gave them shelter in his house for $100 apiece—fourteen men in two bedrooms. The men chipped in 1 million TL a day each—about 70 cents—for food, cooked and ate together, and remained inside for the most part. Roberto had left Africa for a better life, but he was now trapped in one of the poorest neighborhoods of Istanbul. He was not free. The Turks frightened him. The police made him tremble. Neighbors looked at him with suspicion, he thought. Day in and day out, he stayed behind closed doors and dreamed of his grand escape.

He contacted smugglers and other African migrants preparing to leave Turkey. Different routes were studied. Some suggested leaving for Bulgaria. Others told Roberto about Greece and the advantages of landing somewhere in the European Union. After days of discussion, a decision was made.

In a convoy organized by a Nigerian human smuggler, eighteen Africans left Tarlabaşı for Bodrum, a rich town by the Aegean Sea, with some of the best beaches in Turkey, expensive nightclubs and restaurants, luxury hotels, and fancy villas and yacht clubs. The final destination was the Greek island of Hios, only a few miles away. The Africans arrived in the dark of the night and rested in a secluded safe house away from the town center. A day passed. When the sun set the next day, they quietly left their hideout and walked to the beach. This was June 28, 2002.

Far from the glittering lights and the loud music of the nightclubs, a boat waited for the Africans. They sat tight in the boat as it left the shore, slowly entering the deep waters of the sea. Soon the migrants were in Greek waters. The island was in sight: "We were so close. We could see the city lights." As he recounted this part of his story, Roberto was more excited than before; his voice was louder than ever. He wanted me to understand that after years of waiting, he had been so close to Europe.

Before they reached shore, a Greek coast guard boat spotted the Africans. Its powerful lights lit up the sea and their tiny vessel. Relieved to be in Europe, the Africans waved and cheered. They were to be taken in and registered as asylum seekers, Roberto thought. Suddenly their joy turned into confusion as the coast guard boat speeded up and crashed into the small boat carrying the Africans. The boat sank.

"They ran us over with a boat as big as this restaurant. We shouted, begged for help," Roberto said, gesturing. Looking at me with reddened eyes, he said, "Men and women jumped off the boat into the sea. Everyone was screaming. We cried for help. There were other boats around us. No one came to our rescue. Twelve of us died. Five others and I survived. I knew how to swim."

The survivors held on to pieces of the wrecked boat for five hours. Many fishing boats passed by. Pantomiming waving to an imaginary boat, Roberto told me, "We shouted for help, 'Hey, hey, hey.' " No one came to their assistance. After five hours in the water, Roberto and the other survivors were rescued by a tourist boat and handed over to the Turkish authorities in Bodrum.

Sitting before me in the café, Roberto pulled out a carefully folded newspaper clipping, opened it, and laid it on the table. "This is me in the picture." The daily *Radikal* reported the incident on June 29, 2002. Six frightened Africans wrapped in towels were shown in a picture. The story reported twelve Africans dead in an "accident" at sea. Six "Somalis" survived. There was no mention of the Greek coast guard boat. "Did you tell the reporters about the Greek boat?" I asked Roberto. He said the Africans had explained the tragedy at length. Later a friend told me, "The papers are careful. They don't want to be stirring up trouble between Greece and Turkey." These were sensitive times in the relations between Turkey and Greece. After many years of tension over Turkey's occupation of the northern part of the island of Cyprus, a new era of rapprochement had begun between the two countries, which were taking part in multilateral negotiations for the resolution of the Cyprus question. At the same time, Turkey was actively engaged in obtaining a date for its formal accession negotiations with the European Union, and angering Greece, an EU member, was not advisable.

After nearly a month in police custody, Roberto and the other survivors escaped and returned to Istanbul. Escape was easy. Keeping the Africans in jail was a burden for the local gendarmes, who had to feed them and give them medical care. For the most part, the gendarmes closed their eyes to the illegal migrants' efforts to escape, preferring to let the authorities in Istanbul deal with the problem. Like many migrants before them, Roberto and his African friends walked out of detention without attracting any attention. They were free to go.

Roberto didn't drink alcohol or smoke cigarettes. He didn't follow many of the Africans who lived in Tarlabaşı to the clubs off Istiklal Street where they danced all night ("We feel equal to others on the dance floor," a Nigerian told me). Roberto didn't talk about women, either. He remained focused on one objective: someday reaching the United States of America. "This is the country I have been dreaming about all my life. I want to get married, have children, and live there for the rest of my life," he told me. "I do not know how to explain it. America is the end of everything."

I once told Roberto about the possibility of my leaving the United States and moving to another country. He was baffled, unable to believe my seemingly irrational statement. He stared at me for a few

Old man with the scale greeting me in Istanbul in September, 2002

Shahrokh Khan

Afghan refugee in Patras

Woman in an Istanbul Ghetto

Afghans in a tent city in Greece

Roberto

short seconds, then let out a short scream, laughed loudly, shook his head, and said, "I will do anything to be in America."

I was Roberto's sole non-African friend in the world, and his "big brother." I was the "white guy" he trusted, and one of the few people in the world he told the details of his life history to. He would call my cell phone but hang up before I could answer—a free way to let me know he wished to talk to me. I would return the call immediately. We would meet, drink tea, and eat a small meal at times. He sent me a text message when I left Istanbul for a brief visit to Van, wishing me "a safe journey."

Returning to Istanbul, I found Roberto restless, unhappier than before. "I have to leave," he said every time we met. Istanbul felt suffocating to him. He wanted to work and pay for his food. "I can do many things." Not able to work, he had to rely on handouts for food. "I am not a beggar," he often said.

"He is a very nice man. He feeds me," he said about a Ghanaian in Istanbul who housed and protected him.

"God bless you. This will feed all of us for a month," he cried when I gave him a meager amount of money one time. Wishing not to burden me, he would choose the cheapest food when I took him out for a meal.

He began planning for another journey. "I will not stay here. I hate Tarlabaşı," he told me. One day in November 2002, Roberto called my phone. When I returned his call, he said, "A friend called me from Bulgaria. He will take care of my journey to Bulgaria. He contacted a reliable smuggler in Istanbul. We have to wait some time. The smuggler will call me when the time is right." The smuggler was to be paid upon Roberto's safe arrival in Sofia. There was no risk of trickery and cheating, he told me. All arrangements had been made for his secure departure.

A week passed. The smuggler didn't call. Roberto remained hopeful. "He has to get a group together for the journey."

On November 22 Roberto wanted to meet with me, so we rendezvoused at the McDonald's later that afternoon. Roberto was unusually jubilant. He was childlike, excited. We embraced. "I am leaving Turkey," he said. The smuggler had called that morning. A group of twenty-five was to leave Istanbul for the border with Bulgaria. Roberto was told to prepare for the journey.

"I will take bread and water and be ready for a few days of trekking. Once on the other side, I will separate from the rest in case the gendarmes spot us. I will hide in the bushes, wait till everyone is gone, and run in the morning. I will walk, walk, walk. . . . I will get there. I know I will."

I cautioned Roberto and told him of the risks involved in the journey. Still, he was determined to leave. "I will not come back to this country. I will take a knife with me and kill myself if I get arrested at the border."

That was the last time I saw Roberto in Istanbul. The next morning, he was on his way to the border.

Nur

The year 2003 brought the arrival of a large number of Sudanese to Turkey. Leaving Sudan for Libya, some boarded large ships and arrived in Istanbul via the Mediterranean and the Sea of Marmara. Others traveled to Lebanon and Syria and entered Turkey through its southern borders, aided by human smugglers at different stages. Once in Istanbul, they were taken to safe houses in Aksaray and Kumkapı.

I met a group of ten Sudanese, new arrivals in Istanbul, in April 2003. I had gone to IIMP to see Helen Bartlett about the case of an Iranian asylum seeker, but my plans changed when I arrived and found the office dealing with the Africans' arrival. "Will you talk to them?" she asked me. I entered the room where Bartlett's assistant was with the Sudanese, registering them and preparing hospital visit forms for those in need of immediate medical care.

Holding their young children in their arms, they had stayed in the darkness in the hold of a ship, crowded in with many other people, for fourteen days and nights. On the orders of the human smugglers, the parents fed sleeping pills to their young babies. For fourteen long days and nights, the babies did not utter a sound. They remained asleep, protecting the adults on their voyage to the West.

Standing at the door, I watched the men and women in the room. Some struggled over the English-language forms before them; others were resting. There were women in head scarves, men in worn-out clothes. Switching between Arabic and English, a tall man—who looked to be in his late twenties, a bit overweight, with sparse facial hair—helped the others with their registration forms. When he noticed me at the door, he came toward me with a warm smile. "Abdul," he introduced himself, shaking my hand. Taking me around the room, Abdul introduced me to his wife, Nidal. Wearing a baggy long-sleeved shirt and jeans, her hair hidden under a head scarf, Nidal greeted me and offered me a chair. Speaking broken English, she pointed to a small hyperactive boy, jumping up and down, picking up chairs twice his size, moving things around. "My son, Muhammad," she said. Eleven months old, Muhammad had big eyes, chubby cheeks, curly hair, and a disarming smile.

Nidal showed me a book of drawings and artwork she had published in Sudan. From time to time she would pick up her boy, who was creating havoc in the room. At one point I set Muhammad on my lap, but soon he was on the floor again, moving the chairs around and amusing the adults.

Getting help from her husband to translate, Nidal told me of her job teaching in refugee camps in Sudan. She taught the children orphaned by the war that began in 1983, merely the latest in a series of conflicts that had begun shortly after joint British-Egyptian rule ended in Sudan in 1956. When the colonizers departed, they left

Nur and Nidal

behind a history of favoritism and differential treatment of their sub-
jects. After independence, the favored Arabs of the north imposed
Arabic as the national language and wished to control the other, non-
Arab ethnic groups in the south. Aided by a long, collective memory
of enslavement by northern Arab traders, the non-Arab, non-
Muslim south rejected the policy of Arabization of the new independent country.

   In 1983 the fighting escalated when the National Islamic Front
government instituted an even more forceful Islamization of the society, including strict imposition of sharia law. Ordinary people,

both Muslims and Christians, Arabs and Africans, were assaulted. Many had their homes destroyed and families murdered, and they became displaced. Others left due to the poverty and famine caused by the protracted war. Two decades later, the dead totaled more than two million, with many more displaced and homeless. Nearly four million people—80 percent of the estimated population of southern Sudan—became displaced at one time or another since the mid-1990s, with about half leaving the country. The rest fled in search of a safer place within Sudan's borders, and the country became home to the largest internally displaced population in the world.

Both Nidal and Abdul taught at a refugee camp for the internally displaced. Pressured by the government, they were asked to help convert the Christian orphans to Islam. When they refused, Abdul was detained and tortured. "I am a Muslim and Arab. But I would not take part in this," Abdul told me, showing me a big scar on his left leg from the beatings and torture in detention.

It was during my conversation with Nidal and Abdul that, looking across the room, I noticed a small, beautiful woman holding a little girl in her arms, smiling and staring at us with radiant dark eyes. She wore a gray and white head scarf knotted in the front. I nodded at her and pulled out a chair, inviting the woman to join our conversation.

Her name was Nur. A Sudanese with a bachelor's degree in management, she had left Sudan with her husband and her one-year-old daughter. "This is Samah," she said, indicating the girl in her arms. Large discolored spots covered the child's skin, a reaction to fourteen days of constant drugging.

Having told me about her education and job in Sudan—the basic questions I asked her after introducing myself   she looked me in the eye and said, "Where is your family?" I spoke a little of my history, and then she asked, "When was the last time you visited Iran?"

For the first time after months of meeting with migrants, I had before me a woman who inquired about *my* life, *my* place of birth, and *my* reasons for being away from home. Not consumed with her long journey at sea, she asked about Iran, its people and culture, its natural beauties. I told Nur about the beautiful mosques in Isfahan, the Caspian Sea, and the mountains surrounding Tehran. She listened to my words attentively, asked more questions, and said, "I hope to visit Iran someday."

In coming to Istanbul, Nur left behind an ailing old father and a brother waiting for Nur's financial support from Europe. Three years before leaving Sudan, she was married to her cousin Yussuf, a manual laborer with no education. Their entire extended family were members of the Nuba ethnic group, nomads who migrated with their animals as the seasons changed.

I asked Nur about her childhood years in Sudan. In broken English, using her hands and asking for help from a friend, Nur described to me her home in Sudan: a triangle-shaped tent made from dried grass. "The material was very strong. Rain could not go through it . . . very strong," she explained. "When it rained, we moved for the animals," looking for new pastures to graze. "We lived quietly. Every week, we went to a big market to sell our animals and buy new animals. We had a simple life. We had a big family. We lived together. In the evenings, we made music and danced. That was our custom," she explained. Gracefully moving her fingers and hands, she told me about their dance routines, the anklets the women wore, and the musical sound the anklets made when the dancers pounded the ground with their feet.

Few people in Nur's extended family continued their education. "The boys in my family only finished the primary school. After that, they helped their fathers with the animals." That was the story of Yussuf and Nur's brother. Grazing animals was all they knew. Nur was an exception. She was the top student in her class, and her father and grandfather went against the old tribal traditions and decided to send her to high school, and later to the university. She was sent to Khartoum to live with a friend of her grandfather's and attend school. Nur became the first person in her family with a university degree.

Two years after her marriage to Yussuf, Samah was born. A year later, they traveled to the Red Sea town of Suakin. "We were put in a small room in the bottom of a big ship. No one saw us." The smuggler was a ship employee. "Nobody could go outside. The small people [children] could not cry." Two weeks later, holding little Samah in her arms, Nur and the other Sudanese joined the migrant community in Istanbul.

Like so many migrants who arrived in Istanbul, Nur applied for asylum with the UNHCR, but following the male-dominant culture of her place of birth, she filed for protection as Yussuf's dependent. It was Yussuf and his case that would determine the family's chance for asylum and their future. The UNHCR staff in Ankara interviewed Yussuf for two hours. He failed to understand the questions asked or to make a convincing case for asylum. The case was rejected.

Hoping for another chance, Nur requested the opening of a new case based on her own life history in Sudan. In an appeal letter that she wrote to the UNHCR with my help, Nur described her reasons for leaving Sudan.

I have experienced persecution because of my tribe, and my non-willingness to join a political organization supporting the government of Sudan. I am from the Nuba tribe, a minority group of people with darker skin and life habits different from the ruling group in the country.

While studying in the university, I was pressured to join a Muslim student organization, the United Muslim Students. Not wishing to be political and not knowing the exact activities of the organization, I refused to join. This was not taken lightly. They continued to pressure me. I refused time and again. The

refusal to join came to haunt me when I graduated from
university and applied for a job in my town.

   I applied for employment in a government-owned com-
pany. . . . My application was declined. . . . I applied for a
teaching position in Kosi near my home. Once again, I was de-
nied employment. Instead, I was dispatched to a small town far
away from my home. Once there, I developed a serious throat
illness. I begged to be allowed to return home for medication.
My request was rejected.

   I taught for three years. While I worked harder than other
teachers, I was paid only once in three months. Meanwhile, my
illness became more severe. As a result, I was finally allowed to
teach in Kosi. But the same problems followed me there. My
headmaster made me work many hours more than other teach-
ers, harassed me, and shouted at me. The teachers scorned me. I
worked for four years under unbearable conditions. . . .

   Life was becoming unbearable for me. In my own country,
I did not feel normal.

The UNHCR rejected her request for refugee status, deciding
that the discrimination she suffered in Sudan did not amount to persecution.

With this rejection, Nur lost the chance to enter Europe legally.
She began planning and waiting for the right time and right border
to cross. This was late October 2003, and Nur was three months
pregnant.

I first visited Nur's house in Aksaray on a rainy evening in November 2003. Walking up the narrow stairway, I knocked on the heavy
metal door on the third floor. The door opened, and a young
Sudanese welcomed me to the stuffy living room.

Nur lived with other Sudanese, Sri Lankans, Ethiopians, and Er-
itreans in a two-bedroom flat that served as a safe house. In a room

shared with five others, she slept on a single bed with Yussuf and Samah. Others used the bed as a couch during the day. The bedrooms were small but tidy, and with four beds to each room, there was no space to move around. Fourteen men and women shared a single bathroom and a kitchen smaller than nine square feet.

Located in a back alley in Aksaray, the house was rented out to migrants by a Sudanese "connection"—a smuggler working with a network of bigger smugglers operating on the route to Greece. There were fewer than a dozen Sudanese and Somali "connections" in Aksaray and the neighboring quarters of Kumkapı. They sheltered migrants in tenements, and delivered them to big smugglers from Turkey and Georgia in groups of five or more. Joining men and women organized by other "connections," the migrants were transported to the Meriç River in groups of twenty, or put on boats for a sea voyage to one of the nearby Greek islands.

The migrants deposited money with their "connection." This was advance payment for safe delivery. Leaving one "connection" for another or trying to outsmart the smuggler was not advisable—at least it cost the migrant a noticeable part of the deposit, and at worst it could lead to violence.

Inside the flat, men and women greeted me with smiles, shook my hand, and gave me a place on a bed. A young man, a seventeen-year-old Sudanese, ran to the corner store and returned with a can of soda for me. All were eager to tell their stories.

A man in his late twenties, Khalid, coughed nonstop as he introduced himself. "Welcome, brother. Thank you for coming," he said. I asked about his cough. "I cannot sleep at night," he said, as the coughing kept him awake. He had no money to buy medicine. Showing me a prescription as a sign of the authenticity of his ailment, he asked for help, a chance to buy his medicine or perhaps see a doctor again.

Muhammad, a tall, skinny young Sudanese, showed me his inhaler. Suffering from chronic asthma, he had no means to visit a doctor and buy a replacement. He left Sudan three years before coming to Istanbul. For eight days and nights, accompanying a caravan of clandestine migrants, the young man crossed the desert to Libya. Some died before they could make it out of the desert. Muhammad lost two friends to dehydration. "The sun," he said, pointing to the sky, showing me the killer of his friends.

A sixteen-year-old boy in a white T-shirt sat on the bed across from me. When I asked why he left Sudan, he giggled with a friend but offered no reply. When I took out my camera to take pictures of the flat and its residents, the boy followed me around and wanted to appear in every picture. I asked him again why he was in Aksaray, away from home. No answer.

Lydia, also sixteen, with beautiful eyes and long braided hair, cracked open the door to the bedroom by the entrance. Looking out from the small opening, she watched the rest in the living room. "May I take a picture?" I asked her. She smiled, remained in the opening at the doorway, and waited. A teenage girl from Ethiopia joined Lydia in the frame. They looked shyly at the camera lens as I snapped their picture, then they returned to the bedroom, shutting the door behind them.

Weeks had passed since Nur's case had been rejected. The tight border control by the Greeks meant that leaving was not possible. In the meantime, Samah's skin rash had returned. She was in and out of doctors' offices and hospitals. The hospital visits were free of charge, but medication was not. "I cannot buy medicine for Samah," Nur told me after one of her hospital visits. "This is not a good place for a child. She is always sick."

The residents of the flat took care of Samah. When boredom and sadness prevailed, Samah lightened up their mood. They took her out, played with her. They bought her candy and milk. Samah rarely cried. Quiet and calm, she observed others. Nur believed Samah sensed the adults' mood. Staring at them with her big eyes, talking to them in her child language, she would make them smile. They would pick her up, put her on their laps. Samah would laugh and kiss them.

After I left the flat in the safe house, a Sri Lankan—short, clad in a sari and head scarf, and older than the others—ran after me. She was going to open a case for asylum with the UNHCR and wanted me to help her win her case. I explained my lack of power to influence her case. "Help me," she repeated.

On my second visit, not much had changed. There were a few newcomers mixed with those who had lived there for weeks or months. Some were boys and girls as young as sixteen, others men in their thirties. Many suffered from illnesses: respiratory problems, infections, and tuberculosis. Many smoked.

"This is the first piece of food I had today," a young man told me, showing the small piece of bread in his hand.

Minutes later, Khalid arrived with a large garbage bag filled with day-old bread from an Aksaray restaurant. The hungry migrants were overjoyed. Big chunks of bread in their mouths, they laughed and posed for my camera. "They gave us their leftover food during Ramadan," Khalid said. "We could eat once a day. But now, we can only get some bread from them at times. All we eat is bread and tea."

I asked Khalid to accompany me to a nearby corner store. Picking up potatoes and other staples, Khalid turned to me and said, "Can we buy some milk and two bananas for Samah?" Now a year and a half old, Samah hardly ate any nutritious food. "She loves bananas," he told me.

The shopping finished, we went back to the safe house with bags of potatoes, eggs, and tomatoes. "We can have a warm meal tonight," a young Sudanese said. Some rushed to the kitchen to prepare the meal of the day; others sat on the beds in the living room. Keeping me company, they told me of their stories and their cases, asked me for advice about how to win the heart of their interviewers at the UNHCR.

I was told the story of Hassan, the most recent arrival from Sudan. Born to a Syrian father and a Sudanese mother, Hassan was stateless. He came into this world in a small village in northern Sudan. A village elder made a note about his birth in a book, but no birth certificate was issued. His father left Sudan for Syria when Hassan was only ten years old. His mother passed away when he was seventeen. Sudanese officials refused to issue him a passport to visit his father in Syria. He was not a Sudanese, they told him. Paying a smuggler, he left Sudan and entered Syria clandestinely. He sought refuge with his father, now married with children in Syria.

"You are not my son," the father said, telling Hassan that in fact he was the son of a Sudanese village man. Rejected by the man he had thought was his father, Hassan bought the service of a smuggler, crossed the border to Turkey, and thus arrived at the safe house in Aksaray.

"Is Hassan's a good case?" Nur asked me.

While Nur waited in the safe house, her old throat ailment returned. A swollen gland in her throat grew large. Doctors recommended surgery. More than four months pregnant, she was diagnosed anemic. Her situation deteriorated over time.

"She gets very sick during her pregnancy. Her legs swell. She becomes very weak," a friend told me, pleading to find a way to save Nur.

With her ailment and pregnancy, and carrying Samah, trekking would have been deadly; even many healthy and strong men had failed in the past. Still, Nur was ready to try her chances. "I'll walk a long distance if I have to." She wished to leave the overcrowded flat in Aksaray and save Samah and her unborn child.

December came. More Sudanese arrived. The flat in Aksaray became more crowded. Then they discovered that the Sudanese "connection" had failed to pay the landlord the rent for three consecutive months and Nur and all the other waiting migrants were evicted. Fourteen men and women and a child became homeless in Aksaray. Another Sudanese "connection," a "kind man" who rented a house in neighboring Kumkapı, came to their rescue. They moved to a tenement already housing twenty-five migrants. Nur invited me to the new safe house.

"We are forty people there. The place is much dirtier than our old flat. There is no room to sleep. Please come to see our new place."

The "connection" questioned my motives and trustworthiness but at last gave his consent for my visit. On the appointed day I met Khalid and another Sudanese by the McDonald's on Aksaray Avenue. After a fifteen-minute walk through the back streets, we were in front of their building. "This is our home," Khalid said, introducing me to the half dozen or so Africans—the "connection" and the migrants—standing in front of the building.

"Press?" an African asked.

"A friend," I replied.

Shaking my hand, he welcomed me to the building.

A long stairway faced the entrance to the building. To its left stood a communal kitchen. There were no other rooms on the first floor. Walking up the narrow stairway to the second floor, I found myself in a small space, a platform crowded with bags and a tall man sleeping under a blanket. On the third floor I saw a single room in which men were playing cards, killing time. A man was sleeping on a bed. The room was full of blankets, backpacks, and plastic bags. Men and women moved in and out.

On the third floor was a narrow room facing the street. More than ten Sudanese and others sat tightly squeezed on three single beds and a blanket on the floor. Familiar faces—Muhammad, Yussuf, and others—came to greet me. All sat in their winter coats. Nur welcomed me to her home. Samah played with the adults. Three women from a nearby house were visiting the crowded room as well. Jokes and laughter erupted. A young Sudanese, perhaps in her teens, sat in her hooded sweatshirt and windbreaker, smiling gently and quietly watching the laughing crowd.

A man inquired about life in Europe.

"Tell us about Greece," a woman asked.

"Do they have doctors for the refugees?"

"Tell us more. You have been there. You can help us by telling us more about there."

"How are the police in Greece?"

"Do they give asylum to Africans?"

"How are the camps? Can we work there?"

"Have you heard the news about a possible peace accord in Sudan? That will be bad for us. No country will give us asylum."

"Please bring other people to see our condition."

The men and women in the room were from a variety of ethnic groups in Sudan, with different religions. Their warlords fought in Sudan, but here in Kumkapı they lived in peace. "We are all friends. No fighting here," Nur said.

Three days after my visit, the police raided a nearby house, confiscated cell phones, beat a few men with their batons, and left. After that, all visits to Nur's house were banned. Assembling outside the building became prohibited. Unnecessary movements in and out of the house had to stop.

"I have to find a way to go to Greece," Nur repeated in moments of despair. "Will you put Samah in your bag and take her with you?" she asked me before one of my trips to Athens. Others laughed and exclaimed, "Take us with you. We won't make any noise."

My flat in Istanbul was on the top of a hill, within walking distance of the Bosphorus and the Sea of Marmara. Standing by my building on clear, sunny days, one could see the Prince Islands and gaze at the endless blue waters of the Sea of Marmara. "There, look over there, that is Greece. I can see it," Yussuf said every time he visited my flat. "These are the Greek islands. Let's swim. We'll be there soon." Nur and others laughed.

Everyone wanted to leave for Greece, but traveling had become exceptionally difficult after the summer of 2003. Many attempted to leave, but most were arrested and sent back to Aksaray and Kumkapı. Failure was common. In winter, all attempts were halted. The Turks and the Greeks were determined to crack down on human smuggling from Turkey. For Turkey, the tightening of the borders in 2003 was a response to criticisms from the European Union about Turkey's inability to stop illegal migration. A 2002 European Commission document stated the following:

> Some progress has been made with regard to visa policy. . . .
> New border posts have been set up and sea patrols have been introduced. Nevertheless, the Commission has asked Turkey to adopt a strategy to control and manage borders. . . . Turkey is still a country of destination and transit for trafficking in human beings and its legislation falls short of the necessary minimum rules to eliminate this illegality.[3]

Turkey submitted an application for full membership in the European Union (then called the European Economic Community) in 1987. More than a decade later, in 1999, the European Union accepted Turkey as a candidate state. When I arrived in Istanbul in the fall of 2002, Turkey was waiting for a vote by the European Union to assign a date to start formal negotiations for its accession to the Union. The vote came in December 2002, and no date was assigned; December 2004 was set as the time for a new vote. Turkey became entangled in a web of new policies and official practices in order to prepare for the next vote. The constitution was amended, and new laws were passed to change Turkey's human rights image and meet the European Union's criteria for membership. Among the new practices were Turkey's efforts to block illegal crossings to Greece.

Turkey used additional human and financial resources—domestic funds and grants by the European Union—for controlling its borders. The gendarmes practically sealed off the land borders in northern Turkey, and so the smugglers instead focused on the sea route in the south. But even that became difficult, as the gendarmes or police arrested most migrants before they took to the sea.

Similar policies and procedures were carried out on the other side of the border in Greece. For the Greeks, stopping the flow of illegal migrants was a part of a long-term European Union migration policy. But in the months preceding the summer of 2004, a new and more immediate concern shaped Greece's approach to its borders with Turkey. The 2004 Summer Olympics were around the corner, and the Greeks wanted to clean up Athens before the games. They spent millions of euros on paving roads, cleaning building facades, renovating parks and city squares, and restoring the city's historic sites.

Preparation for the games also required tightening security. To many, that meant dealing with Athens's growing migrant population—Kurds, Iranians, Afghans, and others. Most had come illegally from Turkey. Many had registered with the police and were waiting for a response to their asylum applications. And many gave the police fake identities.

The Greek government did not provide any benefits to most registered asylum seekers. Some lived in city parks or squatted in abandoned buildings. Many survived by hawking in Athens and the surrounding villages. They laid out their merchandise in fancy, expensive shopping districts, places often visited by tourists and other foreign visitors.

In a move unusual for Athens, normally a tolerant and friendly city, the municipal police began chasing and issuing summonses to the street hawkers a year before the start of the games. The city police more regularly stopped dark-skinned men and asked for their papers. And the coast guard closed its eyes to the activities of the men and women who wished to leave Greece clandestinely for Italy.

While allowing some to leave the country, the Greeks tightened their control of the land and sea borders with Turkey. The Greek city and border police had been known for treating migrants well, but all that seemed to change in the fall and winter of 2003.

It was February 2004, and Nur was in the sixth month of her pregnancy. There were no signs of any change in her situation in Istanbul. My phone rang one day, and Nur said, "Can I see you today? I am going on the journey in two days." I invited Nur to my flat. Early in the evening, she arrived with Yussuf and Samah. A somber mood dominated our meeting. Samah was asleep in Yussuf's arms. Eating our last meal together, we talked about Greece and Nur's hope of receiving proper care for Samah and her new baby in Europe. Looking at my girlfriend, Leyla, Nur said, "I am calling the baby Leyla. When the doctor told me that my baby was a girl, I decided to call her Leyla."

Not able to pronounce it right, Samah called her unborn sister "Lula." The men and women of the safe house followed suit. "Everybody calls her Lula," Nur said, smiling. The migrants bought clothes for the unborn child and extra food for Nur. "This is for Lula. Eat it," they would tell Nur. Some brought her milk. "Drink it for Lula," they would tell her.

In two days, Nur was to leave Istanbul for Çeşme, an ancient town by the Aegean Sea and a popular resort for wealthy Turks and European tourists. Aboard a small boat, she was to reach Hios island, hide from the police, and take the night ferry to Athens, where she and others would register with the police and apply for asylum. Reaching Athens was an important step: when migrants were intercepted at sea, they were returned to Turkey by the Greeks, and many were deported after having reached one of the islands, but once the migrants were in Athens, the Greeks did not deport anyone without registering them and reviewing their cases. "I hope to give birth to Leyla in Athens," Nur said.

The time came to leave. "Thank you for everything," Nur said, standing at my flat's door. We embraced and said farewell. "I will call once I reach Greece."

Days passed and I did not hear from Nur. There was no phone call from Greece. Friends called, inquiring about Nur and her family. Anything might have happened: arrest by Turkish authorities, detention in Greece, deportation, an accident at sea. After a week had gone by I received a call from Nur, who was in Istanbul.

"Where are you, Nur? Are you okay?"

"Everything is good."

"What happened?"

"I am alone. Samah and Yussuf are not with me."

A group of twenty-two Sudanese had left Istanbul in a taxi and a large minibus, she told me. Yussuf and Samah had been in the minibus, while Nur and four others traveled in the taxi. Reaching Taksim Square, the Sudanese had been chased by a police car. The van drove away. The taxi was pulled over.

"They are taking me to the hospital," the pregnant Nur told the police. The officers laughed. They did not believe her story. Then the negotiations got under way. The police demanded 50 million liras (about $35) apiece from the migrants as the price for their release. The money was put together and given to the negotiating officer. The Sudanese were free to go, but, having lost the van, they had to return to Kumkapı.

Nur had waited impatiently for a word about her baby's whereabouts. Four days later, a call from the smuggler informed Nur of the safety of Samah and Yussuf. They were in Greece, housed in a detention camp (formerly a dance hall) on a Greek island. "Samah misses me. She calls for me all the time. I have to join her in Greece."

With Samah and Yussuf away, for the first time since arriving in Istanbul Nur was restless and scared. She was illegal, with no job or money. "I don't want to be begging. I will work if I can find a job. But what can I do here? Nobody would hire me. Maybe I should send another appeal to the UNHCR." But Nur was aware of her chances with the UNHCR. "Can you help me contact human rights lawyers here? Maybe they can take me to my daughter."

The men and women in the safe house encouraged Nur to leave and join her daughter and husband. "I want to ask for your advice," she said to me. "What should I do? Everybody says I should take the journey. I can't sleep at night. I sit on my bed and think about the future of Samah and my new baby. I don't want to give birth in Istanbul. I have nothing here. My baby will need food and a safe place."

Not long after her first failed escape from Istanbul, she decided to undertake a new journey. The Sudanese community in Kumkapı came together to help bring Nur to her daughter and husband, with the "connection" housing Nur in Kumkapı agreeing to take Nur to Greece free of charge. She was approaching her delivery date, however, and travel was increasingly difficult and hazardous.

Days went by, and then finally I received a call from Nur.

"I am going on the journey tomorrow. I will call you from Greece."

Nur left Istanbul with nineteen other Sudanese on April 22, 2004. Near the city of Bodrum, the Sudanese were dropped off in the woods and asked to wait to be picked up by a boat that would take them to Hios. The migrants waited for three days and nights without food and water. Twice they were rained on. They sat in the mud, hoping for a quick departure. No one came. Cold and hungry, and having lost all hope, they left the woods, walked for four hours, and reached Bodrum. Nineteen Africans clad in shabby clothes on the streets of a popular vacation resort by the Aegean Sea were quickly spotted and rounded up by the gendarmes, and after two days and nights in custody, they were handed over to the police. Three days later they were put on a bus to Istanbul. "The gendarmes were very kind," Nur said. "They allowed me to stay in the office and gave me better food than the others."

But in the end Nur was back in Kumkapı.

On June 4, little Leyla was born in a hospital in Istanbul. I was away from Istanbul for two weeks, but a Sudanese migrant called me from the hospital. "Thank God Leyla is born. She is beautiful. Nur is fine," he said.

Nur and Leyla were housed in a hotel in Kumkapı for two months, the cost paid by friends in IIMP. I visited Nur immediately after returning to Istanbul. There were many Sudanese migrants crowding the hallways outside her room. They brought food and flowers for Nur. Some had brought chocolates and other candy. The Sudanese community was celebrating the birth. Nur's face was glowing. A picture of Samah taken on the occasion of her second birthday was framed and placed next to Nur's bed. "She is in Greece," Nur said, staring at the picture. Holding Leyla in her arms and moving closer to the picture, she said: "Take a picture. All of us are here now."

Despite Nur's physical condition and the poor food she had eaten while pregnant, Leyla was a healthy baby. She quickly gained weight and grew bigger. Two months after her birth, sitting in my flat, Nur looked at Leyla and said with a beautiful smile on her face, "I have good milk."

I picked up little Leyla and held her in my arms. Nur leaned back, watching us, still smiling. "Lula . . . Lula," she said, using her other daughter's nickname for the baby. "I miss Samah too much," she continued.

Samah was spending the last days of her three-month detention in a camp in Greece. Soon she was to be freed with her father, but Nur was worried. "I cry every day. I cry and cry, because I think about many things. I worry about Samah. Will she get lost when they leave the house? Can Yussuf find a job? Yussuf will not be able to take Samah to his work. He cannot leave her in the house. I worry all the time. What will happen to Samah?

"I dream sometimes. I dream I reached Samah in Greece. When I wake up, I go and stay by the sea for many hours. There is a big sea between Samah and me. Samah is in Europe, and me in Asia. Sometimes I think maybe Yussuf lost Samah. I telephone Yussuf and cry. I tell him, 'If Samah is lost in Greece, I will come and eat you [hurt you].' " Her laugh was bitter and painful.

"Does Samah know that Leyla is born?" I asked Nur. She told me they had spoken on the phone after Leyla's birth. "Samah always touched my stomach and talked to Lula," Nur said, remembering. "Sometimes I called Samah over and asked her to kiss Lula. She put her lips on my stomach and said 'Lula.' " When the women in the safe house had bought her candy, Samah would come over to her mother, hold up the candy bar, and say, "Lula, Lula."

When they were freed from the camp, Samah and her father traveled to Athens. Hoping to save Samah from the dire conditions she was likely to face, I contacted the UNHCR office in Athens. A meeting was arranged for Yussuf and Samah. A friend and a compassionate UNHCR staffer later wrote to me, "Samah is a wonderful child. I gave her a pack of biscuits and instead of her eating them alone—as is the norm with children—she opened it up and gave one to her dad and one to the friend who had been with them all the way from Patmos. Really something."

The summer of 2004 came to an end with Nur still in Istanbul, hoping to someday cross the sea and embrace Samah and Yussuf. I was preparing to leave for the United States. We met in my flat one last time. I had hoped to leave Istanbul after Nur's successful journey to Greece, but now that did not seem likely. Nur was aware of the difficulties ahead. Still, she maintained her usual positive outlook. "Everything is good," she repeated.

As I prepared to say farewell to Nur, I did not wish to leave her behind unprotected, poor, and away from her husband and daughter. I was worried about Nur, and perhaps that is why I began questioning the rationality of her choices. Would she not be better off back in Sudan? "Do you think your situation is better here, Nur? You are separated from your daughter and your husband. We both know it may be a long time before you get to see Samah again. You know the risks of traveling. Do you wish to go back to Sudan?" I asked.

Her reply was thoughtful. "Here I have nothing. I have no

money. I have no house. But people are very nice to me. I feel like a human being when I come to your house, or when I speak to people in the church [the NGO helping the migrants with social services]. That was not the case in Sudan. There were many tribes in Sudan— this is number one, this is number two. [But] here everybody is equal. I have hope here. Things are bad, but I think someday they will be different. Everything will change when I travel to another country. This will not be the same all the time. But nothing will change in Sudan.

"Sometimes I dream that I am back in Sudan. I am teaching. When I wake up, I am very sad. I think maybe this will happen and I won't see Samah. I cannot see Yussuf another time. I am afraid too much for this."

After weeks of confusion in Athens, Yussuf found a migrant family who agreed to care for Samah for 100 euros a week. Having secured a place for his daughter, he began working irregular jobs. Nur was relieved.

In October 2004 I received an e-mail from a mutual friend about Nur, who had made another attempt to leave Istanbul for Greece.

Nur went traveling last week and got on a boat, and almost reached Greece, but the captain opened the doors and pushed them all in the sea . . . and she spent three hours in the sea. . . . She was a little hysterical when I saw her, and Leyla is sick and they are back in Kumkapı.

I phoned Nur on October 24.

"How are you, Nur?"

"Everything is okay," she said at first. But then she admitted, "No, I am not okay. Too much problems."

For the first time in our friendship, the word *problem* was used recurrently in our conversation. Frustrated with her situation, she was ready to leave again, but she was not willing to risk her daughter's life once more. "The sea is problem," she said.

"I want to go by the river [crossing Meriç River to Greece]. But everybody is too much afraid of my daughter. They are afraid that my daughter will cry. Going by the river is too much money. If Leyla cries, the police send everyone back. I went to the pharmacy to get the syrup, but the doctor was afraid for my daughter. Leyla has heart problems. The medicine may kill her."

I asked Nur again to inform me of her situation. Our phone conversation ended with her words.

"I don't know. I don't know what to do. I only think about travel now. Too much control. Too much laws. Every time, I dream of reaching Greece and calling you from there. But that never happens. I tried many times. They sent me back each time. I am thinking about this too much."

Not long after our last conversation, Nur made another attempt to leave for Greece. Eventually I received an e-mail from Istanbul: Nur and Leyla were safe in a camp on an island in Greece. Days later, they joined Yussuf and Samah in Athens.

PART TWO

Sofia

Roberto, 24A Montivideo

A week after my last meeting with Roberto, the young Angolan I had met in Istanbul, an e-mail arrived from him. "Hello Big Brother, I made it safely to Sofia. For now, I am in a UN camp outside Sofia. The address is 24A Montivideo. Everything is fine. I am taken care of. May God always bless you."

Arriving in Sofia, Roberto had been instructed to turn himself in to the police and register for asylum. The police transported him to the State Agency for Refugees, a government-run registration and reception center. Located on 24A Montivideo, this was a refugee camp housing new arrivals whose cases were under consideration for asylum. Roberto was housed in a room with a Nigerian.

The United Nations did not have a camp in Sofia or anywhere in Bulgaria. Growing up in countries torn by civil war, Roberto saw the UN as the sole guardian of refugees. It was the UN and its partners that organized camps, provided food and health care, and gave temporary assistance to the refugees. To Roberto, every refugee camp was a UN camp.

In our last meeting, I had vowed to Roberto to visit him on his next stop on the journey west. He had crossed his first border, so on November 27, 2002, I boarded a night bus to Sofia.

Shortly past noon on my first day in Sofia, I took a taxi to 24A Montivideo. Leaving the city center and turning onto a wide boulevard, we drove past row after row of communist-era housing projects: identical tall apartment complexes with cracked windows, broken doors, and facades crying for repair and new paint. There were plastic bags and beer cans littered across dry, neglected lawns, large potholes and bumps on the road. The sky was cloudy, dark gray. Fighting the penetrating dampness and the cold weather, men and women walked with their heads down. Not a single passerby smiled. Old men in shabby winter coats dug into garbage bins; they walked away with objects I could not identify from afar.

Looking withdrawn, my cabdriver drove along the boulevard and the narrow roads. After passing small, impoverished-looking farmhouses and patches of woods, the taxi stopped in front of New Sofia University, a private institution built after the fall of communism. I paid the fare and began my search for the camp.

Behind the narrow road leading to the university, past an abandoned building surrounded by barbed-wire fences and empty lots covered with overgrown grass and garbage, stood a half a dozen or so neglected tall communist-era buildings. One among them was 24A Montivideo, I was told in broken English by a police officer standing by the university gate.

Turning left by the fences, I walked toward the first building on my left. There were no street signs, or none I could understand. A lone stray dog shambled by. A short middle-aged woman left the building. I said hello, and speaking slowly, carefully enunciating my words, I said, "Montivideo, refugees, Africans . . ." Giving me a strange look, she adjusted her scarf and kept walking. I passed the building, turned right, and stood by the entrance to a row of buildings to my right. After a few minutes of waiting, I noticed a young woman and two children in the lobby. I smiled and waved, and the woman opened the door. I said my words, but she rushed away, pulling along her children.

Moving in and out between the buildings, I suddenly noticed dark-skinned men assembled in small groups on an open field some two hundred feet away. Walking closer, I recognized Roberto standing by the skeleton of an unfinished building, hands in his pockets, wearing a hooded windbreaker.

I waved, called out his name. Immediately he left the field and came toward me with his African friends. Standing outside 24A Montivideo, we embraced. "How are you, Roberto?" I asked. Holding my arms, he laughed. We embraced again.

Friends slowly clustered around us. All were expecting me, Roberto's guest from Istanbul. Among them were Nigerians, Iranians, Afghans, and Iraqis. Shaking hands, they told me their names. An Iranian kissed Roberto on the cheek. "Take a picture," he said.

"He is a good football player," an Afghan said about Roberto.

"These Afghans are good guys," Roberto said in return.

Noticing the gathering in front of the camp, more men joined. They welcomed me. Introducing himself and shaking my hand, a short Afghan in his twenties embraced Roberto. "These are very strong men," Roberto said.

Crossing the border between Turkey and Bulgaria, Roberto had become an admirer of the Afghans when an Afghan traveler saved his life. Roberto left Turkey with a group of twenty-five migrants. The smuggler took the group to the border, gave them maps and directions, and said goodbye. The men crossed the Meriç River. "We walked in mud. There was mud up to my knees. We climbed up steep hills and walked again for hours."

Roberto collapsed twice. "I gave up. I couldn't do it anymore. I didn't have the strength." His shoes full of mud, his pants soaked and heavy, and tired of trekking, Roberto could not move another inch. He sat down and said farewell to his dreams. In a moment of helplessness, he spoke to his God, pleaded for help, and begged for strength. "I saw death. I asked God to help me." An Afghan traveler came to his rescue, forcing him to move. "He kicked me in my back. 'Get up, Get up,' he shouted." The Afghan stayed with Roberto, helping him gain his strength. "The Afghan men hiked the hills as if walking on a paved road. They were so strong. They were fast," he repeated. "The journey is tough. Only the strong can survive. The Afghans are very strong."

The initial jokes and laughter gone, the men told me about their life in the camp. All boasted about their registration cards and their ability to walk in public as free men. Having escaped the constant harassment by the police in Istanbul, they cherished their freedom. "Istanbul was hell," a Nigerian said.

"They give us bread," Roberto said—as always, he was concerned with food. In Bulgaria, he was sheltered and provided with heat, a shower, food, and above all security. Carrying a registration card, he was no longer afraid of the police. Pulling out his card, he showed me his name. "This is me," he said with a big smile.

It was getting dark, and many residents of the camp retreated to their rooms. The temperature was dropping, and a cold wind started up. Roberto, a few of the other men, and I took shelter in the unfinished building on the field across from the camp, as no visitors were allowed inside the camp. For long minutes we stood silently, staring at the tall guarded building before us. Finally I broke the silence.

"Will you stay here?" I asked, moving back and forth between the men with my eyes.

"We are bored," an Afghan admitted.

"I do not feel normal here," Eric, Roberto's Nigerian friend, added.

"We want to work," Roberto said.

There were no jobs for the Africans or other asylum seekers in Bulgaria. Indeed, there were not many jobs for the Bulgarians in Bulgaria. Eighteen percent of the labor force was out of work. Many Bulgarians lived in poverty.

Two and a half million Bulgarian pensioners received 70 leva ($35) monthly from the state. "My parents [pensioners in their late sixties] had to change the heating system in their home from electricity back to coal," a Bulgarian professor teaching in northern Cyprus told me. Even so, the pensioners were better off than the 2.1 million Bulgarians who survived on less than $1 a day. More than 70 percent

Selling flowers on Boulevard Maria Luiza, Sofia

of Bulgarian households regularly reported difficulties in balancing their monthly budget.

The Bulgarian poor were everywhere. The security guard at the Sun Hotel on Boulevard Maria Luiza, where I stayed, a polite young man in his early twenties, worked eight 24-hour shifts a month for 120 leva, 30 leva less than the rent for a small two-bedroom apartment in Sofia.

Across from the Sun Hotel, six women sat by their buckets of carnations and roses from early morning to an hour or two past sunset. At times they conversed among themselves. There was occasional laughter. One among them   an old woman in glasses and a colorful head scarf—especially caught my eye. She seemed withdrawn and hardly engaged the others. For many hours a day, every day, she sat on a street corner holding two bouquets, smiling timidly, hoping to sell flowers and stay alive.

Every day at eight-thirty in the morning, sitting by the windows of my hotel's café, drinking my morning coffee, I watched the old woman. Every day she stood with the same posture and the same somber look. One morning I bought a bouquet of red carnations from her, and a big smile appeared on her wrinkled face. The next day, and every day after that, I crossed the street and greeted the woman with a bow. She smiled. That too became a routine.

One cloudy day I was walking through the back streets of Maria Luiza toward the main post office. It was an hour before noon, and the streets were quiet, the restaurants empty. I stood by a Chinese restaurant with red plastic tablecloths and large Chinese inscriptions on the window. An old man smiled. Bowing to the man, I continued my walk, passing by restaurants and corner stores, humble private homes, and men and women going about their business.

There was no noise other than the singing birds and the occasional sound of an engine from a passing car. Then, turning a corner, I heard the gentle sound of an accordion from a place not far away. I followed the sound.

A momentary pause in the music disappointed me. Then came the next tune, now louder than the first. I moved in the direction of the music. A block away, I saw a man sitting on a chair in front of a small green space, opening and closing his arms with the rhythm of the sound. The man was all bundled up; two thick blankets covered his legs. He wore a thick light brown winter jacket. A long black hat made of sheepskin covered his head and forehead all the way to his eyebrows. He was unshaven and had a thick white goatee. A pair of hexagon-shaped sunglasses with big light-green lenses disguised most of the rest of his face. He did not smile and made no moves other than what was needed to play his accordion.

I stood in front of him, taken by his music and amused by his appearance. I could tell that he was staring at me through the green lenses covering his eyes. I took out my camera and asked for permission to take a picture. He stopped playing. Lifting his right arm and rubbing his thumb and index finger together, he requested money. I put money in the box in front of him on the ground. The music started. A controlled smile on his face, he posed for the picture.

Every day, walking through Maria Luiza, I would return to the spot where the man played his accordion. For long minutes, I would stand near him, immersed in the sound of his music. I would always put some change in the box. He would greet me with the same smile.

After three weeks in Bulgaria, Roberto had still not visited the town center in Sofia. In Istanbul, the only big city he had seen outside of Africa, he had walked in fear and avoided leaving his tenement when possible. Now in Bulgaria, Roberto lived among the men and women in transit. The camp, its surrounding space, and a nearby village were all he had seen of Sofia. I wanted to meet Roberto away from the camp, away from all that made life abnormal. Three weeks after his escape, I took Roberto, Eric, and another Nigerian friend out for a stroll in the capital.

On their first trip to the city center, the men took the wrong bus and got lost. They arrived at our meeting place, the main post office in Sofia, an hour late and hungry from the long ride. We proceeded to a modest self-service restaurant on Boulevard Maria Luiza. Chicken and rice was the food of choice for the three African migrants. "This is my first hot meal since I left Istanbul," Roberto said. We had our lunch in silence. Heads down, the men finished their food in a few short minutes. I insisted on a second round, but they refused. "Later, perhaps," Roberto said.

Rested and with full stomachs, we began our tour. At one end of Boulevard Maria Luiza, a short walk from my hotel, stood a spacious square bordered by the Sheraton Hotel, modern banks, ancient ruins, and a popular fast-food joint called Goody's. A large space across from the Sheraton housed an old church, newsstands with foreign dailies and magazines, and vendors selling flowers and postcards.

Sitting on the church steps, a half dozen old women with swollen faces and legs and yellow teeth begged from the churchgoers and the passersby.

The big hotel with fancy cars parked in front of it fascinated the Africans. One by one they posed in front of the Sheraton, standing near the doorman and pretending to enter the building, and asked me to take pictures. "Take my picture here. Make sure it shows the [hotel] sign," Eric instructed. When he was living in Tarlabaşı, he had visited an Internet chat room one day and met a girl from Iran. He had spent many hours, and a lot of money, talking to the girl. She had sent him her pictures. "She is very beautiful," he said. He wanted to send her a picture of him in front of the Sheraton. "She loves me," Eric said. He wished to leave Bulgaria for Greece. "She wanted to visit me in Istanbul, but I asked her to wait. My situation there was not good. I will ask her to come to Greece."

Walking away from the hotel, we watched well-dressed men and women leaving a wedding ceremony at the church. Having suddenly noticed the old women begging on the church steps, Roberto moved closer. Dropping some change in their plastic cup, he bowed to the women. Then we slowly walked to Boulevard Vitoshka.

Boulevard Maria Luiza and Boulevard Vitoshka were the two faces of Bulgaria after the fall of communism. During the day, Boulevard Maria Luiza was a busy street with cheap restaurants and cafés jammed in among shops selling electronics and computers, mobile phones, and other products. Bulgarians and immigrants crowded the cafés during the day, but the shops and restaurants closed early in the evening. After that the boulevard looked deserted, except for the prostitutes dressed in their work outfits, standing on the sidewalk, waiting for business.

"Be careful when you go to your hotel at night," an Iraqi woman, an accepted refugee, had warned me about Maria Luiza. "Don't talk to the women who may be looking at you and smiling. Put your head down and go straight to your room."

There were many small hotels on Maria Luiza and the back streets surrounding the boulevard. These were specialized hotels renting rooms on an hourly basis. They were a part of Sofia's postcommunist sex industry. Men entered the hotels, rented a room for a few hours, and asked the receptionist to call in a "girl." That was a part of the service such hotels gave their customers. "We don't do that here," a young receptionist at my hotel told me. "One night, a man came and rented a room here. I gave him the keys and showed him the room. A few minutes later, he called and asked me to call for a girl. I told him that he was welcome to have any guests he wished. But *he* had to make the arrangements."

Only a ten-minute walk from the heart of Boulevard Maria Luiza was Boulevard Vitoshka, which many Bulgarians called Sofia's Champs-Elysées. This was home to Sofia's fancy restaurants and cafés, bars and nightclubs, and boutiques selling clothes with prices many times higher than the monthly income of most Bulgarians. Young men wearing gold chains and watches cruised in their Mercedes-Benzes and BMWs. Well-dressed men and women crowded the boutiques. At nights, those who had made a fortune after the fall of communism packed the clubs and restaurants. Among them were the mafia, the new entrepreneurial class, and high-priced call girls.

With the collapse of communism, the Communist Party and its high-ranking officials were removed from the official channels of power. A new system of control emerged. The mafia replaced the party. Old influential members filled the cracks in the power vacuum.

The mafia had a presence everywhere in Bulgaria's new economy: gambling, prostitution rings, insurance companies, banks, food processing, and agriculture. Economic extortion became a matter of everyday life. The mafia collected tribute—a rent of some sort—from those living off the free market.

The day I strolled along the boulevard with Roberto became a lasting memory. For weeks to come, I remembered the big smile on his face. Walking with his head up, he looked at the passersby, lingered by shop windows, and showed his friends new electronic gadgets he had never before encountered. "This Sofia is a very nice city. It is clean. Better than Istanbul," he would say every few minutes.

For more than an hour we strolled up and down the short boulevard and through the surrounding streets. At one point, noticing a vendor, Roberto bought a souvenir, a cheap address book.

"Who is this for, Roberto?" I asked.

"It's for me," he said. "I want to put your phone number in it." For the first time since he left Africa in the bottom of a ship, perhaps the first time in his tormented life, Roberto became a tourist.

The early evening hours were soon upon us, with light rain falling. Umbrellas opened and passersby were rushing to get home. The temperature had dropped. The Nigerians were ready for tea or coffee in a warm, dry place, but Roberto wanted to be out on the streets. "I don't know when I will have the chance to be here next," he said.

"Look at me, guys, I'm walking on the streets without fear," he said nearly five times that day. "Look at me, guys, I'm a free man, not afraid of the police."

Gently I steered Roberto toward a café on Boulevard Vitoshka. We ordered hot drinks. Roberto leaned back in a comfortable chair, stared at the café's red interior, watched the well-dressed men and women around our table, and said, "This Sofia has a lot of clean and nice restaurants."

The hot tea and warm air had relaxed the men. They looked content and thoughtful. Following a few quiet moments, Roberto broke the silence with an abrupt declaration.

"I will go to America someday. This is my dream. I will get there someday."

America was the "ultimate," as he called it. The Nigerians disagreed. A duel of dreams erupted. America, Canada, the Netherlands, and other countries were mentioned, disputed, challenged, and debated.

"I do not want to go to America," Eric said.

"You hate America," Roberto replied.

"I do not hate America."

"I like Canada," another said.

"Not for me. I will go to America," Roberto said again.

"I do not want to forget my roots. Most Africans who go to America forget their roots. You call them and ask for help. They say they have nothing. They cannot help," Eric responded.

"Canada! I like Canada," repeated the other Nigerian friend.

Roberto was suddenly quiet. He was perhaps thinking about America. "Human-rights-wise, Canada may be better," he said after a few minutes. "But America is where things are happening."

"I would like to have my base in Sweden or Canada. I will leave here for Greece. I will go to Italy, Spain, and Sweden. That will be my base," the quiet Nigerian said.

Making the final statement and ending the battle, Roberto said, "You go to Sweden, I will go to America."

Roberto and his friends had their eyes on a home elsewhere in the world. They were visitors passing through Bulgaria, aimlessly strolling on the fields around the camp, gathering by the fence, playing ball now and then, returning to their rooms, and repeating the same routine, day in and day out. Remaining in Bulgaria was not a choice for Roberto and the other migrants. Bulgaria and the camp at 24A Montivideo were transit homes on the way to the West. There was still a long road ahead.

Like Roberto and his friends, many Bulgarians dreamed of leaving for elsewhere in Europe. Bulgaria was to become a full member of the European Union in 2007. As a prelude to that, Bulgarian citizens were allowed to enter the EU for three months at a time without having to apply for a visa. Many young Bulgarians took advantage of their new privilege to work in busy European cities and earn euros. Many were waiting for full membership to leave their country and resettle elsewhere in Europe. "I will leave the day after I finish my studies. There is nothing for me here," an art major at Sofia University told me.

Two waitresses took turns working at my hotel's café. Mariana was twenty and in love with an American Marine who had visited Sofia for two weeks before returning to the States from his post in Europe. "I have a fiancé in the United States," she told me. The Marine had returned home, and she waited for the day when she would marry her love and live with him in the United States.

She lived with her parents on the outskirts of Sofia. "It takes me one hour to get home," she told me. The money she earned from the café helped the family manage their expenses. On her days off, she slept until the afternoon, ate, and watched television at night. Summers she worked in a hotel in Cyprus to save money for her family and her dream journey to the United States.

The other waitress, Anna, a twenty-two-year-old university dropout, had left school to work and save money; she planned to return in the future. She put in five 15-hour shifts a week. "I work during my holidays. My parents do the same. Most Bulgarians work during their days off," she told me. Like many her age, she wished to escape Bulgaria someday to find a "normal" life elsewhere in Europe. "You see all these nice cars on Boulevard Vitoshka. I cannot even dream of buying an old Soviet car. There is nothing here for me. I will leave here someday."

While the younger Bulgarians left home for elsewhere in Europe, others remained behind and painfully endured their deteriorating economic condition. Among them was a cabdriver I met on one of my visits to Sofia.

He was a short, chubby man with a kind face. He stood by his freshly waxed, brand-new taxi, waiting for customers. After negotiating a price I climbed into the front passenger seat.

"What brings you to Sofia?" he asked. I told him about the subject of my book, and he got very excited.

"I was a writer too," he said. "That was many years ago. I wrote poems. People liked my poems. I enjoyed writing."

"Why did you stop?"

He fell silent, and the glee disappeared. Finally he faked a smile and said, "They did not approve of what I wrote."

One day, men visited him from the Durzhavna Sigurnst (DS), the secret police. He ceased writing. A scar on the upper left side of his face was a reminder of the days of his literary life and the way it came to an end. "Were you tortured?" I asked, staring at his scar.

"Nothing important," he said.

Once again, he drove silently. Looking out the window, I imagined the driver in his youth and thought about the men who had tortured him, who had made him end his literary career. We were now close to my hotel. I wanted to talk to him some more, ask him questions about his life before and after the change. Breaking the silence, I said, "How is the taxi business?"

The driver smiled, paused a few moments, turned toward me, and said, "It could be better if the mafia allowed."

Encouraged by his frank answer, I asked questions about the mafia. How widespread was the mafia influence? Did they use violence? How did they operate?

"Even the newspaper man on the street corner has to pay off the mafia. Nobody is free," he replied, looking straight ahead.

"How much do you have to pay?" I asked.

"Please do not ask," he pleaded.

I stopped questioning him.

"I understand the subject of your book," he said as we pulled up to my hotel. "I also tried to leave many times when I was younger. But leaving wasn't easy in those days. I would leave tomorrow if I were young," he added as I paid the fare and said goodbye. "I am fifty-eight years old, too old for this."

Elahe and Mohsen

While the taxi driver was resigned to remaining in Bulgaria, others, natives and transit migrants, lived with the hope of someday leaving the country for good. Among them were Elahe and Mohsen.

I met Elahe, a refugee from Iran, on November 29, 2003, in the office of the Red Cross in Sofia. Elahe was short, with a gentle, round face. She had straight short hair, small and chubby hands, and slanted eyes. That day she was wearing black pants and a puffy winter jacket.

She was accompanied by an Iraqi and an Afghan woman. I asked the women if I could use their names in my stories. The Iraqi wished to disguise her identity, but Elahe told me, "I have nothing to hide. Use my name." She wasted no time telling me about her disgust with Bulgaria and its treatment of the refugees.

"Elahe has had a very hard life. That is why she is so negative about everything," the Afghan said.

"She has not been able to adapt to the situation here," the Iraqi woman told me later that day, walking me to my hotel.

Elahe arrived in 1991, and after nearly a decade of living in Bulgaria with her husband and four children, she was given humanitarian refugee status. Her husband, Mohsen, was the primary applicant in their case for asylum. The Bulgarian authorities did not believe that Mohsen had a justified fear of persecution if he returned to Iran, but they gave him and his family refugee status on humanitarian grounds. Unlike other refugees who had achieved their status under the 1951 refugee convention, Elahe and Mohsen were not eligible to become Bulgarian citizens. Their status was temporary.

Before leaving the Red Cross office, I exchanged phone numbers with Elahe. She insisted that I visit her home for dinner. "Our home is not worthy of you, but you won't have a bad time. My husband will be very happy to meet you."

Three days later I phoned Elahe. "Please tell me your favorite Iranian dish. I will make it for you. This is the least I can do," she said.

We made a plan to meet at my hotel, and she arrived at half past four. "Will you wait for me? I will return shortly. I have to buy a few items from the market," she said. Not long after, she was back in front of the hotel. Walking fast to make sure that I would not have to wait long, she arrived with plastic bags full of meat, cheese, beans and peas, and vegetables and fruits. Apologizing for being late, she said, "This is the only place in the city I can afford shopping. I come here when I get paid. I buy a two-week supply of meat, rice, vegetables, and everything." Elahe, along with other migrants and poor Bulgarians, shopped in the large open market near my hotel, behind Maria Luiza. The vendors there sold their products at prices substantially lower than those in supermarkets and the fashionable new stores.

Helping her carry the bags, I fetched a taxi. Her home was a twenty-five-minute drive from the center. Sitting in the back next to Elahe, I asked about her day.

"My husband, Mohsen, is ill. He has not been able to work for a few years. We get help from the government. In return, I clean the floors and the rooms in a municipal building. This is better than where I was working before. At least the others don't see me here." Before, she had been assigned to sweep a city park. "They usually give these jobs to the Gypsies. I was very embarrassed doing that," she said with tearful eyes. I was to discover that Elahe frequently broke into tears.

The taxi passed through various suburbs and finally arrived in a mazelike area crowded with neglected and unattractive communist-era apartment buildings. Seeing me stare at the buildings, Elahe said, "This is where my home is. I live in a doghouse."

Elahe's building had not been painted or repaired for years; its facade was disintegrating. Behind the broken front door, a long, dark corridor led to two elevators. One was out of order. There were no working lightbulbs in the hallway. The plaster was falling off, and the walls were blackened by dirt.

The "doghouse" was a small one-bedroom apartment on the eighth floor. Mohsen opened the door, welcoming me to the apartment. "My husband, Mohsen," Elahe introduced him. Mohsen was unshaven and had gray hair and a big belly. He was wearing gray sweatpants and a blue and gray sweatshirt. Following the Iranian custom, we hugged and kissed twice on the cheeks.

A jubilant and skinny eight-year-old boy rushed to the door as Elahe's thirteen-year-old daughter took the bags of food away. "Welcome, you have brought us honor," Mohsen said, directing me to the small living room with old and mostly broken furniture. There was an old carpet on the floor, three chairs, a rickety dining table covered with a discolored plastic tablecloth, and an old sofa. Elahe and the children slept in the bedroom; Mohsen took the sofa. Facing the sofa stood a television on a bookshelf.

An opening in the wall connected the living room to the kitchen. The kitchen sink was in disrepair; a plastic bucket on the bathroom floor served as the sink. Wire was used to hold the refrigerator's broken door shut.

A leak from the apartment on the ninth floor had destroyed the walls of the bathroom. There were many missing tiles. The plaster was almost gone on one side. A big hole exposed the pipes and the old and dirty bricks. Layers of rags and plastic covered a large metal box. There was a leaking shower, a toilet bowl, and a sink, but the sink and the toilet were clean and shining.

I was offered a chair at the table, which was used mainly for serving tea and fruits. Dinner was served on a piece of cloth on the floor. While Elahe worked in the small kitchen preparing a number of delicious Iranian dishes, Mohsen kept me busy with stories of his life. Occasionally Elahe would step into the living room to listen to our conversation for a few moments, then return to her cooking. "You must be very hungry. Dinner will be ready soon," she would say each time. An appetizing aroma came from the kitchen.

Mohsen and I had many things in common: both of us had been educated in the United States, spent time in Texas, and enjoyed smoking a *nargile*. He had an old *nargile* that he had inherited from a friend. That night, smoking and drinking cup after cup of tea, Mohsen reminisced about his youthful years in the States.

He had left Iran for the United States in the mid-1970s. Unlike today, the United States then had an open-door policy toward Iranians. Visas were easily obtained once a student was accepted to a college. Mohsen was among the scores of young Iranians who took the opportunity, and he enrolled in a small college in Texas, studying civil engineering.

Those memories brought a smile to his face. "Those were good days. We were young and full of energy." Mohsen worked different jobs to pay for school. "Studying was easy," he remembered. Elahe emerged from the kitchen. Looking mischievous, she said, "Mohsen had many girlfriends there." Early on in their marriage, she said, "I grabbed a knife and took out the eyes from the photos of his American girlfriends. I took them out one by one and then dropped the pictures in front of him." She was laughing as she told the story. With his hands over his belly, smiling, Mohsen said, "Senseless jealousy. I never desired another woman after I married my wife, never misbehaved."

Elahe disagreed. She told me stories about Mohsen having "long conversations with other women" at parties. "Is this worthy of a married man? You be the judge, *dadash* Behzad." But it was clear that his wife and children loved Mohsen, and he them. "I love my children. They are everything I have," he said. Later that evening, going through family albums after dinner, Elahe pointed at a picture of her husband and said, "Look at Mohsen here. Look how thin and handsome he was." Turning to her husband, she said, "You still look good." Mohsen smiled, and for a moment it seemed that they both had forgotten his large belly, his heart ailment, his inability to work and feed his family. But in fact time had changed both husband and wife. Elahe had once been a beautiful young woman. Now she was overweight and tired; she had lost the liveliness and the joy she revealed in her pictures. "Look at us now," she said as she stared at the pictures of their youth.

The photo albums were the proof of the better past that the couple had once enjoyed: dinner parties in Iran, a nice house, and trips to Europe. "This is our house." Elahe looked proud as she showed me the picture of the house she had left behind in Iran. The house was spacious. It had a large living room that was filled with the classic furniture favored by many middle-class Iranians.

There were pictures of dinner parties with colorful dishes of saffron rice, saffron chicken, meat curry, green salad, and potato salad laid out on a long dining table. Iranians like to photograph such tables before the guests begin on the food, and in turn the guests admire the hosts and compliment them on the lovely food before they eat. As the pictures suggested, Elahe was a good cook and a generous host. She wanted her guests to eat plenty. "I made this for you," she said to me, putting another portion on my plate every few minutes.

"No one can cook like my wife," Mohsen said. Biting her lip and smiling like a shy schoolgirl, Elahe turned to her husband, looked at him for a short few seconds, and returned to the album. It was evident to me that she had gone through the pictures many times in the past, showing them to visitors and friends. That was the past she envied and wished to return to. But that did not seem possible.

It was way past midnight. I said farewell to the family and took a taxi back to my hotel.

I returned to see Elahe and Mohsen once more before I left Sofia for Istanbul. Dinner was again memorable. This time, having prepared the food earlier, Elahe joined Mohsen and me in the living room. We cracked open roasted pumpkin seeds, ate grapes, drank tea, and talked. There were many complaints about life in Bulgaria. "Bulgaria is hell," Elahe said. I wanted to learn about the family's past in Iran, the reasons for putting up with life in this hell.

Mohsen prepared his *nargile,* putting it in front of me on the table. "Here, Behzad, you start." He leaned back on the sofa, took a deep breath, and began his story.

Mohsen was born months after America helped overthrow the democratically elected government of Mohammad Mossadegh in August 1953 and reinstalled the shah, Mohammad Reza Pahlavi. "My father was a member of *Jebhe Melli*"—the National Front, the political party of Mossadegh. One year after his birth, his father was jailed for his earlier participation in a nationalist political movement against the shah. "I did not see my father again until I was five years old."

Affected by his father's imprisonment and the overall politics of his family, Mohsen developed a dislike of the shah's government, a feeling that grew stronger when he left Iran for his studies in the United States. In the 1970s the United States, Germany, and a number of other countries in Europe were centers of anti-shah activity. United in an umbrella group, the Confederation of Iranian Students (CIS), with branches in many countries and thousands of members, young Iranians organized rallies and marches and joined with non-Iranian political parties to expose the crimes of the shah's government. The CIS encompassed a diverse group of anti-shah activists, including Marxists, Muslims, and nationalists. CIS members would contact Iranians who had just arrived in other countries for their studies. Most Iranian students abroad were familiar with the CIS, whether they were active members, sympathizers, friends of members, or just distant observers. Texas had large Muslim associations connected to the CIS. Mohsen was influenced by them.

When the shah was overthrown in February 1979, student activists with different political tendencies returned to Iran. Mohsen had become an admirer of Ayatollah Khomeini and his uncompromising stance against the monarch. That brought him closer to Islam. He returned home to help the revolution.

Elahe's history was different. "I am not a political person like Mohsen. I never liked politics. My sisters and brothers were very political, but I stayed away from all of that. I always hated Khomeini, but out of respect for Mohsen, I never said anything. I even hung up Khomeini's picture in my house, but deep inside, I liked the shah. I can say that now," she said.

"I love my religion, but I was never a fanatic. I did not support everything that the government did," Mohsen said defensively. He did not follow the ayatollah's cultural message—for example, Mohsen admired good wine and enjoyed listening to the banned music from the time of the shah. "I liked having a good life."

Excited by the establishment of an Islamic state in Iran, Mohsen joined Jahad-e Sazandegi, the Construction Crusade, and moved to Kurdistan. The Construction Crusade was set up by the Islamic Republic as a replacement for the late shah's Education Corps and Health Corps. Many young Muslims joined the Construction Crusade with the hope of helping the poor in Iran's remote and rural areas. "I wanted to help my country and its people," Mohsen told me. But the Crusade was quickly transformed into a spying organization, a propaganda tool, and an institution to further the power of the central government.

When Mohsen joined the Crusade, the government was engaged in a bloody war in Kurdistan. Villages were bombed, and scores of activists were rounded up and put before the firing squad. To the local population, Mohsen and others working with the Crusade were enemy. In 1980 he was arrested by Kurdish guerrillas. He was released as a part of a prisoner-exchange deal the guerrillas made with the government.

"How was your experience? How did they treat you?" I asked.

"I told them that I was only there to help. I had nothing to do with what the government was doing in Kurdistan. I was only working there."

Soon after his release, Mohsen left the Construction Crusade. "Did you leave because of what happened to you?" I asked.

"No, I couldn't work with them [the Crusade] any more. They were not interested in really helping people. They rejected all my proposals."

Mohsen's concern with developing workable methods of irrigation and his efforts to convince the Crusade to save and redirect wasted groundwater in Kurdistan had not been welcomed by the central government authorities dispatched to Kurdistan, he told me. Recalled to Tehran and questioned, he did not return to Kurdistan.

"I could not do anything there. I didn't return to Kurdistan. Instead, I moved to Sistan and Baluchistan [the poorest province of Iran, bordering on Afghanistan] and started a private contracting business."

In Zahedan, Mohsen had made most of his money from contracts with the army. He built warehouses and other structures. His earlier contacts with the government proved useful in his new line of work. "I was a builder, a very good one. I made a lot of money."

It was in Zahedan that Mohsen had met Elahe, a local girl from a middle-class family of four. Mohsen was a U.S.-educated civil engineer and a successful private contractor, and so when he asked Elahe's father for his daughter's hand, he was accepted. Soon they were husband and wife. These were the golden years of Mohsen's career. He built "two nice homes" for them, Elahe told me, registering one under his name and one under hers. Mohsen smiled, nodding in approval. The couple had traveled abroad, and visited different parts of Iran. "We used to travel twice a year. We stayed in really nice hotels," Elahe said.

A war had started between Iran and Iraq soon after Mohsen returned to Iran from the United States. More than a million lives were lost on both sides. This was a war against the "enemies of Islam," the ayatollah had told the Iranians who selflessly fought in the war. In

1989 the war ended abruptly as the result of an order by Khomeini. After eight years of devastating conflict, a peace agreement was signed with the "enemies of Islam" without any explanation given to the public. Anticipating a period of rising domestic tension in response to the peace agreement, Ayatollah Khomeini ordered the mass execution of political prisoners across the country.

One by one, prisoners had been pulled out of their cells and shot to death. There were men and women, important leaders of oppositional organizations, and their young followers. The opposition had to be destroyed. Independent groups reported the execution of between five thousand and twelve thousand inmates. That was the end of Mohsen's tolerance of the Islamic state, he told me. "I wrote *shab-nameh*, secret flyers distributed clandestinely at night, and spoke against the mullahs," he told me. He became radicalized. "I called for the overthrow of the Islamic Republic. It was dangerous for me to stay in Iran. I had to leave."

In the winter of 1990, Elahe and her family had left Iran for Turkey. Staying in a hotel in Aksaray, they contacted a human smuggler, an Iranian recommended by friends, and paid him $12,000 for their safe delivery to Germany. A week after receiving the money, the smuggler disappeared. Elahe and her family remained in Aksaray. Long weeks passed, and finally they contracted with a new smuggler. Once again, Germany was the destination. Bulgaria was to be their first stop. In spring 1991, Elahe and her family were transported out of Turkey into Bulgaria. But this smuggler cheated them, too, disappearing and leaving them in Bulgaria.

Mohsen and Elahe had come to Sofia with money, and they made many attempts to leave Bulgaria. All failed. Slowly their hopes withered away. Their families sold their two houses and their furniture, sending them money that they used to live and pay the smugglers. In the beginning, they lived in relative comfort. They hosted friends, sheltered those in need, lent money to those wishing to move up, and in some ways tried to reproduce the life they left behind in Iran. "Our door was always open to friends. Everybody knew us. We had people staying with us for weeks. We helped many leave this hell and go up, but all of them stabbed us in the back. They did not even call to thank us. That is how people are," Mohsen said.

The visitors had continued to arrive. Friends continued to stay at their place. Soon there was less money to spend, less ability to host big dinner parties. With that came the family's slow isolation. Old friends disappeared. "Everybody became busy all of a sudden. His friends did not even come to visit when Mohsen was in the hospital. We were of no use to them anymore," Elahe said. Mohsen would call friends. There were no return calls. "It is during the hard times that you know your real friends," Mohsen lamented to me.

Out of money, Mohsen had looked for ways to feed his family. These were hard times in Bulgaria. The sudden turnaround in the economic system had begun to have an impact on ordinary people's lives. Jobs were cut. Many were laid off. Teaming up with a friend, he made sandwiches and sold them in the city parks on weekends and holidays. For almost a year, he made kebabs for a small Syrian-owned restaurant. "I worked hard every day and brought a lot of money to his business. The business picked up. We had a name. He had promised to make me a partner after one year. But when the time came, he went back on his word. There was no deal. I left the job."

Despite these setbacks, Mohsen made every effort to provide a comfortable life for his family. Then he developed a heart ailment. He could not even work. As time passed, he rarely left the apartment. Mohsen felt useless. The harshness of life in exile, his ailment, and unemployment had transformed him. "He now has a hitting hand," she told me. "I cannot do this anymore. I do everything I can to make my family happy. But he hits me after a minor argument," she told me. This was February 2003.

I returned to Sofia in July 2003. Mohsen's health had deteriorated. There was fluid in his lungs, and his heart had enlarged. He needed a major operation, for which the family did not have any money. The doctors were not convinced that they could save him even with the operation. To find the money for her husband's medical needs, Elahe cleaned people's homes, begged the Red Cross and other NGOs, cried in their offices, pleaded for their mercy. She was the sole bread-winner of her family.

The family owed 1,400 leva ($700) in heating bills. They were penniless. Paying the bill was not possible. Elahe contemplated ending her life. That too was not possible. "I looked at my boy and realized I could not go through with that. What is his fault in this? He needs a mother." She had to live, she told me.

One evening in their apartment, smoking a *nargile*, Mohsen turned to me and said, "I will sell everything we have [a broken re-frigerator, two gold rings, a gold bracelet or two] and send them. I cannot even buy an ice cream for my boy. He knows the situation. He doesn't even ask. I have to go up [to the West]. We are finished here." Mohsen wanted to hire the service of a human smuggler and send his wife and children to Hungary. But the smugglers charged $1,000 per person for safe delivery to Hungary, and all his family be-longings would not generate even $500.

"Why do you not go back to Iran now? Many years have passed. You can take care of your health problems," I told him.

"Do you think I would have stayed here another day if I could re-turn to Iran? I cannot go back, Behzad. Look at my life here. Do you think I like to stay? Even my sister asks me to go back. How can I re-turn? They will kill me."

Before I left Sofia the next morning, Mohsen came to see me at my hotel. He had a hard time walking. Out of breath, he had to stop every few steps. He was pale and weak. We embraced, vowing to meet again.

Mohsen was admitted to the hospital in January 2005. He was in a coma when I called in February. "The coma is temporary. The doc-tors are hopeful," Elahe told me.

The Dogs

It was the afternoon of December 4, 2002, two days after my walk on Boulevard Vitoshka with Roberto. I returned to 24A Montivideo to visit him, but he was out shopping for a winter coat in a nearby village. I decided to wait.

Walking around in front of the camp, I noticed a twelve-year-old Iranian boy I had briefly met during my earlier visit. I greeted him, and we exchanged a few words. "You are lucky to live in America," he said.

For the next ten minutes, I answered questions about "America": chances for finding work, the country's immigration policy, the attitudes of American people toward foreigners, and life in New York City. Looking excited, he asked about amusement parks, movies, and music. Mentioning names I did not know, he told me about the American bands and singers he liked the most. As with many Iranians, action movies were the boy's favorite. His hero was Arnold Schwarzenegger. He had seen *The Terminator* many times and knew the lines by heart. Like most children his age, the boy had watched a host of American action movies on video. "I have seen everything," the boy boasted. Despite the strict censorship of the Islamic Republic and its near ban on American films, some in Iran specialized in clandestinely copying and distributing Hollywood movies. The videos were widely distributed throughout Tehran, home-delivered to customers based on their specific tastes and requests.

It was my turn to ask questions. I asked about life in Sofia.

"Are you happy here?"

"No," he replied, playing with his Nike hat. Pausing and looking reflective, he said, "There is no work here. The salaries are not good. My family has to leave Bulgaria."

"Where would you like to go after here?" I asked.

"I would like to go to America. They say there is work in America. Whatever that is, it must be better than here. America is big."

I gave him my tape recorder and asked him to talk to the readers of my book. He laughed, grabbed the small tape recorder, and posed like an important star, but soon he became somber. "Would you like to talk?" I asked. I turned on the tape recorder. Staring at the small machine, he looked up, gave me a brief smile, and began talking.

"Hello, my name is Daniel. I am twelve years old. I have been here for a year and three months. I traveled legally from Iran to Turkey. I came to Bulgaria with the help of a smuggler. We tried to go to Greece. We were going down a cliff when my mother fell down and broke her leg. She almost fell off a cliff. There was a river at the bottom in the valley. It looked like a narrow water hose from the top."

The boy stopped. "See you in America," he said before leaving and saying goodbye.

By now, a large group had gathered around me. Having earlier seen me with Roberto, they came to greet me. Some asked about my work with migrants. Like the Iranian boy, others asked about life in "America."

"Why are you writing this book?" an African asked.

I told them about my plan to document the experiences of the migrants on the journey to the West: the illegal border crossings and everything they endure.

They came closer to me. "I can tell you about the borders," an Afghan said. An Iranian followed, then a Nigerian, then others. As one spoke, others nodded in agreement. I taped some testimonies, but some migrants feared having their voice recorded and asked me to turn off the machine; I complied and committed their accounts to memory. Standing on the field across from the camp to escape the curious eyes of the camp's security, some of the migrants talked about their experiences. Then, when it came his turn to talk, and scared of speaking in public, an African suggested we move further into the woods behind the open field. There we hid among the trees and the shrubs as more tales were told.

"We saw the dogs. They're trained for special purposes. They're very big. I tried this border [the Turkish border] many times, five

Hiding among the trees and shrubs across from a refugee camp in Sofia, migrants tell stories of their journey.

times. We saw the dogs each time. The last time I succeeded," an Afghan said. Looking to be in his early twenties, he was skinny with soft black hair. Like most Afghans in the camp, his skin was toughened and prematurely wrinkled from exposure to harsh weather, and perhaps hard and tedious work. Looking around, he came closer to me, and said in a low voice, "I witnessed this myself. There was a man from Iraq. The Bulgarian police shouted, 'Stop.' The Iraqi did not understand. He took one step, only one step. The police took him in a car and sent two dogs to the car. After some minutes, they asked us to take him out of the car. I remember our clothes were soaked with blood. The Iraqi was badly hurt."

Encouraged by his testimony, an Iranian came forward, took the tape recorder from my hand, and began speaking. "There was a man named Saeed Yunes," he said. "The dogs bit off half of his hip. He was a middle-aged man from Iraq. But they had no mercy on him. He was in the hospital for fifteen days and then left for Iraq. I saw him in Turkey, in Atatürk Hospital in Istanbul."

"I am a citizen of Afghanistan," a short, unsmiling Afghan said. "I have been living in Bulgaria for seven or eight months. I came here illegally from the Turkish border. At the border, I saw them set two dogs on someone. He passed out from fear of the dogs. They [the border police] really behave in a barbaric way. They beat you ruthlessly. I was deported to Turkey three times. The Turkish guards are better. They take all your money, but they don't beat you like the Bulgarians. They feed us and take care of us. As some of my Iraqi friends said, if a war breaks out between Turkey and Bulgaria, they will be the first ones to volunteer to defend Turkey."

"My name is Manoocher," an Iranian said. "I came to Bulgaria from Turkey almost a month ago. We were twenty-three people. There were twelve blacks with us. They undressed the families with women and put a baton in their private parts. As Muslims, we were ashamed to witness this. They do not like Afghans and Iranians. They beat the blacks very hard. Ask one of the UN agents to cross the border from Turkey to Bulgaria to see if there are dogs on the border or not. That is the only way for them to find out about this. Let them come through the border themselves."

"My name is Eric," Roberto's Nigerian friend said. "These dogs bit two of my brothers. The border police ordered the dogs to bite my brothers and said they don't want them back in Bulgaria again. They would shoot them to death if they were seen on Bulgarian soil again, they told my brothers. I saw the bites myself. . . . We took them to the hospital when my brothers came back to Turkey. They should remove that dog from that border."

I was about to leave for my hotel when Roberto returned from the village. In contrast to the ease I had seen in him on Boulevard Vitoshka earlier in the week, the Angolan refugee now looked intense, anxious, and uneasy. His face showed the same kind of fear and restlessness it had in Istanbul. His eyes were red. Embracing me, he pulled me aside and whispered, "I will leave for Greece tonight. A

friend has made all the arrangements. I will be trekking the mountains."

Roberto had gone to the village to buy warm clothes for his journey—a jacket and boots. Winter was approaching.

I followed Roberto to a waiting area inside the camp. Mostly we
stood without speaking, but from time to time he would break the
silence with abrupt whispers. "The mountains are cold," he would
say.

"Be careful, Roberto," I would reply.

Suddenly I saw before me Daniela Veleva, a camp official, and her
translator, both polite and smiling like diplomats. The translator
wore a well-trimmed beard, a sport jacket and pants, a vest, and a
necktie. He introduced himself and said, "We would like to ask you
to leave the building. We were told you have been speaking to the
refugees."

"I was here waiting for my friend from Istanbul," I told Veleva.
"The refugees wanted to talk to me about their situation here."

"No outsider can meet and talk to the refugees without the presence of one of our staff. You should leave now," Veleva said through
the translator.

Staring at the authorities and me, Roberto seemed more anxious.
I asked to be allowed to finish my conversation with my friend. "You
should leave now," they repeated.

"If you wish, send us your questions. We will study the questions
and reply to them in time," Veleva suggested.

"I want to hear the refugees' stories about the border. I need to
speak with them in person," I said.

"We may set up a meeting with our staff and one or two refugees,"
she responded.

"But the refugees will not speak openly in front of the authorities.
They will fear consequences. This is normal."

"You cannot speak to them here. This is for their security."

"Can I meet with them outside, on the field around the camp?"

"You cannot meet them anywhere around here."

Showing me the door, they came closer to me, separating me from Roberto. He looked confused. I looked him in the eye and embraced him. "Please be careful," I said quietly.

Followed by Veleva and her translator, I left the building and entered the courtyard. Turning around, I waved at Roberto. Hours later, I called Roberto's mobile. The phone was off.

Many things changed in Bulgaria after the fall of communism, but many things stayed the same. Communist Bulgaria tightly controlled its borders with the outside world. They were militarized, sealed by barbed wires, soldiers, and attack dogs. Escape was not possible. Those daring to leave were shot. With the fall of communism, the Bulgarians were allowed to travel, get passports, and visit the world, but the borders remained tight after the change. This time, the soldiers and the dogs were used to prevent travelers such as Roberto and other migrants from entering and leaving Bulgaria.

The reason for this was that with its accession to the European Union in 2007, Bulgaria's borders with countries such as Turkey were to become EU borders. Bulgaria was on its way to becoming an eastern frontier of the European Union. As was the case with other candidate states, sealing off its borders was a requirement for Bulgaria's accession. "Better management of the Union's external border controls" was an important help "in the fight against terrorism, illegal immigration networks and the traffic in human beings," according to the Presidency Conclusions from the December 2001 European Council meeting in Laeken, Belgium.[4]

In Bulgaria, illegal migration was regarded as a national security threat. Although the use of dogs to assault border crossers was not endorsed in any official document or statement, the dogs were promoted as a surveillance weapon.

I asked Louise Druke, the UNHCR representative in Sofia, for help in speaking to NGOs and state officials. She picked up the phone and arranged for me to meet the relevant people.

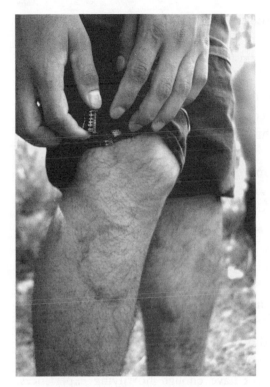

Migrant assaulted by
Bulgarian border police

My first meeting was with Iliana Savova, director of the Refugees'
and Migrants' Legal Protection Project of the Helsinki Committee in
Bulgaria, the main nongovernmental organization providing legal
support to the asylum seekers. Savova was an unsmiling, businesslike
woman with straight, light brown hair and an attractive face. She directed me to a large office, where she stood, arms folded, leaning
against a desk.

"We only have a short time," she said. "What can I do for you?"

I hadn't been offered a seat, but decided to sit down on a sofa anyway. I told Savova about my interest in border stories, and began to
explain what I had heard about the dogs at the Bulgarian border with
Turkey, when she interrupted me.

"This does not happen on Bulgarian soil."

Surprised by the interruption and her abrupt answer, I told her of some of the refugees I met in the camp and their stories.

"There was only one registered case of such violence [in Bulgaria]," she said impatiently. The single case of violence had occurred on the Romanian border, not the border with Turkey, she said. The incident, she added, had come about as a result of a scuffle between the border crossers and the police. The police had called in the dogs to put down the scuffle.

"Many cases of rape and domestic violence remain unreported. Does that mean rape does not occur?" I responded.

"But this is different," she said, even more impatiently. "We're the NGO helping the refugees. We're not the state. They [the refugees] should feel secure with us."

"These stories are told by many people," I said. "Could there be some truth to them?"

"Bullshit. These are stupid lies," she told me, "fabricated" by the "traffickers" and their networks. Angry for having "wasted fifteen minutes" talking about this "nonsense," Savova said, "Only non-genuine refugees, those who need to lie to get attention, make up such lies. Genuine refugees have enough horrifying experiences. They don't need to lie."

I was hesitant to pursue the issue further, but not wishing to end our meeting at that point, I asked about beatings and other abuses at Bulgarian borders.

"Look," she said, "police violence happens everywhere. It happens in Sofia. It happens all over the world."

"We have to fight it everywhere," I replied.

"It happens in Turkey, not in Bulgaria."

I told the director that I was well aware of the situation in Turkey, but I was in Bulgaria now, dealing with the Bulgarian violence.

By now, the director's annoyance at my questions had increased to the point that the conversation was at a standstill. I moved to a new question, my concerns about the deportation of border crossers from Bulgaria.

"This is my real concern," she said, "not the dogs."

"What percentage of the asylum seekers are sent back once caught at the border?"

"All of them."

She told me of the fast-track procedure used at the border with Turkey. The arrested border crossers were detained and dropped on the Turkish side of the border, often in less than forty-eight hours.

"*This* is my problem," she said.

I asked about the fate of the asylum seekers once they reached Sofia. Did the authorities register them and consider them for asylum? The answer was negative. There was no guarantee for registration even in Sofia. The asylum seekers were, by law, entitled to the right to register their case with the State Agency for Refugees. The agency provided an interpreter knowledgeable in both Bulgarian and the national language of the asylum seeker. The interviewers, interpreters, and the others involved in the process worked as a team. Extortion and bribery were common. But, of course, none of that could be proved, Savova emphasized.

I left the Helsinki office wondering why the director believed the stories of bribery but not those of the dogs and brutality at the border. A day later, December 5, 2002, I met Ivan Sharenkov, the director of the Legal and International Coordination Department of the border police.

I arrived on time, introduced myself to the guard at the entrance, and waited. A friendly young woman greeted me in the lobby. Speaking nearly perfect English, she was to be my interpreter for the meeting. Ivan Sharenkov would be late, she informed me. I was guided to his assistant's office for general orientation about the department's activities.

I opened the door. A sudden rush of air lifted papers from a desk; documents went flying, and a heavily made-up middle-aged woman chased them around the room. A man stood by an open window, using a large folder to fan a cloud of cigarette smoke out of the office. He invited me in and offered me a cigarette. I declined, and he began to smoke. With a wide smile showing badly discolored teeth, he apologized for the chaotic introduction. I watched his movements, body gestures, and speech mannerisms in the few minutes we were together in the office. The cigarette in his hands, the smoke dancing in the air, and the strict party line he gave me all reinforced the movielike images of old Communist Party bureaucrats in my head. The young woman translated the assistant's words and giggled at his jokes. The assistant briefed me on the state approach to asylum seekers and provided basic information that I had already obtained in my short visit. Polite and friendly, he offered his help in case I had any requests or further questions.

My meeting with his boss, Ivan Sharenkov, lasted only about ten minutes. Well dressed, sharp looking, and charming, he was young and balding. Smiling, he offered me a seat as I briefly explained my research and interest in the borders. Sharenkov advised me to send a formal request to the director of the border police, presenting my stories and questions in writing. In due time, my request would be studied and responded to. "Instead of going over long stories now," he said, "it is better to submit everything in writing."

While postponing the dialogue to an unknown time in the future, Sharenkov gave me some by-now very common advice about conducting my research. Make a distinction between "the so-called economic migrants" and "genuine refugees" in need of protection, he advised me. He warned me that the stories I'd heard from the migrants were false—and this was before he had even heard them. "The traffickers and smugglers make up these stories and spread them around. The border crossers then repeat the stories everywhere."

I concealed my outrage and shock by smiling and thanking Ivan Sharenkov for the advice. We shook hands and said goodbye.

PART THREE

Athens

Roberto

A few days after Roberto had told me he was about to embark on his journey to Greece, I got an e-mail from him: "Hello, I arrived in Athens fine on Friday night. I am okay at the moment. There are many stories to tell you later. Hope you arrived in Turkey safely. May God bless you always."

Two months later, in February 2003, I was standing with him by the magnificent Acropolis as Roberto tearfully recounted the story of his journey through the snow-covered mountains to Greece.

"We kept on climbing the mountains that had no end. Everywhere was covered with snow. We were caught in a storm. We climbed throughout the whole night, throughout the whole day, until the next morning.

"On the way down, a Nigerian boy lost control and fell in the snow. We carried him for quite a while. It was difficult to walk. Everyone had to save himself. Look, he dropped down there; he could not make the journey anymore. We left him there, thinking that he was going to die. There was nothing else we could do. We continued descending.

"Then two other Nigerians dropped. Kenneth, you know him. You must know Kenneth; he escorted you from the camp to the taxi by the university in Sofia. I carried him on my shoulders for a long distance, twice as long as where we came from today." By this point we had walked more than a mile, from the National Garden to the Acropolis. "He could not move his legs. I said, 'What is it, Kenneth?

Move, move, we cannot stay here.' But he had lost his strength; he could not walk anymore. I carried him. It was snowing hard. I could not see anything. Kenneth was heavy. I could not move anymore.

"Behzad, I had to continue and save my life. I left Kenneth in the snow. I left him there to die. I *had* to do it to save my life. Otherwise, I would have died with him.

"He was a good boy. I liked him a lot. Ever since, he has been in my dreams at night. I see the mountains. I see him covered with snow. This Kenneth was a good boy, Behzad."

For most of the migrants in Turkey and Bulgaria, illegal crossing to Greece is their only chance of entering the European Union. Greece is a frontier state. Following the general EU migration policy, the Greek government has been making every effort to fortify its borders with Turkey and Bulgaria. Like Spain, Italy, and many other nations in Europe, Greece has been using the war against terrorism as a platform for combating illegal migration.

As a consequence, our country, at the crossroads between South-eastern Europe and the Eastern Mediterranean, is being called upon to play a crucial role, as a first line of defense of the European Union in its fight against illegal immigration, which is directly linked with terrorism and various forms of organized crime. The geographical proximity of Greece to areas that are in the limelight of the world political stage, as well as its geophysical structure, with thousands of islands and thousands of kilometers of shoreline, render the task for a more efficient protection of the EU's external borders particularly burdensome. In fact, it is the entire Schengen area and not just the member states bordering third countries that becomes thereby vulnerable to illegal immigrants and asylum seekers, or even terrorists who attempt to enter illegally.[5]

Greece has minefields on its northern border with Turkey. It has increased the number of its patrols and signed bilateral deportation agreements with its neighbors to allow the immediate return of arrested border crossers. Violating its commitment to the 1951 Convention Relating to the Status of Refugees, Greece habitually deports those arrested at its border, without providing them with a chance to apply for asylum. On a number of occasions, Iranians deported to Turkey were consequently transferred to Iran, where they faced persecution. Article 31 of the 1951 convention forbids all these actions:

> The Contracting States shall not impose penalties, on account of their illegal entry or presence, on refugees who, coming directly from a territory where their life or freedom was threatened in the sense of article 1, enter or are present in their territory without authorization, provided they present themselves without delay to the authorities and show good cause for their illegal entry or presence.

Those like Roberto who escape deportation register with the police in Athens and apply for asylum. Greece rejects most of its registered asylum seekers, however. It has one of the lowest recognition rates in Europe. In 2002, a mere 1 percent of all asylum seekers were granted any form of protection, either refugee status based on the 1951 convention or humanitarian asylum. Across the European Union, on average 15.8 percent of migrants received refugee status under the 1951 convention, and an additional 11.1 percent were granted humanitarian refugee status.[6]

In 2001, across the European Union, 32 percent of Iraqi asylum seekers were accepted as convention refugees. From 1980 to 1998, Greece granted refugee status to only 430 Iraqis. In 2002, only 100 applications out of a total of 9,278 Iraqi asylum cases were granted asylum. During the first six months of 2003, the asylum applications of 2,171 Iraqis were rejected and only 22 were recognized.[7] The situation was not better for the Afghans or the Iranians.

Once they have registered in Greece as asylum seekers, the migrants usually must wait many months for an interview with the Greek immigration authorities. Another, longer wait often follows the first interview. While waiting, the registered asylum seekers must survive on their own means. There are very few social services provided by the government. Shelter is only available for some families with children and a few others. There are no monthly payments for food and other basic needs. Many migrants work illegally and save money for the next stage of the journey.

Roberto registered with the police when he arrived in Athens. Recuperated from the physical fatigue and the emotional trauma of the journey, he began hawking goods on the street to make a living. For years he had dreamed of working as a free man in the West. The dream was now realized. He was no longer frightened to show his face in public, and no longer scared of the police. For the first time after leaving Africa, Roberto was allowed to labor, earn money, and live without waiting for handouts from others. A new Roberto was born in Greece: the entrepreneur.

Carrying the official white paper that identified him as an asylum seeker, Roberto roamed around Athens with his head up. "I even ask the police for directions," he boasted to me. "Greece is a good country. People are very kind. I can go anywhere I want. I can work."

He was a free man, albeit an African, in a European capital. Like hundreds of other Africans, he sold merchandise in a village three hours by train from Athens. Roberto was now a part of a transnational street merchant community, the men and women who were an annoyance to local shopkeepers and boutique owners, but a blessing for bargain hunters. Proud of his new identity, Roberto took me along shopping for merchandise from the Chinese-run shops in the back streets near Omonia Square.

Standing behind him, I watched Roberto bargain with the shop owners, test the merchandise, and buy supplies for his next trip to the village. Moving from one shop to another, he would buy clocks, watches, picture frames, and eyeglasses. Looking like a seasoned merchant, he would examine the products, touch them, and say, "I can sell a lot of these. The Greeks love them." The work was tedious. Every night he walked many hours between bars and restaurants. "You have to be strong to do this work," he said. But the money was good, the profit margin high. He sold a 2-euro Chinese watch for 9 euros, a 70-cent pair of glasses for 5 euros, and a 2-euro alarm clock for 8 or 9. In less than a month, Roberto saved 500 euros.

It was midafternoon, and walking in and out of the streets and shops had made us hungry. We decided to take a lunch break. "Wait, I will take you to a good place," he said. Food was always a primary concern for Roberto; in Istanbul he had eaten only once a day, and in Sofia he had relied on the meager ration provided by the State Agency for Refugees. But all that had changed in Greece. "I eat anything I want. I can even buy myself new clothes," he boasted, showing me the new pair of boots he had purchased from a store near Omonia Square.

Roberto took me to an Egyptian fast-food restaurant in the neighborhood. Roberto was a regular customer at the place, and he proudly and happily introduced me to the owner. Then he showed me the assortment of sandwiches and other food and said, "Take what you want." I ordered a falafel sandwich. Roberto asked for two chicken kebab sandwiches. "I eat once a day, but I eat well. I need to be strong. This will keep me going for the whole day."

Having finished our meal, I asked for the bill, reaching for my wallet to pay. "Not here," Roberto said, holding my wrist. "This is my town. You always paid for me in Istanbul. Here, I pay for you."

As we strolled the streets after lunch, Roberto said hello to friends, introduced me to other Africans, and showed me stores for bargain shopping. "Come here if you want to make long-distance calls. Mention my name. The calls are much cheaper from here," he said, taking me to a small African shop with a few phone booths. Having just arrived in Athens, I wished to obtain a local number and buy a SIM card for my cell phone. "I will take you to a good place for that," Roberto said. Calling my number after we got the card, he told me with great pride that no longer would he need to call my phone and hang up before I answered as a cost-free way of letting me know he wanted to talk to me. "I can afford to call you and talk to you now." Indeed, in Athens, Roberto frequently called me from his newly purchased phone, a modest secondhand Nokia that he had bought in Omonia Square.

Cell phones are invaluable devices for migrants of all nationalities, allowing them to be connected to the rest of the world. Living on the margins of the society, the cell phone gives them a sense of normality. It helps them fight their isolation. Roberto was no exception. In Bulgaria, he told me, he had shared a SIM card with a Nigerian friend. Climbing the mountains between Bulgaria and Greece, however, he had lost his cherished cell phone. "It fell from my pocket and rolled down in the snow," he had told me.

Omonia Square, in central Athens, is the hub for newly arrived migrants. There they meet others from their country or region of the world, get help from strangers, learn the rules of the game, and obtain the necessary information for their new life in Greece.

A metro stop from the Parliament building and popular Ermou Street with its expensive boutiques, Omonia Square and its surrounding areas are the heart of the migrant world in Athens. Throughout the day, migrants from Iran, Iraq, Albania, and other places in Africa and Eastern Europe crowd the square, selling T-shirts, socks, watches, shoes, and cigarettes. Many languages are spoken in the square. Greek is a rarity.

A short walk from the square, in the back streets, is a Third World in the heart of Athens. Not many Greeks are seen. A neighborhood of a few blocks, the area is brilliantly divided into separate zones. Together, they form a quasi-federation of African, Pakistani, Bangladeshi, and Iraqi Kurdish areas, among which the migrants move freely.

A day after I met Roberto there, I returned to the square on my own. The streets were bustling with activity. Pakistanis hurried along, carrying big plastic bags. The Africans congregated on their street, mingled with the Kurds, called contacts in other European countries, and tried to arrange escape to Greece for brothers and sisters trapped in Turkey and Bulgaria. Although there were no police in sight, the neighborhood appeared safe, a haven in Europe for dark-skinned immigrants.

The African zone is a narrow side street filled with barbershops, African restaurants, electronics shops, and stores specializing in inexpensive long-distance calls. Africans of all nationalities crowded the street. Some women wore colorful traditional African outfits, and others were dressed in fashionable Western clothes.

A group of Kurds stood at an intersection a block away from the African street. They smoked cigarettes and reminisced about life in Kurdistan. "This is northern Iraq," Babak, a young Kurd from Halabja, told me, referring to the Iraqi Kurds all around him.

A well-established division of labor divided commerce between different nationalities. The Egyptians made food—falafels and kebabs—for the hungry Kurds and others. The Kurds sold illegal cigarettes. The Pakistanis sold phone cards. The Chinese supplied the Africans and other buyers with cheap imports—Chinese-made watches, radios, alarm clocks, underwear, and anything else that was of any use. Elsewhere in the city or in the nearby villages and towns, the Africans resold the merchandise to the Greeks at a profit.

There were rarely feuds, turf wars, or other conflicts between the men and women of different zones. One exception was the occasional wars among the Kurds. The men from each city—Halabja, Mosul, Kirkuk, and other places—lined up with their people to fight those from other towns. But the alliances always changed when Albanians attacked a Kurd. All Kurds united and fought the Albanians with butcher knives and other weapons.

These were wars for control of the streets and to gain respect. In December 2002 some Albanians attacked a number of Kurds with chains and clubs. The Kurds regrouped, retaliated, and randomly assaulted Albanians, beating some nearly to death. But the feud was resolved, with the Albanians staying out of the Kurdish turf. "They respect us now," Babak told me.

Like the Kurds, the Albanians arrived here in the 1990s. By February 2003, between half a million and two million Albanian migrants were living in Greece. The Albanians came after the collapse of communism in 1991 and the economic and political chaos that followed. Many factories shut down, and hundreds of thousands lost their jobs. A mass exodus occurred. One out of every six Albanians left their country in the 1990s. Many fled to Greece, an EU country sharing a land border with Albania. A large number arrived illegally.

For the most part, the Albanians worked on farms and in the construction and restaurant industries, performing the low-skill manual labor shunned by most Greeks. Among those fleeing to Greece were criminal elements and members of an emerging Albanian mafia. Joining the Greek mafia, they soon controlled the sex industry and drug trafficking in Athens and other big cities. The media reported various acts of violence by the Albanians. As a result, they were stigmatized, viewed by the public as the source of all criminal activities.

"Our streets were safe before. Women could walk home alone, and without fear, late at night. The Albanians changed everything," a middle-aged taxi driver told me. "The Greeks were not a racist people. We became racist after the arrival of the Albanians," a journalist told me. Other migrants echoed the same sentiments. "They steal and do all sorts of bad things," an African said. When Roberto lost his secondhand Nokia, he warned me, "An Albanian stole my cell phone on the train. Be careful in the streets here."

In our first meeting in Istanbul, Roberto had told me about his mother and how he lost her at age nine, when she disappeared the night he left Angola. He grew up as an orphan, living with other men and boys.

When I met him in Athens, one of the first things Roberto told me was "I just found out that my mother is alive. My brother located her." I found this news utterly shocking, but Roberto said this in an emotionless voice and then proceeded to start telling me his story of crossing the snow-covered mountains.

Staring at Roberto, I stopped walking and interrupted him. "Roberto, tell me more about your mother. Where is she? What is she doing?"

"She lives in Nigeria and is married to a Nigerian man. You know women," he said with a bitter smile on his face.

"I am very happy for you, Roberto," I said.

Roberto's only reply was to repeat "She is married to a Nigerian man."

Months later I again asked Roberto about his mother and her whereabouts.

He said exactly what he had said before, with the same bitterness: "She lives in Nigeria and is married to a Nigerian man. You know women."

"Have you spoken to her, Roberto?" I asked.

"No," he said. "She is fine, my brother tells me."

Roberto's mother did not call him. He did not contact her. That was the last time I asked Roberto about his mother.

For years, I knew, Roberto had longed for the love and compassion he was deprived of after that night of shooting and madness in Angola. Now, having discovered that the woman whose gentle hands had given him love in the early days of his childhood was alive, he felt paralyzed and unable to reach out to her. For Roberto, the newly discovered woman was a stranger. His mother had died the night he left his home in Angola. In some ways, he felt betrayed by the fact that she had lived. Why had she not looked for him and his brother? Roberto had no answers.

He had lived without a mother or female love for most of his life.

He had traveled with other men, worked with them, and escaped with them. He spoke warmly of the men who had given him shelter and fatherly love. Women never came up in my conversations with Roberto. The journey was the only topic he wished to discuss.

"I cannot think about women. I have to focus on my journey, Behzad. Finding a woman takes a lot of time. You need to go to clubs regularly and spend a lot of time and money there. After a while, women may get to know you and talk to you. But that takes a lot of time. I want to focus only on going to America."

As a black man in foreign lands, he had learned to avoid contact with "the white people, especially the white girls," he told me. They intimidated him, frightened him. One day, strolling in central Athens, I witnessed his fear firsthand.

I asked two passersby for the shortest way to the Acropolis. They were young, Greek, and female. After a momentary initial hesitation, the women stopped. Speaking kindly, they showed me the way. I thanked the women and turned to Roberto. He wasn't there. I found him busying himself with a magazine at a nearby newsstand, looking paranoid and scared.

"Behzad, I never ask anything from white girls," he said when I asked him why he had walked away. "I prefer to ask directions from the police. You know, they talked to us because you were with me. They would have never talked to me. They are scared of the black men. I am very careful with them."

But a short while later all of that had changed. In a village near Athens, Roberto met a woman he fancied. Feeling safe and human for the first time in many years, he allowed his instinctive desires for female companionship and love to come to the surface. The woman broke that taboo for Roberto. He felt liberated from his old fears, freed from his isolation. He looked shy and wonderfully charming when he spoke about the woman. He even giggled.

Roberto traveled to the village twice a week to sell merchandise. He would leave Athens every Sunday with a bag full of watches, clocks, eyeglasses, and other goods. He would rent a room in a hostel in the village. Every evening he would visit all the village bars and restaurants, holding his merchandise, looking for customers. It was in one such bar that Roberto met her. She was a bartender, a Greek woman in her thirties. She would treat Roberto with kindness, offering him free food and a beer every time he visited the bar. Roberto did not drink, but once in a while, to be polite, he would take a sip or two.

He learned a few words in Greek. She spoke a word or two of English. They smiled and used body language to express their friendship and appreciation of each other. Roberto had been in Greece for nearly three months, and the bartender was the only white woman he had spoken to in all that time. She was nice, and was friendly to him. "She teases me," Roberto told me with childlike glee on his face. At one point he even envisioned staying in Greece, marrying her perhaps. He was ready to settle down.

"How about America?" I asked, reminding him that in Sofia he had said that all he wanted was to get to America.

"Greece is a good country. I will stay here if she takes me," he said.

Unlike other white women, the Greek bartender did not frighten him, did not remind him of his black skin. That was a new feeling for Roberto. She treated him as she would anyone else. He was an equal.

I left Greece and did not see Roberto for four months. Returning in June 2003, I met him at a café near a friend's apartment. "He lets me stay at his place, but I would like to get my own place soon, a room somewhere. I want to have a quiet place to myself." I remarked that Roberto had lost weight. "I work too much. I eat only once a day," he said. The business was good. He was saving money. "I don't go out to clubs. I work and save. That's all I do."

I asked Roberto about the Greek woman in the village. "Oh, the Greek girls are friendly. They talk to you, pull you over, and joke with you. That is all. When you ask them for their phone number, they all give you the same answer: 'I have a boyfriend,' " he said, laughing. Indeed, that was the answer the bartender in the village had given Roberto. All the other women he befriended had boyfriends, they told him. They were kind and friendly to the African vendor, but there was a limit to their willingness to associate with him. Roberto was aware of the invisible wall separating him, an African street vendor, from the women who received him with kindness. He had crossed the mountains between Bulgaria and Greece, lost two friends to the storm, and survived, but crossing this new border proved more difficult. Nothing seemed to be helping. At times he broke down, weeping and feeling sorry for himself and his marginal place in the world.

He told me about an experience that made him understand the true limits of his existence. It happened in Athens in the spring of 2003. Tired of the work in the village, for three weeks Roberto joined the other African hawkers in Athens. He sold merchandise on the busy streets of the capital. On his way home after long hours of hustling on the streets, he would pass by the same café, night after night. One evening, exhausted from a long day of hawking around, he was invited to join a table of two men and three women. They befriended him, joked with him, bought him food, and spent many hours talking about mundane things. Roberto was thrilled and went back every night. The gatherings eased the pain of his long hours of work, relaxed him, and made him feel included, part of a normal crowd, a nonrefugee crowd.

A woman in the group paid the most attention to Roberto. A wealthy Greek residing in England, she was in Athens for a short visit to family and friends. Roberto enjoyed her company. She was friendly and kind.

One night Roberto returned to the café at midnight to find out that the woman was leaving for London the next day. Saddened by the sudden departure of a friend, and hoping to perhaps see her again in London someday, Roberto asked the woman for her phone number. Smiling, she refused. It was the same story all over. But, hoping to thank Roberto for the hours of laughter and good time, the woman offered him 100 euros, a kind of pay for the amusement Roberto had brought to her life.

Shocked and shattered by the offer, Roberto refused to accept the handout. She insisted. Roberto again refused. In the end, though, he succumbed; he took the 100-euro bill, returned to his room, and wept. He remembered his days in Istanbul, the days of waiting for other people's handouts to feed his hungry stomach, the days of living like a beggar, the days he wished to forget and leave behind.

Roberto did not spend the 100-euro bill. "I cannot use this money. I am not a beggar, not a good beggar anyway. I work very hard here," he said with tears in his eyes. The 100-euro bill brought back painful memories for Roberto. It reminded him of his African origin and proved to him that Africa had followed him to Europe. "I hate Africa. The Africans are animals. I will never go back," he told me, banging his fist on the arm of his chair.

That was my last meeting with Roberto.

Babak

He rolled up his sleeve and showed me the tattoo on his right arm—a single capital *M*.

In moments of near madness, alone and drowning in sorrow in a room filled with cigarette smoke, he tattooed the first letter of her name with cigarette burns. He put the lit cigarette on his naked skin and held it there until the smell of burning flesh and the pain became more than he could bear. Night after night, cigarette in hand, he burned himself until the letter *M* was fully constructed and the girl was eternalized on his right arm. He suffered from infection, oozing pus and bleeding, but he carried the girl with him, from Iran to Turkey, and later to Greece. Nothing could separate the two.

His name is Babak. He is a Kurd from Halabja, Iraq. I met him

one cold day in mid-February 2003, the day after Roberto introduced me to the world around Omonia Square. Babak trusted me
from the outset, revealed his innermost secrets, and told me stories
he had not shared with others, because I was an Iranian and he was in
love with Iran, its music, and a girl he had left behind when he
crossed the mountains to Turkey.

Across from an Egyptian fast-food restaurant, Babak and another
young Kurd sold cooked chicken liver sandwiches. Their capital con-
sisted of a shopping cart, a portable gas burner, and an aluminum
pot. Cooking their chicken livers in cheap vegetable oil, they fed the
hungry Kurds with greasy liver sandwiches. Two older Kurdish men,
who appeared to be in their thirties, stood behind the food stands.
Leaning against the wall, they conversed with others, checked the
performance of the businesses, and provided Babak and the other
food vendor with fresh pita bread when the supply ran out.

The day I met Babak, the area was packed with Kurds from northern Iraq. Men had assembled in small groups, smoking cigarettes
and rubbing their hands together to keep warm. A few sold black-
market cigarettes for 1 euro a pack. An older Kurd argued with a
Bangladeshi over a nonworking phone card he had purchased earlier
that day. Gathered around him, other Kurds played with their mobile phones and killed time. A group of Pakistanis, or perhaps
Bangladeshis, passed through the intersection with big boxes full of
merchandise.

I approached the spot where Babak sold liver sandwiches. Taking
a chance, I said a word or two in Persian to the men standing by the
food stands. A man eating his sandwich responded in Persian. It
turned out he was a Kurd from northern Iraq. Like many Kurds in
Athens, he had spent a few years in Iran before leaving for Turkey
and later Greece. I told the man about my reasons for being in
Athens, and slowly others assembled around us, eager to speak to the
Iranian in the crowd about their good days in Iran.

Babak selling chicken liver sandwiches in Athens

I was talking about Iran when I noticed the unshaved and scruffy young food vendor quietly listening to our conversation and nodding. Clad in a dirty blue jacket, an old sweater, a scarf, jeans, and an Adidas cap, he stood behind his pot of cooked liver. His teeth had dark yellow stains from smoking and lack of hygiene. His hands were coarse and there was dirt under his fingernails. Leaving his food cart, he came to me and said: "*Salam, be Aten khosh amadi*—hello, welcome to Athens." Surprised by his perfect Persian accent, I asked if he was Iranian.

"No, I am Iraqi, a Kurd," he said excitedly. "But I love Iran."

Lighting a cigarette, he offered me a liver sandwich. I declined. "A soda?" he asked. I had had a few cups of tea not long ago, I told him. Still smiling, he stood near me, listening to my conversation with the other Kurds.

A few minutes later, during a pause in the talk, he looked at me and said, "I want to ask a question that may be out of place." He came closer and said shyly, "Can you help me find Dariush's phone number?"

"Dariush?" I was puzzled. Noticing my confusion, he said, "The singer, the famous singer. Can you help me find his number? I would like to call him and tell him how much I love his music."

A pop singer from the time of the late shah, Dariush was an icon in Iran when Babak was a child in Halabja. In the 1970s, during the last years of the shah's regime, Dariush and a number of other pop singers personified the rage and unhappiness of a large segment of the Iranian youth. Using symbolic and metaphoric lyrics, he spoke of the pillage of national resources, state censorship, and the feeling of being suffocated and trapped. He touched the souls and hearts of the outraged, demoralized, but not yet politically active youth in Iran.

Dariush left Iran for California after the revolution in 1979. There he sang songs about the pain of exile and his longing for his homeland. His words touched the souls of the displaced Iranians living outside their country.

Standing on the street in Athens, eyes closed, Babak sang Dariush's songs for me, with a perfect Persian accent. Between songs, he interpreted the words, explaining the real meaning behind the symbols. He understood the world described in Dariush's music and identified with the singer's longing and the nostalgia.

When he finished, I promised to help him find the singer's e-mail address. He was thrilled. Warmly shaking my hand, he thanked me by singing another song from Dariush.

> *The house, this soulless house,*
> *has a thousand memories for me.*
> *The house, this empty house,*
> *reminds me of those days*
> *that its wall was full of windows,*

Afghan migrant assaulted by Greek coastguards

Tarlabasi, Istanbul

Nur and Samah

Afghan migrants in their shantytown in Patras

Roma children in Sofia

Africans in an Istanbul safe house

*Sudanese migrant in
an Istanbul safe house*

Cheering for their team in the African Soccer Cup
organized by migrants in Istanbul

Afghan migrant holding a postcard of
the mountains of his hometown, Kandahar

and until the horizon,
our neighbors were the sea and the stars . . .

My father used to say
in times long gone,
we threw out our hatreds in the snow, the rain, and the wind
and we built the house with our hearts . . .

Then came the pillaging flood.
It ran through the river,
broke and took away the bridges,
went through the house,
destroyed the house,
killed my old father,
maddened my mother.

Now, I am left with these ruins,
full of rage
and hatred . . .

I write the last word on the soil:
Who would come to put their hands on mine
to rebuild our house again?
Who would come to put their hands on mine
to rebuild our house again?

Three days after our first meeting, Babak took a day off from sell-ing sandwiches to meet me in a café in a trendy and newly gentrified neighborhood and tell the story of his journey. Placing his cell phone and two cigarette boxes on the table, he removed his hat and lit his first cigarette.

"Where should I start?" he asked, taking a long drag on the ciga-rette.

"Halabja," I replied.

On March 16, 1988, Halabja, a Kurdish city in northern Iraq
with a population of eight hundred thousand, had been bombed by
Saddam Hussein's air force. The aircrafts arrived at one-hour inter-
vals and dropped bombs containing a deadly cocktail of mustard gas
and several nerve agents. The buildings remained intact, but five
thousand people, many of them children and the elderly, died.

The attack on Halabja was the climax of the eight-year-long war
between Iran and Iraq. Oppressed by Saddam Hussein, many Iraqi
Kurds sided with Iran during the war. Receiving support from Iran,
they fought against Iraqi forces, hoping to gain their long-dreamed
political autonomy. Helped by the Iranian Revolutionary Guards,
the *peshmergeh* forces of the Patriotic Union of Kurdistan (PUK) entered Halabja on March 15, 1988. The next day Saddam Hussein responded with chemical bombs.

Babak remembered the day of Halabja's bombing.

"We had our lunch. I was in the courtyard of our house. My
brothers were drinking tea. Then the planes arrived. Their noise was
deafening. They were nearly touching the ground. The planes
dropped their bombs everywhere. We ran to hide in our neighbor's
basement. A man covered in blood was lying flat on the ground at
our doorstep. There were more bombs, very close, two blocks away
from our neighbor's basement. These were the warning bombs. The
chemical bombs came soon after.

"We left the basements and escaped to the mountains on foot.
There were dead people everywhere. More planes came. I heard
more bombs. Everyone was running. I saw many dead bodies; many
were children. Mothers left their children behind to save their own
lives. I saw people with swollen eyes. Some had gone mad; they were
laughing uncontrollably before falling down and dying. Many had
burnt skin. There were those who could not breathe. They died of
suffocation. There were different types of bombs.

"We lost my father. We didn't know what to do. My mother cried.
I wanted to return and look for my father. But we had to go on. We
continued to run."

Escaping the falling bombs, Babak and his family trekked through the mountains to Iran. Descending to a valley on the other side, they crossed a minefield and walked to the Iranian side of the border. The Iranians welcomed them and gave them refuge in a border village. More Kurds arrived from Halabja. Babak's mother inquired about her husband, but no one had any news. "My mother wept. We thought he was dead," he recalled. But not long after reaching Iran, the father arrived at the village. The family rejoiced. They had survived, and once again they were together, albeit in a foreign land.

For the next four years, until Babak was nineteen, they worked and lived in the safety of Iran's Kurdistan. There he found new friends and a new home. "The Iranians were very kind. I still have many friends there," he said. All his life, he had lived in a small town in the Kurdish area of Iraq. Now he was in a different country, and he found that exciting. Although a refugee, he was welcomed as a guest, and the Iranian Kurds' friendliness and hospitality intrigued him.

Once again, however, war changed Babak's life. The Iraqis invaded Kuwait in 1991. The Americans attacked Iraq. Once again, the Kurds saw an opportunity to gain their national rights. The Americans promised support, but in the midst of the war they retreated. Saddam Hussein was allowed to stay in power, and his forces attacked the Kurds. More than a million Kurds fled to the mountains separating Turkey from northern Iraq. Thousands died. Finally, the Americans intervened and helped create a no-fly zone and a quasi-independent state in northern Iraq, which allowed many Kurds to return, including Babak and his family, who went back in 1992.

Many things had changed for the young man, and to his dismay, Babak was no longer content in his place of birth. Halabja was too small, too mundane. He tried different jobs to earn a living but left each because of boredom. "Nothing could satisfy me," he said. He traveled to different towns and worked with relatives who owned their own small businesses. That too did not satisfy him. He was restless. At times he would spend days in the mountains to try to calm himself: "I love the mountains, but even that did not help." His restlessness concerned his family. "Everybody in my family had something for themselves. My older brother had finished the university and my sister married a doctor. They were pressuring me to finish high school." But four years had passed since his high school education was suddenly interrupted, and Babak no longer wished to return.

Not long after he returned home, a new wave of violence began in Kurdistan, with the Patriotic Union of Kurdistan, led by Jalal Talabani, and the Kurdish Democratic Party (KDP), headed by Massoud Barzani, battling for political supremacy and control of the lucrative smuggling trade—Iraqi oil going through Kurdistan on its way to Turkey and the international markets, food and consumer goods of all types entering Iraq from the outside. Northern Iraq was divided into two independent and separate zones of control, with Talabani and the PUK in the east, Barzani and the KDP in the west. Hoping to defeat his rival, Barzani asked for military help from Saddam Hussein. Talabani requested assistance from his main protector, Iran. Both courted Turkey.

Babak became a *peshmergeh* for the Kurdish Democratic Party. "I did it mainly for the pay. I needed to work," he said with indifference. Babak was not a warrior, and soon he left the *peshmergeh* forces. He also left Iraqi Kurdistan, disappearing without saying farewell to his family; only months later would he call them to let them know he was alive. "I didn't tell them because I knew they would want to stop me. They wanted me to stay, but there was nothing there for me. I had to leave."

In the fall of 1996, Babak went back through the mountains to Iranian Kurdistan, where he was embraced by his friends. He stayed for a few months, but there too he was bored and restless. Most of his friends were unemployed. Drugs were everywhere. Young men his age spent their days sleeping, standing on street corners, wasting away. This was not the life Babak had left home for. The original attraction he felt in his first visit to Iran had disappeared. Everything felt small and mundane. There was no excitement. He had to move on, and the next stop was Tehran.

✳

Tehran was unlike the small towns Babak had known in Kurdistan. Life was too fast. There were twelve million strangers, traffic jams, noise, men and women hustling to survive. Babak was quickly overwhelmed and lost. An illegal Iraqi in Tehran, he was lonely, penniless, and frightened. Not knowing Persian, he did not understand the words spoken by the others around him. At times he contemplated returning to northern Iraq. Young and full of energy, Babak was trapped. Then came a miracle.

A contact Babak had met earlier introduced him to a man needing an additional worker on a construction site. The young Kurd began working construction, helping build a three-story apartment for his employer's family. Having found a job, he gave all his energy to the new work. "I worked hard and learned everything that there was to learn." He built walls, painted, dug wells, and did plumbing. After a few months in Tehran, Babak became fluent in Persian. He joked with coworkers, made friends, and won the trust of his boss and those around him. "There was nothing I couldn't do," he boasted to me.

Touched by Babak's honesty and hard work, his boss took him under his wing. They wove a relationship unlike that of a boss and a hired hand. Babak told him about his experiences and sought his advice. His employer was a man of relative wealth and comfort, as he owned a medium-sized garage. He was a Muslim with traditional values, "a very good man," as Babak would repeat many times.

To Babak, this man was a friend, a boss, a savior, a mentor, and a respected elder. The boss gave him fatherly love. Babak respected him and looked up to him for guidance. "He would come to my room and we would play chess and talk for long hours," Babak told me. When he felt lonely, his boss kept him company. When he was in need of money, the man gave him a hand. And when he felt weak and threatened by the others, the boss stood up for him and protected him. "He gave me everything," Babak told me.

Feeling loved and protected, Babak settled into his new home, away from the madness of northern Iraq. He was thriving in his job. His boss and his coworkers admired him. Tehran had all the excitement and energy he had been missing in Halabja and the small towns of Kurdistan, and the city no longer frightened him—he knew its neighborhoods, its movie theaters, its music shops. It was in those days that he became acquainted with the music of Dariush.

One day, Babak had to visit his boss's home for a matter related to work. When he rang the bell, a girl covered in a colorful *chador* appeared at the door and smiled. Babak stood motionless. "I don't know what happened to me. I was paralyzed and couldn't move or say a word. I didn't even say hello."

She said a word or two, still smiling. He saw her beautiful lips move but didn't hear her words. Staring at the girl, he felt he was melting away. Long moments of silence followed. With the shy smile on her young face and a few strands of hair peeking out from her *chador,* she took Babak's breath away. She turned around to walk away but mischievously glanced back over her shoulder and looked him in the eye, creating the most cherished memory of Babak's life. This was the first and last time the two met alone, face-to-face. "I had never seen anyone so beautiful in my life. I cannot explain how I felt at that moment. My legs were trembling. I forgot everything, my words."

Babak stared at the girl until the father appeared at the door. This was the beginning of Babak's new odyssey.

Many things changed that early afternoon when he saw M. For the first time in his life, he had found love. "I couldn't stop thinking about her," he said to me in Athens, puffing on his cigarette. Returning to the privacy of his room, he had sat on his single bed, smoked cigarettes, and thought about the girl. "I stayed up the whole night thinking about her. I was angry for not having spoken to her. Closing my eyes, I saw her smile at me." He remembered her graceful walk and the gentle touch of her fingers on her forehead tucking her hair back under her *chador.*

Suddenly he thought about the girl's father, and guilt overwhelmed him. Babak had grown up in Kurdistan, a place where friendship and loyalty are among the most cherished values. To love the daughter of an elder who had saved him from loneliness and poverty and had allowed him the sanctity of his home was a betrayal of that trust.

Soon an imagined wall grew between Babak and his boss. For the first time, he could not share his secrets, and that only increased his guilt. Seeing his boss at work, playing chess with him in the confines of his room, Babak felt tormented.

Caught between love and friendship, Babak lived in agony for months. He toiled long hours to forget his predicament, then sat alone in his room, dreaming and worrying. He began to waste away. "I became like a skeleton. People thought I was sick, but I could not tell them the reason. I said I was missing Kurdistan." In his room, he listened to the words of Dariush, smoked cigarettes, wept, and played the songs over and over.

Could he ask his friend for the girl's hand? Babak would ask that question every night in the quiet of his solitude, and the answer never changed—it was always no. He imagined his boss's anger at him. Deep inside, behind the feelings of loyalty to his elder friend and patron, it was the insecurity and the "inferiority" of his social position that kept Babak from revealing his love to M and her father. "I was a construction worker, an illegal refugee from Iraq. I had no future. I was nobody. He would have never agreed to that. He would have laughed," Babak said. "She was a university student. He had dreams for his daughter." Tradition and social class separated him from his love.

He loved M more than anything in life, and in ways he couldn't explain. He was convinced that she loved him as well.

She would pass by the construction site where he worked, staring at him for a few long seconds. To Babak, that was a sign of her love.

"I know it from the way she looked at me. I could feel that in my heart. She would pass there only for seeing me. I know that, Behzad. She loved me too. I thought about talking to her, telling her about my love. I was sure she would have expressed the same feelings for me."

That was Babak's dream, but at the same time it was what he feared. If she returned his feelings, he could no longer be with her only in his dreams and thoughts. "I would have had to take her, run away with her, and go somewhere no one could find us." This he could not do to his friend. "How could I steal his daughter from him?"

Day in and day out, he wrestled with the question, imagined the outcomes of different alternatives, and succumbed more and more to depression and despair. That was when he began tattooing the first letter of her name on his skin with a lit cigarette. Soon that letter was an inseparable part of his body. "She was to be always with me," he told me, staring at the tattoo.

Not long after, the construction of the three-story building was finished. Babak no longer worked for his friend, no longer saw M passing by the site, smiling at him. Being so close but not even seeing her was unbearable for him. Sometimes he would linger on street corners near M's house for hours, hoping to glance at her in passing. He would return to his room, close his eyes, and see her in his dreams. Soon this too was unbearable. "There was nothing left of me," he told me. He worked other construction jobs in Tehran and in Ghazvin, a city eighty miles north of Tehran, but he could not forget his love for M.

One day, the young Kurd packed his belongings and took a bus to the mountains separating Iran from Turkey. Babak left the land and the people he cherished not because of war, falling bombs, or poverty but to forget his love. He touched the letter *M* on his arm and remembered the face of his love as he trekked the mountains. He would remain loyal to his friend.

Soon Babak was in Van. M was behind the mountains. The two did not meet again, and Babak started a new life in Turkey. This was winter 1998.

Unlike others who crossed the mountains to Turkey, Babak had no plans for a journey west. Istanbul was as far as he had planned to travel. He got a job as a laborer in a small factory and learned to speak Turkish, charming his boss and the other workers. "I was a good worker. Everyone liked me," he said about his job in Istanbul. Working hard at the job and making new friends, he wished to forget M, but the memory of the day at his boss's house remained with him. He bought a television, a sound system, and other things that he hoped would help make his life comfortable and normal, but he remained restless.

A Romanian woman visiting her sister in Istanbul temporarily changed his life. She befriended Babak, and Babak found her a job at the factory where he worked. Soon they were living under the same roof. But that did not last for long. "She was very jealous. We fought all the time," Babak told me. As time passed, her jealousy increased. At times, Babak would slap her hard, punch her, scream, and leave the apartment for days. Regretting his behavior, he would return to her, and the couple would live in peace for a short while, until another incident would lead to a new cycle of fighting, physical abuse, separation, and reconciliation. In December 2002 Babak realized, "I could not take this anymore. I had to leave." He packed again, left his Romanian lover behind, and headed for Greece. I met him at the intersection shortly after.

In Athens, Babak shared a squat with ten Kurds. They lived without electricity, water, or heat. They snatched water in big plastic buckets from a nearby restaurant, and bathed for 3 euros apiece at a local hostel. At first he was embarrassed to take me to his home. "It is not worthy of you," he said. A day before I left Athens, having gotten to know me better, he invited me there for drinks and music.

An abandoned building in central Athens, the squat had three floors and six rooms. The number of squatters changed all the time. Men left, others replaced them, but they were all migrants on the journey west.

Entering the front door, a room to the right was occupied by Babak and Jamal, a twenty-two-year-old cousin from Halabja. Like Babak, Jamal spoke perfect Persian. "Where did you learn Persian so well?" I asked.

"I listened to music," he said. On his own, and without a teacher, Jamal listened to lyrics of Persian songs he loved and asked his grandfather, an Iranian-born Kurd, for translation. Music was his guiding light. Like Babak, he worshiped Dariush.

"I love Iran," each said a number of times.

Babak and Jamal's room was cluttered. A single bed and a coffee table stood at one end. There were a few blankets in another corner, and two television sets—one didn't work, the other had a large piece of aluminum foil as its antenna. Spread across the room were many plastic bags full of discarded groceries and fruit the men had collected from behind a nearby supermarket.

There were two small windows opening to the street. Neither had any glass. One was covered by plastic fixed to the frame by duct tape. For the most part, the walls were covered with flowered wallpaper. Damaged by water, the wall across from the windows was covered with cardboard. Across the room, posters of Hollywood stars and seminude women were plastered on the walls. Shirts and pants hung on nails sticking out of the walls.

We spent many hours drinking, chatting, and listening to the music of Dariush and other singers of exile. A guest of the squat, I was treated to bags of potato chips, apples and pears, bananas, sunflower seeds, and all that Babak and his housemates had at their disposal.

Many men visited us in the room. Some stayed long enough to smoke a cigarette. Others said a word or two and disappeared.

Across the hallway, another small room housed sixty-year-old Uncle Mustafa, who joined us with his pack of cigarettes. After smoking many, Mustafa disappeared for a while, returning an hour later with a shopping cart full of spoiled fruit and vegetables from the nearby supermarket. We had a feast.

Uncle Mustafa lived in Greece with no plans for the future. He was quiet and kind. For most of the day, he remained in his room, smoked cigarettes, and drank white wine. Like others, Uncle Mustafa had left northern Iraq for Iran.

"Why didn't you stay in Iran?" I asked Mustafa.

"*Hazz-e safar dashtam*—the road was calling," he replied.

The evening continued with more white wine and Persian poems. Babak read verses about love, nostalgia, and uprootedness and interpreted the poems like a seasoned scholar.

> *There will be no humans, if there is no love*
> *There will be no life, if there are no humans*
> *Do not ask me what happened to love*
> *My answer is nothing but shame*

For the first time, Babak told me of the death of his parents, which had occurred while he was living in Istanbul. "The love Dariush talks about is a general love: love for a person, love for one's home and country, and love for one's parents," he said. "I am ashamed for having left and not saying goodbye to my parents."

"Will you return to Kurdistan, to your family, if Saddam goes?" I asked.

"I will never return. There is nothing for me there anymore. I have to go up," he replied.

Purya

It was a cloudy afternoon in late February 2003. Longing for a breath of fresh air, I walked with Babak through a busy outdoor fruit market near Omonia Square. There were Albanians, Roma, Iranian, Iraqi, and Afghan transit migrants who sold winter coats, shirts, hats, socks, and illegal cigarettes. They laid their items on the ground on pieces of white cloth, used the word or two they knew in Greek to entice their customers, and left after a full day of work. Rain and cold did not stop them.

There were vendors selling fresh fruits and vegetables, cheese, and olives. The aroma of fresh celery, cucumbers, beets, parsley, dill, oranges, and red and green peppers kidnapped me from a day of stories about falling bombs, borders, and broken hearts. I bought a few pieces of cheese, some cucumbers, and a few tomatoes. Looking at the merchandise put out on the ground by different vendors, I stopped near a man who looked to be in his late twenties and was selling winter socks and hats. He said a few words in Greek, perhaps telling Babak and me about his low prices. Nodding, I smiled, and continued my conversation with Babak in Persian. I was telling Babak about the dogs and the beatings at borders in Bulgaria when I was suddenly interrupted.

"I have seen the dogs with my own eyes," the vendor said in Persian. "The Bulgarians nearly beat me to death."

Turning around, for the first time I looked at the man standing before me. He was barely five feet tall, with an unshaven, bony face. Wearing a wool winter hat, a big blue windbreaker, blue jeans, and old and dirty white sneakers, he looked unassuming, forgettable. His small body got lost among the other vendors and hustlers and bargain shoppers.

I introduced myself. Shaking my hand, he said his name, Purya. His skin was rough. His hands were those of a workingman.

Iranian migrant family at the market on Athenas Street

A vendor to his left sold inexpensive shoes and slippers. To his right, a Roma sold colorful fabric. All had laid out their merchandise on the ground. Many shoppers passed us by. Coming toward Purya's bundle of winter socks, a Greek man bent down, picked up a pair, examined them, and began talking to the Iranian vendor. Babak and I stepped aside. After a minute or two, the Greek man left without making a purchase. "Too expensive!" the Iranian said, shrugging.

I asked about Bulgaria. Purya started to tell me stories, but another potential buyer stopped by. He too left without making a purchase. I mentioned the dogs, but we were interrupted once more. "I'm sorry for these interruptions," Purya said, lighting a cigarette after selling three pairs of socks for 1 euro. "Are you new here?"

I had been asked that question many times in the past few days. That was the first question the migrants asked of a new face among them. The question was usually followed by "Did you come from Turkey?" or "Did you come from the sea?"

"I'm new. But I'm not a migrant," I answered. "I am traveling collecting stories." I told him about the places I had visited. Then I asked him, "Will you tell me about Bulgaria?"

"I have nothing to lose," he said.

We exchanged phone numbers. "I will call in a day or two," I said. We shook hands, and I departed.

I returned to my hotel room and read my notes about Bulgaria. I read the testimonies over and over. Anxious and excited, I called Purya the first thing next morning. We made a plan to meet the following day at noon. I suggested the large self-service restaurant on the top floor of a department store on Omonia Square.

Purya arrived on time. Somehow, he looked even smaller than he had in the market. Wearing the same hat and windbreaker, he was carrying a big bag full of merchandise. "I will set up after two o'clock in the afternoon. Not much happens there in the morning."

Like the Turks, the Greeks had a high appetite for cigarettes. Rules prohibiting smoking were meaningless in most places. Tourists, migrants, and others followed suit. Purya put two packs of cigarettes on the table, lit a cigarette, and smoked nonstop for the next two hours.

I hoped to get all the details of Purya's story. "I can take notes or tape your voice. I will go whichever way you are more comfortable with."

He didn't want his voice to be recorded. "Take notes. I'll speak slowly and repeat if you want me to." Lighting a new cigarette, he began his story.

In the summer of 2001, Purya left Iran for the West. "I had reached a dead end. My life was not going anywhere. I wanted to start fresh somewhere else."

Purya had finished high school in 1993. "I started working right away. I wanted to move out of my father's home and start a new life." He worked many jobs, none more than a few months. The pay was low, not enough to even rent a small apartment anywhere in Tehran, he said. "I worked three months in my last job, but my boss did not even pay me." The 1990s were difficult years in Iran. The war with Iraq had bankrupted the treasury. The decline in oil prices aggravated the situation. Facing severe financial difficulties, many businesses could not pay their employees on time. Fearing unemployment, the employees remained at their jobs, hoping for better times and the payment of their overdue salaries.

Purya left his job, borrowed money from friends and "loan sharks at 50 percent interest," and started a small business, making and selling cheap plasticware. The business failed. Unable to pay his creditors, he knew he would soon have to face the law. Many like Purya were spending time in jail for failing to honor loans of less than a few thousand dollars.

Purya had heard of young Iranians toiling in Europe. After a few years of working and saving money, many had returned to Iran, bought homes, and started their own businesses. "I wanted to try my chances." Selling what he had collected in the past few years, and with help from his father, he began his journey.

A local smuggler helped him cross the mountains separating Iran from southeastern Turkey. Unlike many from Iran, he did not stay in Van, did not apply for asylum with the UNHCR. He had a plan to proceed with the journey and reach Europe in the quickest time possible.

Preparations were made in Iran for Purya's safe delivery to Istanbul. With no complications, no time wasted, Purya was in a hotel in Aksaray four days after leaving Iran. The first day in Istanbul, he called the number he had been given by his smuggler in Tehran. A man nicknamed Ali Video made the preparations for Purya's entry to Bulgaria. "He got me a passport with a Bulgarian visa." Ali Video paid off the bus driver. The driver paid off the passport control officers at the border. This was routine. At the border, everyone left the bus and queued to have their passports stamped. "I did not even leave the bus. The bus driver took my passport and got it stamped."

Purya was dropped off in Plovdiv, a city halfway between the border and Sofia. A Bulgarian officer was to meet him at the train station in Plovdiv. The officer drove Purya to a nearby village, where he spent the night in a safe house. The next morning the officer "came with a police car and drove me to Sofia, and helped me register," Purya said with irony. He became a registered asylum seeker with a Bulgarian identification card. Purya did not intend to remain in Bulgaria; he began a search for a reliable smuggler to organize the next stage of the journey.

He arrived in Sofia with ease, did not encounter the border guards, and did not see the dogs. Determined to have the same ease leaving Bulgaria, Purya contacted a smuggler specializing in sending migrants off to Greece. The man, nicknamed Abbas Ahani, or "Iron Abbas," was a trusted smuggler with a high rate of successful delivery. Many had used his services in the past. His record was solid. A deal was made between Purya and Abbas Ahani. The smuggler was to be paid $1,000 upon Purya's safe arrival in Athens.

After two months of planning, the time had arrived for the journey. "I took a small backpack with a few pieces of clothes and went to Sandanski," a town only a few hours' walk from the border with Greece. In a safe house in a village close to the border, he joined a contingent of migrants. "We spent the night and the next day in the house, and started walking the next night," at ten o'clock. After four hours of trekking, they were to reach a village on the Greek side of the border, where they would be picked up by a Jeep and taken to Thessaloniki. A contact person was to put them on a bus to Athens before seven in the evening the next day.

A group of twenty-two migrants—nine women from Central Asia and Eastern Europe, and thirteen men from Iran and other Middle Eastern countries—left the village for Greece in the dark of night. They walked two hours and reached a long line of barbed wire. A creek covered by dense fog lay beyond the barbed wire, and beyond that were tall trees for as far as the eye could see. Covering their hands with their jackets, they pushed up the barbed wire. One person at a time, they crossed, walked through the creek, and entered the woods.

They trekked through the woods. "My clothes were torn. I was tired. We walked without stopping." The migrants were determined to reach Thessaloniki. They walked for many hours but did not reach the village they had been told of by the smuggler. "We walked through the afternoon, but there was no end to the woods, and no sign of the village. We were lost."

Fear was slowly overcoming the migrants. "Some were thinking about returning to Bulgaria." That was not possible. They had gone too far, moved in too many directions. "We didn't know the way back, or the way to Thessaloniki." They walked aimlessly.

Finally, at nearly six in the evening, "we saw men in uniform." The Greek border police arrested Purya and those traveling with him. But "I was happy," Purya said. Turkey and Bulgaria behind him, Purya was in the European Union. He thought of the days ahead in Athens. The original plan had changed, but "I thought I could claim asylum and register with the police. I wanted to start a new life there."

The police had been kind and respectful, Purya recalled. "They fed us and allowed us to rest." The migrants were taken to temporary detention. A few hours later, the police returned. The group was divided into five cars and driven away. "It was raining mildly," Purya remembered. Having a sip from his nearly cold coffee, he looked at me and said, "Everything smelled different. I could feel the European air on my skin. I saw myself in postcards from Europe."

Purya had thought that the police were taking him to Athens, where he would register for asylum. Looking through the window, he enjoyed the scenery and thought about his new life in Europe. Then, reading the road signs, to his surprise, he found out that the car was going in the opposite direction. They were on the road to Bulgaria.

The police drove the migrants back to where they had entered the country. In a state of disbelief, Purya saw barbed wire and "soldiers in Bulgarian uniform" waiting to receive their new prisoners.

Taken into custody in Bulgaria, they were dropped off in a small room where they joined other migrants. "They were blacks and Afghans," Purya recalled. "There was a toilet bowl in one corner. The room smelled very bad." This was to be Purya's home before being transferred to a jail in Petrich, a town at the foot of Belasitsa Mountain. There, the men and women were separated and put in two adjacent rooms. "The rooms were very small," he recalled, and would not allow for stretching or lying down.

"The soldiers woke us up at six every morning. We worked until nine and stopped for breakfast. They gave us one-third of a loaf of bread, and butter. After breakfast we worked again until late evening." Day in and day out, for fifteen days, Purya and others cleared and flattened rocky fields, removed tree trunks, and performed other hard labor. There was no escape from work. Armed soldiers monitored every move they made. "The soldiers would beat up those who couldn't move fast. They kicked them and beat them up with sticks." Even those injured from the beatings worked hard to keep the soldiers away. But the work did not make sense to Purya. "We were clearing fields that did not need clearing. These were not building sites." No roads or hotels were to be built there. The hard work was meant to "teach us a lesson. They wanted us to stop thinking about going to Greece."

After two weeks, Purya and others were taken back to Sofia. "They asked us to pay for the bus fare. Those without money were beaten." Back in Sofia, the migrants were taken to the State Agency for Refugees. Their status was checked, and those already registered as asylum seekers were released.

Limping and bruised, Purya began to recuperate, and also planned for his next escape. The beatings and the hard labor had failed to discipline him. A month later, he was on the road again. He had the same smuggler, used the same route.

Purya left Sofia with a new group of border crossers. Near the border they began their walk to Greece, passing the barbed wire and approaching the creek. Prepared this time for a long walk through the woods, Purya trekked with strength and determination. Having gone through the route earlier, he was resolved to stay out of the sight of the Greek police until he reached Athens. "I would separate from the rest of them and proceed alone if I had to," he said.

"It was dark. There were no stars in the sky. We walked without making any sound. No one spoke. Occasionally we heard the singing of the birds, or the howling of animals. We proceeded toward the creek. Then, all of a sudden, we heard the clicking sound of rifles. Everyone froze for a moment. We looked ahead and saw Bulgarian soldiers with their rifles pointed at us. There was chaos. The soldiers chased us with big dogs. We ran back toward the fence. Everyone was running as fast as they could. The soldiers were screaming. The dogs were barking. I was frightened, I couldn't breathe. I ran without looking.

"Their barking was deafening. They were enormous. Their eyes were shining. I kept running until I fell in a ditch."

Like many migrants going through Bulgaria, Purya had been told that dogs could trace him only by following the smell from his nasal passages. Covering his nose, he would leave no trace. "Hold your nose with your hands and stay motionless. The dogs become disoriented; they will not find you. Don't be scared. Breathe from your mouth," his smuggler had told him. Purya was skeptical, but facing the immediacy of the situation, he had no choice; he did what the smugglers had taught him.

"I was sitting in the ditch with water up to my chest. I took off my jacket and put it over my head, held my nose, and waited without making any move. The dogs ran around me, jumped over the ditch, barked, and did not see me. I felt their heavy breathing. I was frightened to death," Purya remembered.

It was a cold night. A hard rain started falling. The chaos continued for long minutes. There was more screaming. Slowly the screams
became less frequent. Then there were no more barking dogs. "I
heard the sound of a moving car."

Arresting everyone except Purya, the soldiers left for the night. He
was too frightened to move, however; wet and cold, he stayed in the
ditch until daybreak.

"I left the ditch. My muscles were numb. I couldn't move my legs.
Not knowing where to go, I stood shivering. Everything was wet. My
whole body was covered in mud."

He walked aimlessly, stumbling, falling, and rising to his feet. He
was hungry, but there was no food to eat. Thinking that the soldiers
had left with their dogs, he stood in the open, hoping for someone to
save him. But the soldiers had returned in the morning, looking for
Purya.

The border authorities had a complete list of the migrants on their
way to Greece. "They must have been informed by someone," he
said. Missing one person, they returned to the area, hid behind the
bushes, and waited for Purya to show up. Knowing that their victim
had not left the area, they waited patiently.

Shortly after leaving the ditch, wandering in total confusion,
Purya heard the clicking sound of a rifle and a sudden burst of shout-
ing and barking. "I wanted to cry when I saw the soldiers."

Purya was suddenly attacked, clubbed by the soldiers until he was
nearly unconscious, and taken away. He was back to the same temporary detention center. Engulfed in fear, he thought about the beatings that awaited him.

The Bulgarians had many years of experience in keeping their
borders closed. Trained by the Russians in the old days, they were
masters of interrogation, psychological torture, and physical abuse.
They had a system of disciplining border crossers: the beatings increased proportionally with each arrest, the second time much more
severe than the first. This was Purya's second. The soldiers and their

commander were keen on making this an enduring lesson for him. The beatings were to be only a part of the ordeal. Taken to a back room in the building—there was nothing in the room, he recalled—Purya was interrogated by the commander, repeatedly asked about the number of Iranians in the group, beaten, and questioned again. "The soldiers slapped me. They hit me on the head and kicked me." The commander spoke, the soldiers assaulted. The ordeal continued.

Thinking he was saving the rest of the Iranians from arrest, Purya lied, refusing to provide the demanded information. But the interrogation was a part of the psychological torture. "All the Iranians in the group had already been arrested the night before," as he would find out later that day. Purya was the last to be brought to detention. The commander had completed his list, but he wanted to break Purya's will and make him an example for the others.

The interrogation finished, Purya was taken outside. Behind a minibus, two soldiers held Purya's arms from behind. The third soldier, standing behind him, slammed Purya's face against the minibus repeatedly, then kicked him hard in the ankle. Purya lost consciousness and fell to the ground. When he opened his eyes, he found himself surrounded by migrants from the old room.

"This is the scar. You can still see it." He bent forward, pulled down his sock, and showed me a lasting discoloration on his ankle.

A day after the beatings, following the routine of his last arrest, Purya was taken to Petrich. Unlike the first time, he was now a special prisoner. He was taken to a torture room "for those with multiple arrests," where he was welcomed to the room with heavy strokes of a baton and repeated kicking.

Purya was released after two weeks of detention and beating. He returned to Sofia physically injured and psychologically scarred, but he remained focused. "I could only think of escaping. I was more determined than before." Angered by the beatings, he did not wait to recover from his injuries.

As he told me the story, Purya's eyes filled with tears. I suggested we stop and come back to the story at a later time. But he paused, controlled his emotions, took strong hits from his cigarette, and then told me the story of his third escape from Bulgaria.

After only one week in Sofia, Purya left for the road. Once again arrested, he was soon back in Petrich, cleaning a pig house with an Afghan and another Iranian, removing waste in big buckets. Weakened by the work, "I lost consciousness a number of times," he remembered.

Purya was released after fifteen days and returned to Sofia. Shortly after, he was headed for the border once more. But after three failed attempts, this time he changed his smuggler and his route. The tall mountains separating Bulgaria from Greece were to be his new path. Purya was not a mountain climber, but, determined to escape, he joined a group of twenty for a dangerous clandestine journey through the mountains.

"We stood there facing mountains as high as eyes can see. The other side was Greece. There were no soldiers or police around."

The smuggler, an experienced guide and a man familiar with all the mountain routes, was to take Purya and the others across. He told them he would choose the shortest way, so as not to waste time or the scarce supply of food they were carrying in their small bags. But at the foot of the mountains, they discovered that the smuggler had disappeared. "We did not have any guide. None of us knew which way to go." Long confusing minutes followed.

Different nationalities talked among themselves and then in broken English communicated with each other. Should they trust their instincts? Could they make it to the other side? Should they return to Sofia? It was dark. A decision had to be made. After long negotiations and much debating, they decided to take on the mountains.

Without a guide, they trekked for many hours. Hill after hill, they climbed, fought their fatigue, and did not turn back. They reached the peak. Trekking downhill, they would be in Greece.

On the descent toward Greece, a dispute emerged between different nationalities. Taking the correct route would bring them to Thessaloniki, but no one knew the right direction. Confusion and chaos ensued. After long minutes of intense discussion, the contingent splintered into smaller groups; each group took an arbitrary route. "I stayed with another Iranian and five Bangladeshis."

They trekked the entire night. At daybreak, the small group of seven again divided after a disagreement emerged between the Iranians and the Bangladeshis. Which way was the fast and safe way to Thessaloniki? Travelers of each nationality trusted the instinct of their own kind. Soon Purya and the other Iranian left the group and proceeded alone.

Hungry and tired, the men walked the entire day. Night arrived, and the mountains and Bulgaria were behind them at last. Purya was finally in Greece. "We crossed a road and passed a village. Then we saw the railroad tracks and continued to walk along the tracks till the next morning." These were the tracks to Athens, they thought, though they had no proof.

"It was pouring nonstop. I had a towel with me. I covered my head with the towel. Every few minutes, I had to squeeze it and get rid of the rainwater. I was dripping water. The towel was very heavy. I was tired and could not walk anymore."

Finding a hideout in the woods around the tracks, they rested until noon. Once again, a dispute began about which way they should proceed. The other Iranian chose to go along a road away from the tracks, leaving Purya. "Everything was wet. My clothes were covered with mud. I shaved and cleaned myself. I changed my clothes and threw away my bag and everything else." He continued his walk along the railroad tracks. "I was hungry and cold. My legs were shaking." Purya desperately needed food and rest. He had endured beatings by the Bulgarians and then days and nights in the mountains. Now he was nearly at the end of the road, but he could not endure any more pain.

"I saw the lights of a restaurant." This was four in the morning.

Purya had no idea about his whereabouts, or the risks ahead. "I entered. There was a man at the bar. A woman and another man were drinking coffee at a table." Desperate, he approached the bar, pointed to the mountains, and said in broken English: "I crossed that mountain for four nights. Help me. Please do not call the police."

The man at the bar appeared kind and caring; perhaps he would have wished to help Purya, feed him, and send him on his way. But that was not possible. The man and the woman in the restaurant were police officers in civilian clothes. "The woman made a call from her cell phone and the bartender locked the door." Purya sat at the bar, feeling numb. A few minutes later, he was in a police car, followed by two motorcycles. His journey was aborted, though "the officers fed me and treated me well."

Purya was taken to a jail a short distance from Thessaloniki. It was there that he saw his Iranian traveling partner again. Arrested shortly after leaving Purya, he too had been brought to the jail. "They allowed us to shower and rest." Purya recovered from his long journey, and once again, the following night, he and the other Iranian were driven to the Bulgarian border.

"I thought the Bulgarians would finish me this time. I sat in the car with my head down."

Then a miracle happened. "Rain saved me. All papers were destroyed."

The Bulgarians had a readmission agreement with Greece. They had to accept and readmit the nationals of third countries who had illegally entered Greece through Bulgaria. But this time there was no proof that Purya had ever been in Bulgaria. He had no Bulgarian documents. The soldiers refused to accept him. Purya was saved. Not wishing to allow him in the country, and not able to deport him to Bulgaria, the Greeks had to find another country for him. Turkey was a natural candidate. Saved from the dogs and the beatings by the Bulgarians, Purya was returned to the beginning of his long journey. The Greeks took Purya to the border with Turkey, kept him in jail for two nights, and sent him to the Turkish side of the Meriç River one evening in absolute darkness, without alarming the Turkish gendarmes. "I was back in Aksaray the day after," he said.

Moments of silence followed Purya's last statement. "I have to set up before it gets dark," he said after smoking a last cigarette. He left the restaurant, and I vowed to visit him in the market to hear the rest of his story.

I returned to the market two days later. Standing by his pile of socks and gloves in the nearly empty market, Purya was hoping for a last chance to make some money before ending his day. There were no customers around, however. The only people left in the market were other Iranians and Kurds, rubbing their hands together in the cold, desperately looking for buyers. Most vendors had gone for the day; the vegetable shops were closed, and the market was filled with leftover lettuce, decayed fruits, and empty cardboard boxes. The men stood amid the piles of garbage, watching their merchandise, still hoping for a buyer.

"I have to leave soon," Purya told me in an unusually desperate voice. "There is nothing for me here. Too many hands, not much money. I cannot save anything," he continued.

The market had been slow for weeks. He had sold some merchandise that day, but for the same price that he himself had paid, so Purya had not made any money that day.

"My father would have helped me if he were alive," he said in a somber voice.

This was the first time he mentioned the death of his father. He told me that when he had phoned his family in Iran after his deportation to Istanbul, they had informed him of his father's death. "He had died forty days earlier. I lost the biggest support in my life," he said. He had mourned in the solitude of his single room in Aksaray, and planned for his next escape. "I was not going to stay in Aksaray."

The next six months were a time of reflection, extreme hopelessness, the rebirth of hope, and emotions that constantly changed and altered his plans. With no money to pay the smugglers, he was on his own; he had to cross the borders alone and find the fastest way to Greece. A rerouting was in order. Alone at night, he crossed Turkey's northern border with Greece, only to be spotted by the Greek authorities in the early hours of the next morning.

He was arrested again, but for reasons that can only be explained by chance, and perhaps good luck, Purya was not deported. He was held for two nights, then taken to a detention camp in a nearby village. His transfer to the camp was a welcome sign. He was to be kept in Greece and released after three months. Three months later, the camp guards said farewell to Purya. He walked away.

Months after his release from the camp, he was unhappy and frustrated. I told him of other men, Africans and others, who sold bootlegged CDs and leather bags in busier parts of the city, walked in and out of bars and restaurants, and managed to make a good deal of money and save for the next stage of their journey.

"I can't do that," he replied. "This is humiliating enough. At least there aren't too many people who see me here."

Purya was working hard, saving money for his next move. "I will go. No matter what happens, I will move forward. There is no going back."

That was the last time we met.

Uncle Suleiman's Tent

My meeting with Purya was accidental, with chance bringing me to the spot where he sold merchandise. It was also chance that took me to Uncle Suleiman's tent.

For three and a half years, Uncle Suleiman had lived in one of the official refugee camps on the outskirts of Athens. The camp gave him and others adequate food and hot water for bathing, and so they lived in relative peace while they awaited a response to their petitions for asylum.

Uncle Suleiman's request for asylum was eventually rejected. When I met him, a few weeks before the invasion of Iraq in March 2003, he had just received his deportation letter from the Greek government and was in search of a new temporary home to save him from returning to his place of birth, the town of Erbil in northern Iraq.

It was Nusrat, a twenty-three-year-old Iranian migrant I had met in the office of Médecins du Monde Grèce, who took me to Uncle Suleiman. "I hope you don't mind. I told someone I know about you. She would like to meet you. She lives with her two sons in a camp near here. I can take you there," Nusrat told me on the phone one day. Having never visited a Greek camp, I accepted.

One sunny day in late February 2003, Nusrat and I took a city bus to a refugee camp an hour from the center and a short walk from the Mediterranean Sea. There were no clouds in the blue sky, and the fresh smell of the sea filled the air. This was a small tent city surrounded by low walls. There were a few children playing soccer on a dirt field. A boy rode an old bicycle. A woman in a head scarf stopped and screened us with her eyes.

There were a few short rows of tents, all numbered, some decorated with antennas or satellite dishes. We stopped by tent number four.

"Azar Khanoom," Nusrat called out. Coming out of the tent, a friendly woman in her thirties greeted us. Azar and her boys had been in the camp for nearly five months after their deportation from Germany. They shared a tent with a family from northern Iraq. A piece of cloth separated the tent into two halves: Azar and the boys on one side, Iraqi Kurds—a man, a woman, and a three-year-old—on the other. There was usually peace between them. But Azar

Uncle Suleiman

complained about a lack of consideration. "They watch television and leave the lights on until early morning."

Azar's boys were in school, and this was the first warm day in weeks. We decided to go for a stroll on the beach. I had brought Azar a bottle of red wine. Touring the camp, Azar looked for a corkscrew, but none could be found. "Uncle Suleiman must have something," Azar said, and we walked to tent number one, Uncle Suleiman's tent.

The big smile on Uncle Suleiman's chubby face when he came out of his tent was memorable. His long silver hair shone in the sun. His big belly stood out.

"Please come for tea. I will make you lunch," he said.

"We will come for tea later," Azar said.

Returning to his tent, Uncle Suleiman came out again with a screwdriver. "Will this work?" he asked.

We laughed, nodded, and departed with the screwdriver. On the beach, I used it to push in the cork, and wine splashed all over my clothes. It was splendid wine, and the Mediterranean was awesome as ever.

The camp had twenty-one tents. There were Afghans, Iraqi Kurds, and a few Iranians. Some were relatively new. Others had been there for up to four years, waiting for a final decision. There were a large public kitchen, a laundry room, and private and public bathrooms. Having returned from our stroll on the beach, I asked Azar if I could visit the kitchen, but that made her uncomfortable.

"Single men keep out of the kitchen. They cook in their tents on a paraffin heater." Seeing my confused expression, she explained with a single word: "Muslims!"

Men stayed out of the places where the women spent many hours each day, because the women did not wear the *burqa* or the *chador,* although the Afghan women wore scarves. Parvin, an Iranian woman in tent number ten, also wore a scarf. Azar did not cover her head and roamed freely.

It was a traditional community, and women could not avoid the constant gossip of other women. Azar was the only woman without a husband or other male head of household. Other women watched her moves. They talked behind her back and made up stories about her and those who visited her. But Azar did not believe in taboos. She spoke to other men and visited Uncle Suleiman's tent.

Uncle Suleiman's tent was always tidy and clean. There were four beds, a television set, a sound system, two chairs, two machine-made rugs, a desk, and a paraffin lamp. Clothes hung neatly above each bed. Paintbrushes and bottles of paint on the desk gave the tent the appearance of a real home. The beds were always neatly made; their blankets were tucked in like those in army barracks. Outside, a digital satellite dish was attached to the tent's upper corner. Most tents had their own dishes, televisions, and other home electronics, donated by Greek families or bought from personal savings.

Frequently other camp residents came to visit Uncle Suleiman's tent. Among them were Azar and her boys, Hutan and Hamid. In Germany Azar had had an apartment, and she worked and earned money. But her life had changed when the immigration officers put her and her boys on a plane to Athens. She was not given a chance to pack and take her valuables.

Azar and her boys did not have a television or a sound system. The boys would visit Uncle Suleiman's tent to watch their favorite television shows. Uncle Suleiman was kind; he loved her children, enjoyed their jokes, and welcomed them with open arms. The boys gave him love in return, though at times they irritated him to near madness. They were clever, mischievous, funny, and mature for their age.

"He is fat," Hutan, Azar's six-year-old boy, would say.

"This mister does not do anything. He sits around all day," Hamid, Azar's nine-year-old boy, would join in.

"Uncle Suleiman, show him your paintings," Azar would interrupt the boys. The boys spoke Persian, Turkish, German, and Greek. The only English word they knew and used frequently was *deport*. They did not know the Persian equivalent for this word. I told them I had lived in the United States, and the older boy, Hamid, said to me, "So, you were also deported to Greece." In his world, that was the only way for an Iranian to move backward—north to south, west to east.

Hutan and Hamid scavenged abandoned footballs, bicycles, anything for entertainment from the area around the camp. Unlike many other children their age, they were fully aware of their status; they knew the meaning of life without documents and the feeling of being away from their place of birth and their father.

One day, sitting in Uncle Suleiman's tent, I gave my tape recorder to the boys, asking them to say whatever they wanted to readers in other parts of the world. Excited and curious to hear their voices, they grabbed the machine and began talking:

Hamid and Hutan playing ball in the camp

"My name is Hutan. I am six years old. My mother is hurting. She longs to go to England. Please take us out of this country. Our wish is to go to England. We do not want to be deported. But if you cannot take us, give us a visa."

"Hello! My name is Hamid. I was in Germany for eight months. They came to our home and told us to leave. I was having breakfast. I left without finishing my milk. I could only take one sip. The police took us to the airport and put us on the plane. We flew for three hours. I was vomiting the whole time. We got to Greece. I did not know the language. My mother started speaking English at the airport in Athens. We cried a lot. They brought us here. We would like to go to England because my mother's English is good."

"I am the Hutan who spoke before. I have not seen my father for a long time. Please take me to him."

Hutan's father was an asylum seeker in England. His application for asylum had been rejected, and he was living in London illegally. There was no possibility of a family reunion through legal means. I once asked Azar why she and the boys were not with her husband. She did not give me a direct answer. "Family problems," she said. All I could gather from her answers was that the husband had left Iran long before Azar and the boys.

Uncle Suleiman had shared his tent with many people over the course of three and a half years. Men from Afghanistan, Iraq, and Iran had arrived in and left the camp; they saved him from loneliness, and became a part of his memories. His tent remained the center of gravity, a place that others visited for comfort, advice, and his famous "Arab tea."

A veteran of the Afghan civil war and a Serb who had fought Muslims in Bosnia had lived in Uncle Suleiman's tent in the past two years. Then, early in 2002, a young man arrived to share the living space—Ali, an Iranian in his early thirties. The newcomer revived memories that Suleiman wanted to forget.

Uncle Suleiman and Ali had fought on opposite sides of the Iran-Iraq War in the 1980s. Their governments told them they were enemies. Uncle Suleiman had fought in Ahwaz and helped capture the city for the Iraqi army. Ali was from Ahwaz. At the age of seventeen, he had joined the army and fought to liberate his town. Now, years later, away from the battlefield, Ali hoped to forget the bullets, the howling of the wounded, and everything that reminded him of his youth. Uncle Suleiman wanted to focus on the future, finding a new home. Neither wanted to talk about their common past, but suddenly they were sharing the same space. And the two enemy soldiers grew to be brothers, because they shared the same dream about another place set in the future—their Eden in the West.

Together they watched television, smoked cigarettes, drank tea, and perhaps hared war stories in Arabic, a language no one else in the tent understc d. They became close friends, each the other's support.

Ali was talkative and engaging. He liked soccer. Friends would come to take him to the field, but he would often stay behind, make tea, and talk to me. He worked long hours to save for the journey to Italy. Ali was a construction worker and handyman at a nearby church. The money was reasonable. He had no complaints. The work kept him busy, kept him away from the tent, gave him a purpose, and allowed him to carry on as normal a life as possible. He was friendly and had a good relationship with everyone in the tent, including the Serb and the Afghan.

The Serb had been deported to Greece from France. No one knew why. He was alone. No one spoke his language. Did he have a family back in Serbia? No one knew. He wore black trousers and a blue suit jacket. He would sleep still wearing the trousers and the suit jacket, with a sheet over his head. Waking up, he would greet the others with a smile. He would remain in bed, sitting up, and smiling continuously. This was his routine, day in and day out. The others believed he had lost his sanity.

"He became crazy when they sent him here," Ali told me.

"He does not understand anything," Hamid added, saying hello to him in Greek. The man replied in Greek and smiled again.

The Serb spent much time facing the television screen, lost in his thoughts. He would stare at the images, maintaining his smile even as the scene on the screen changed. I wondered if he ever was in the tent with the rest of us. Perhaps he had never left the battlefields of Bosnia.

The Serb was always in the tent when I visited, but I saw the Afghan only once. The others called him Muhammad. He worked long hours to save money for the next stage of his journey. Having arrived from work, he changed, sat silently with the rest of us, and then left to play soccer with others from Afghanistan and Iran. I did not have a conversation with Muhammad. "He is good," I remember Uncle Suleiman saying about him.

Uncle Suleiman had a wife and children in Iraq. Yet here he was, far away from home, the respected elder of tent number one in a

Greek refugee camp. From northern Iraq he had made a long and painful journey. He knew he would soon be on the road again, still alone, and searching for another tent in another camp in another land that would believe his story, for the Greeks did not believe it. What follows is Uncle Suleiman's tale.

He was born in Erbil. In 1982 he was drafted by Saddam Hussein to fight in the war with Iran. Many Kurds deserted and chose not to fight. Uncle Suleiman was sent to the front; he fought the Iranians and was captured in a battle in Ahwaz, in Iran's southern province of Khuzestan. He became a prisoner of war.

The Iran-Iraq War lasted eight years. He was a POW for nine years. During that time Uncle Suleiman was tortured and brutalized. In Iran's jails, he had often been hit in the face with metal bars. As a result, three of his teeth were missing. Worse happened: they broke his back, an injury that still caused him pain.

Many died in the Iran-Iraq War. Others were emotionally scarred or physically impaired. There were betrayals and changing alliances. Shiite Arabs and Kurds came to the Iranian side. An Iranian opposition group sided with Iraq and fought Iran from Iraqi soil. The Iranians used their Shiite allies to torture Iraqi POWs. The men who broke Uncle Suleiman's limbs spoke his language. They were his countrymen, helping the Iranians to win the war against Saddam Hussein. The Iranians perhaps thought this was an effective way to break the POWs' morale, to make them confess or force information from them. The strategy sometimes worked. I did not ask Uncle Suleiman if he cooperated. The strongest people break down under torture.

After nine years, he was released as part of a POW exchange program. Uncle Suleiman returned home looking much older. "I lost many good years of my life sitting in the jail in Iran," he said with a deep sigh. In celebration of his freedom, wanting to have a normal life, Uncle Suleiman married in Baghdad. His wife gave birth to a boy and a girl. He smiled as he talked about his children, then became quiet. When he spoke again he said, "I wanted to have a normal life like everybody else."

Normality was not attainable. His sufferings were far from over. Iraq's ministry of intelligence, its interrogators and spies, haunted him in his own country. "They would visit my home and take me to their office. They wanted to know if I worked with the Iranians. I showed them my scars, but they would not leave me alone." He was accused of having cooperated with the Iranian government. Life was hell. It was not the reception he had expected.

Unable to cope, he left his wife in Baghdad and moved to northern Iraq, then under Kurdish rule. This was 1996, months after the outbreak of civil war in Kurdistan. Uncle Suleiman could not escape the rivalry between the two warring parties. He was working for the television station in Kurdistan, and he was asked to take sides. "They wanted me to be political. I just wanted to live a simple life." Tired of war and politics, and longing for a life in peace, he left Kurdistan and began his journey of migration. He left northern Iraq for Turkey, then crossed the Turkish border into Greece, where he applied for asylum and hoped to bring his family to live with him.

I met him in early March 2003, nearly four years after he had left northern Iraq, and just after Uncle Suleiman had been told to return to his land of conflict.

A few days after my first visit to the camp, Azar phoned me, inviting me to lunch in Uncle Suleiman's tent. I accepted the invitation. Once again, Nusrat and I boarded the bus to the camp.

Ali and Azar had prepared a feast. Two tables were put together. Chairs were borrowed from other tents. Uncle Suleiman prepared a special dish with his ration of beans and tuna fish. Ali made memorable saffron rice mixed with raisins and lentils. Having asked me about my plate of choice, Azar made an eggplant dish and a delightful curry prepared with walnuts and pomegranate sauce. Sitting around the tables, we ate the food with a hearty appetite. Uncle Suleiman raised his glass of Coca-Cola and toasted his absent wife. Azar toasted her husband in England. The boys drank to the father they had seen so briefly. Uncle Suleiman entertained us with Iranian and Kurdish music. Long before being a POW in Iran, he had been a fan of the Iranian singer Gugush and had a poster of the diva on his wall in Baghdad.

After lunch, the children left the tent to play ball with friends. Drinking a glass of his tea, I asked Uncle Suleiman to take a walk on the beach with me.

"Always ready for a good walk," he said.

I was curious about Uncle Suleiman's years of imprisonment in Iran. Strolling in the narrow streets on the way to the sea, I asked about Iran.

"Why do you want to know that?"

"I want to tell the world," I explained.

He refused politely, and so I changed the subject. The experience was clearly too painful. He had a turbulent past behind him, and now he was worried about a potentially turbulent future.

Uncle Suleiman was frightened by the expulsion order. He had nowhere to go and no money to pay the smugglers for a boat ride to Italy. He was worried about the U.S. invasion of his country, worried about Saddam Hussein's retaliation, worried about American bombs.

He spoke of the U.S. bombing of Baghdad in 1991. "The bombs came at two-thirty in the morning. They attacked neighborhoods. Many died." Walking on the beach, he told me of the Kurds and their betrayal by the allied forces, and about how the Kurds fled to the mountains and died in the thousands. "They left us alone. I am afraid that the same thing would happen again."

Uncle Suleiman told stories about the women who had given birth to children with deformed faces in the post–Gulf War years, after drinking contaminated water and eating vegetables grown in poisoned soil. "The children were punished for being born in Iraq," he said, staring at the blue waters of the Mediterranean. "I will not bring any more children to this world."

※

We did not meet again. By the time I left Greece and returned to Istanbul, the American-led coalition had attacked and occupied Iraq and toppled Saddam Hussein. Iraq was declared safe. Western states closed their gates to Iraqi citizens and encouraged them to return home and rebuild their country. Reconstruction had to begin. And although violence continued in Baghdad and other parts of the country, northern Iraq appeared to be on the road to relative peace and prosperity. Many Kurds returned to their homes in Iraqi Kurdistan.

I do not know if Uncle Suleiman stayed in Greece or moved forward. I do not know if he went home to rebuild Iraq.

Nusrat

My visits to Uncle Suleiman's tent always included exciting bus rides with Nusrat. We would joke and laugh. He would tell me stories about Iran. While in the camp, he would quietly listen to Uncle Suleiman, talk to the boys, or play soccer with them. On our way back to Athens, he would once again be full of stories.

When we first met in the office of Médecins du Monde Grèce, Nusrat was planning his next escape. He pulled me aside and showed me the scar on his chin. This was five months after the coast guard in Patras had picked him up. They told him to lie on his belly on the ground. He was handcuffed from behind. One pulled his hair, punched him in the left eye, and kicked him in the back. He nearly lost consciousness. They put him in a car, took him to a bathroom, closed the door, and began the second round of beatings.

"They beat me for twenty minutes. My chin started bleeding. They hit me with a metal bar and punched me on the face." At that moment a tourist entered the bathroom and, horrified, began taking pictures. Nusrat was saved.

Nusrat was hospitalized for eight days. His mouth was cut in many places. "I could not eat on my own. They had to feed me intravenously." Two weeks after being released from the hospital, he returned to Athens.

Nusrat was a high school dropout, but he spoke the Persian of an educated person. He loved poetry, read newspapers, talked politics, and like many others from his homeland, took pleasure in listening to the music of the Iranian diaspora—Iranian pop made in Los Angeles. Nusrat had a keen interest in medicine. At times during our meetings, he would mention strange diseases and tell me all he had read about them in medical and health magazines in Iran.

"Will you perhaps study to be a doctor?" I asked him.

"No, I only want to keep a healthy body. If I ever make it to England, I will go to the gym and work out every day. That is what I would like to do." He was no longer interested in schooling. "This is not for me," he would always say when I mentioned universities and studying.

His appearance was strikingly different from that of the Afghans, Africans, and other Iranians I met in Athens. He was six feet tall and thin. His short black hair was always well trimmed, neatly combed, and clean. He wore clean, ironed designer shirts, cashmere pants—always black—from Zara International, shining black shoes, and an expensive brown leather jacket.

He ate good food. While many others lined up at soup kitchens and charities, Nusrat regularly treated himself to fancy salads, desserts, and drinks. Tall and athletic, he did not smoke cigarettes or use drugs, but enjoyed the taste of good wine. Nusrat had many Greek friends. They invited him to restaurants and bars, he told me.

Unlike many others I met in Greece, Nusrat did not sleep in parks or squats; he shared an apartment with a Greek man. His friends harassed him, accused him of living with a *baba*—sugar daddy—and performing sexual favors in return for a place to sleep. He dismissed the charges. "They joke with me. But to me it doesn't matter what he [the housemate] does as long as he doesn't ask me to have sex with him." That was the only time Nusrat mentioned his Greek housemate.

For migrants such as Nusrat, finding a *baba* was an easy way of escaping the hardships of life in transit. "This is easy. No reason for working twelve hours a day like me," a street hawker told me. The boys with a *baba* were sheltered. They were paid good pocket money, wined and dined, and dressed in nice outfits. They were young Iranians and Kurds from northern Iraq, men in their early or late twenties. The Kurds came from the villages, the rugged mountains of northern Iraq. The Iranians arrived from small towns, ghettos of big cities, and poor neighborhoods of the capital. They came with a dream. Many failed. They remained in Athens and became the "bar kids" of Victoria Square. Dressing up in their best, they would frequent the gay bars around the square looking for a *baba* or a customer in search of sexual pleasure.

Back in Iran, Nusrat had enjoyed a comfortable life: a supportive and loving family, girlfriends, adequate pocket money, hobbies, and a job he loved. He dropped out of high school in the ninth grade. That was the end of his formal education.

"I wanted to work and be around people," he told me.

He joined "the world of business," working at his father's confectionery store in Karaj, a town thirty miles or so outside Tehran. The money was good. "I was a boss at age eighteen. I managed my father's store." But Nusrat wasn't content. Something was missing in his life.

Though he was no longer interested in formal schooling, he had a longing for reading and learning. He envied the lifestyle of university students, the boys and girls his age who had less money and less power, but enjoyed a richer life. In his free time, Nusrat would visit Tehran University and the bookstores around the main campus, watch the young students, and imagine himself doing the same, entering the main gate with a university ID card in his hand. Then came July 1999.

In the early morning hours of July 8, 1999, the riot police and men dressed in civilian clothes ambushed the housing compound of Tehran University. Rooms were set on fire. Sleeping students were pulled out of their beds, clubbed, and assaulted with chains and knives. Their faces were smashed, their bones broken.

The following morning, July 9, thousands of students in Tehran and across the country responded, taking to the streets to protest the night attack in the compound. For nearly a week, across Tehran and twenty-two other cities, the students demonstrated, barricaded the streets, and fought the riot police and the men who wielded machetes and chain. The streets around Tehran University were the sites of some of the most militant actions by the students and their supporters. Among those protesting was Nusrat.

With excitement, Nusrat participated in the student rallies, chanting and marching through the streets of Tehran. The protests rejuvenated him, gave him new energy. For days, he left Karaj early in the morning and returned only for a short sleep. The next morning, he would be back in front of the main gate of Tehran University.

"I had a natural talent for making slogans," he told me on one of our bus rides to visit Uncle Suleiman's tent. "It came to me very easily. I always loved music. All I did was change the words of the songs I liked. I replaced them with political words. The students loved my slogans, thousands repeated them." Animatedly Nusrat repeated the key slogans of the nationwide student protests of July 1999, both those that he had created and others made by creative students across the country.

I too remembered the streets of Tehran during the week of protest. I had left Iran one week after the protest was put down by the gov-

ernment. Two thousand students were arrested. Tehran and many
large cities fell under the reign of the security forces and the goons
roaming around with chains and knives. Sitting in the back of the
bus, I joined Nusrat in quietly chanting slogans of the week of
protest.

> *"Freedom of thoughts, always, always!"*
> *"Down with Taliban, in Kabul or Tehran!"*
> *"Tanks, artillery, and guns no longer have any power!"*

Keeping our voices down, we reminisced and shared stories, our separate worlds brought together by the tales of a week that had turned
Iran upside down.

When the week of protest ended, Nusrat had returned to the confectionery store with memories that shaped the rest of his life. For
days, he had stood shoulder to shoulder with the students, immersed
in their lives and activities, and shared their energy and excitement.
In the privacy of his room, though, he was aware of his differences
with the students. He was an outsider and did not belong with them.

"I did not know what to answer when they [the protesting stu-
dents] asked me what university I attended and what subject I studied," he told me in a somber voice. "They were curious, wanted to
get to know me better. I often escaped answering."

The summer ended. Students returned to the university. Sporadic
protests erupted, and Nusrat joined a few. Arrested in one protest, he
was released after a night in detention. He was back to the confectionery. The place sucked the young man's energy. To escape the
boredom of his everyday life, he would return to the university, and
stroll up and down along the fence separating the campus from the
streets. But there were no more protests, no possibility of participat-
ing in a life so different from managing the confectionery.

Life went on until one day four close friends from Karaj informed
Nusrat of their decision to leave Iran for Turkey. Without thinking,
Nusrat agreed to join the journey. This was April 2002.

He returned home, packed a small bag, and left without saying farewell. A few days later he phoned his home from Van. "At first, they [his parents] were shocked. But when I called again, they told me to go forward. They were happy that I was no longer in Iran. They did not have to worry about me protesting and getting arrested." Soon after arriving, Nusrat and his friends left Van for Istanbul. They had no intention of applying for asylum in Turkey. Their plan was to move on to Greece.

Istanbul was an eye-opener for Nusrat. "Getting off the bus in Istanbul, I saw the class difference I had never seen before, not only among the Iranians, but the Turks and everyone." In Istanbul, Nusrat and his friends shared an apartment in Aksaray. At night they frequented an Iranian discotheque, but the boys had not left their homes and their loved ones merely to live in Aksaray and visit its nightclubs.

Consulting with other migrants they befriended, they chose a route. Hios island was to be their point of entry into Greece. They would take to the sea without the help of smugglers, they decided. For many long days, they planned, inquired, and contemplated their coming sea journey to the Greek island. Buying floats, or inflatable boats, was the first step in the preparation.

"We bought three floats, two Chinese-made and one Russian, for three hundred dollars. The Russian float was thick and reliable. It had strong oars and cost more. The Chinese ones were flimsy."

They rehearsed their escape in the Aksaray apartment. "We pumped air into the floats, put on our life vests, jumped in the floats, and pretended to be rowing," he said, laughing. "No one thought the boats would go more than a hundred feet."

Two days later, in June 2002, the boys boarded a night bus to Çeşme with the floats packed in their backpacks. "Our bags were big. We were afraid that the police would search the bus on the way to Çeşme. None of us had done this before. We didn't know what was expecting us."

Çeşme was a mystery to the boys. "We didn't know the place, its shores, and the right place to put the floats in the sea. None of us had any experience in rowing." Nusrat and two others could not swim. Scores of young people had died braving the turbulent waters of the Aegean Sea on rickety boats, and Nusrat had been aware of the dangers when he boarded the bus in Istanbul. Many months later, safe in Athens, he looked back at his journey, paused, and laughed.

Arriving in Çeşme in the morning, they checked into a room in a hostel. "We were given the address in Aksaray. We left our bags in the room and went out to look for the right place for departure. We walked along the shore away from the center. We were scared of being caught by the gendarmes. We studied the area, determined the safe location and time for departure, and returned to the hostel." Back in the hostel, they met another Iranian, a lone traveler hoping to leave for Greece. He did not have a float and had no idea of the ways to proceed. The boys invited the Iranian to join them in the journey. They were now six people and three floats, two people per float.

Late in the evening they took their belongings and approached the sea. They had no smuggler, no maps, and no past experience. Their only guides in the sea were the lights on Hios island. It was a clear night, and the island was visible from the shore in Turkey.

They pumped air into the floats, put their clothes in plastic bags and sealed the bags with strong tape, and began the journey.

"The first half an hour was the funniest part of the trip. We didn't know how to row and direct the floats. We were spinning around, laughing," Nusrat said, chuckling again in the retelling. Sitting across from me in a café, using his hands, Nusrat demonstrated the first few minutes of the journey. He pretended to be rowing. Tracing circles with his hand, he demonstrated how the floats spun.

Some in the group were ready to return to the hostel. The others persevered. "We kept rowing, but we were not moving at all." Slowly, one float moved a number of feet away from the shore. The boys had learned the art of rowing. The other floats followed suit. The boys rowed ahead, approaching the lights.

"Weren't you scared?" I asked Nusrat.

"I don't know why, perhaps it was the will of God. I am sure that was it. The sea was very calm. There were no waves, no movements. God wanted to save all the migrants leaving for Greece that night."

A mile or two into the sea journey, the boats became separated. Two of the Chinese oars broke, and Nusrat had to row with his hands. As he demonstrated to me, Nusrat burst into laughter. "I'm laughing now, but we were very scared. I didn't know if we were going to reach the island. We could see the lights, but for some reason, we weren't getting closer. My hands were tired. Everyone was tired."

At seven in the morning, the migrants reached the shore. They washed their faces with the bottled water they had carried from Turkey, changed their clothes, and tore the floats with a knife. No sign of recent arrivals could be left. The oars and the floats had to be destroyed, buried under the sand. Having disguised the evidence of their long journey, the boys proceeded toward the town.

Hios is a tourist island. The streets are always crowded with people. Its long shore is full of cafés, restaurants, and bars. Even during the hot midafternoon hours, men and women, both tourists and locals, congregate in the cafés drinking iced coffee—the drink of choice on the island—and killing time. The tall trees in a park in the center are a haven from the burning sun. Many take refuge there at midday.

After a long walk along the shore, exhausted and hungry, the boys reached the town center. Drained from their night journey, black rings under their eyes, they looked like fugitives. Avoiding the crowd on the main boulevard along the shore, they walked through the back streets and by chance found themselves at the park. Sleeping on a park bench or street corner was dangerous. The town was full of police, uniformed and plainclothes. They sat on two adjacent park benches, resting and making every effort to remain awake. The boys saw three Iranians walking around the park and approached them. The Iranians had just been released after ninety days of detention on the island and were waiting for their smuggler. Athens was their destination. A boat was to take them off the island at ten-thirty at night. Nusrat and his friends joined the group. Purchasing tickets from a travel office on the main boulevard, they strolled on the streets. They had twelve hours on their hands.

"This was the longest day of my life. We could have been spotted and deported, or taken to detention for three months. Trying to walk, I ran into parked cars. I couldn't control myself."

Half an hour before departure time, Nusrat approached the ship. "I had seen this in movies. I wanted to make sure that no one suspected me. I saw an old woman in the line. I took her luggage and carried it to the boat. It always worked in the movies," he told me, laughing. The plan worked in real life. No one suspected Nusrat. "The captain thanked me for helping the old woman. The minute I got in, I left the woman and her luggage and took a seat and slept all the way to Athens."

Helped by his father, Nusrat rented a private apartment and began a life unlike that experienced by other Iranians. Away from his home for the first time, he wept at night and wished he were back in the arms of his family, those who gave him unconditional love. But returning home was not an option. He had to proceed further west.

To save money for the journey, he joined the ranks of street vendors on Ermou Street, selling T-shirts. Ermou Street, off popular Syntagma Square, was a favorite spot for street vendors selling fake designer handbags and for a few Iranians and Chinese selling inexpensive scarves, gloves, and hats. They would come in groups and put out their merchandise on large white cloths on the ground. Athenians and tourists would cluster around them, bargain, walk away, return to buy, and bring smiles to the faces of the hustling migrants.

The scene would change abruptly with the arrival of a police patrol. In a few seconds the white cloths would be folded up and the vendors would run, disappearing from sight. They would return when the police were gone. The vendors would run with bulky and knotted white cloths hanging from their shoulders and then return to the street many times a day, many times a week. They would pay their fines, lose their merchandise at times, but return to the same spot.

This was a daily routine for Nusrat. Playing cat and mouse with the municipal police—"Tom and Jerry," as he called it—he would pack up his merchandise and disappear into the back streets when the police arrived, then return to his site when they left the scene. Day in and day out, Nusrat sold T-shirts and befriended other migrants—vendors from the Middle East, and others from places as far as Africa.

Then came the time to leave for the road again. Nusrat and his friends moved to Patras, a Mediterranean port three hours' drive from Athens, a main exit port for ships leaving for Italy.

Nusrat's attempt to leave Greece from Patras was a failure. When he was released from the hospital after the beating by the coast guard, he returned to Athens. Sometime in mid-March, his family wired him $1,500. A week later, he paid a smuggler all his money and left Athens hiding in a truck with the knowledge of the driver. This was a "guaranteed cargo," he told me. Two days later he called me from Rome.

"You are the second person I am calling, *agha* Behzad. I knew you would become happy. I made it."

PART FOUR

Patras

First Encounter

On the morning of March 7, 2003, I took a bus to Patras, a port 130 miles west of Athens, Greece's gateway to Italy and other countries in Western Europe. The city was preparing for its extravagant yearly carnival, held on the weekend of March 11–13. Dating back to the early nineteenth century, the carnival brought to Patras people from all over Greece and around the world, who traveled there for three days of theater, dance, music, costumes, and its assembly of joyful human creativity. To many migrants from the Middle East and Africa, Patras was the border they had to cross to reach freedom elsewhere in Europe.

My bus arrived minutes past noon. Standing on the sidewalk outside the station, I faced the harbor, trucks, ships, and the vast Mediterranean Sea. A long boulevard stood between the harbor and the city. A fence, twelve feet high and stretching nearly a mile, enclosed the harbor and the world behind it.

I crossed the boulevard and, not knowing my next stop, followed two boys speaking Persian with an Afghan accent, walking on a narrow patch along the fence. There were no activities on the harbor, and not many cars on the boulevard. A few minutes later I was in an open area in front of the fence, by a large closed gate. Six young men wearing old, discolored clothes stood by the fence. Grasping the bars, one gazed at the ships far away. The two Afghan boys joined the crowd. I walked closer and introduced myself.

Saying their names, they shook my hand and welcomed me to

Patras. More Afghans arrived. We were eight, then fifteen. Some were in their teens, but they all had coarse hands and facial skin hardened by exposure to harsh weather. They smiled when they shook my hand. Soon they were passing among them my small tape recorder, telling me their stories. Riddled with anger at the world around them, they spoke about life outside the fence.

In the winter of 2001, the Americans freed Afghanistan from the Taliban. Many refugees returned to their villages, to what was left of their homes. Others, frightened by the renewal of local tribal and religious violence in their homeland and the prospect of poverty in their country, chose not to return and continued their search for a new home in a Western country that would accept them. As the poverty in Afghanistan persisted and its instability continued, still another wave of Afghans joined the ranks of these migrants.

The fall of the Taliban became the occasion for the end of the West's sympathy for displaced Afghans. Afghanistan was declared a safe country, and Western states closed their gates to Afghanistan's poor and war-stricken citizens, encouraging them to return home and rebuild their country. As a result, a population of wandering Afghans emerged—driven from their places of birth and kept behind closed doors elsewhere in the world.

I asked the Afghans about their feelings after the fall of the Taliban.

"America only took care of the problem of the Taliban, but they didn't solve people's problems," an Afghan with a missing tooth lamented. "I don't think Afghanistan's problems will be solved in the next two hundred years." Opening his mouth, he showed me the socket in his jaw. His tooth had broken and fallen out when the coast guard clubbed him and struck him on the face. He had been trying to leave Patras. "Please tell the commandos [the coast guard] not to hit us, tell them not to break our teeth," he pleaded with me.

Impatient to grab the tape recorder away from his friend, a skinny

Afghan refugee beaten by Greek coast guard

Afghan interjected, "From a distance, it appears that things are better in Afghanistan. But there are many problems. None of the countries that promised to help gave any money."

"I will never return to Afghanistan," an intense-looking seventeen-year-old said. He was short, and looked older than his age; his face was red with anger, and it lacked life. When he was thirteen the Taliban had killed his father. At fourteen he had joined one of the small armies fighting the Taliban. He had escaped Afghanistan for Pakistan and Iran a year later; soon after, he was in Turkey. Now he was in Patras, standing in front of the fence, showing me an official document demanding that he leave the country in one month. "They treat us like a football. They kick us. Why don't they take us to the border and send us back? Death is better than this," he said, putting the paper in the side pocket of his winter jacket.

Listening to the words of his friend, a sixteen-year-old boy with his left arm in a cast came forward. I asked him about his arm.

"I was hiding under the chassis of the truck, but the commandos saw me. They came with their sticks and took me out. There were two of them. They hit me hard. For five or six minutes, they hit me with an electric baton. They broke my arm. I was howling. My friends took me to the hospital."

"What will you do next?" I asked him.

"I have to wait. I do not have any money to pay the smugglers now."

I asked if he would return to Afghanistan. He smiled and said, "What can I do there?"

The Fence

A rriving here on buses, the migrants face the fence. From early morning to late at night, they stand behind it, scheme, study it, and dream of leaving. They stare at the ships arriving from the sea, unloading, anchoring for a few days, and leaving the port behind, slowly disappearing.

When it entered the everyday language of the migrants, the word *fence* was transformed. Mispronounced as "fance," it became a part of the tales told by migrants in Greece and places deeper in the European Union. The *fance* was no longer what it signified in English. Rather, it represented the world the migrants were kept out of. In Patras, the *fance* was the border to Italy, the next stop on the journey west. Crossing it was more formidable than crossing snow-covered mountains or navigating rough waters in rickety boats. "At night, we dream of the *fance*," an Afghan told me. The migrants dreamed of flying over the fence like ghosts, passing the coast guard unnoticed, finding their ship of choice, entering quietly, and moving on.

When the night casts its shadow over the city, the migrants walk by the fence away from the town center. Heads down, feeling ashamed of their predicament, they make their way to a makeshift soup kitchen a half hour's walk from the bus station. It is a single truck parked on a vacant lot on the side of the boulevard along the fence. Arriving at the site, the migrants queue up, their plates and plastic containers in their hands. One by one they get their sole meal of the day, and disappear in the dark.

The food might include leftovers from a hospital and a university cafeteria, and fresh macaroni made for the migrants in a church up on the hill, away from the fence. Usually a Greek woman serves the food. There are no people walking by, no buildings, and no sign of life.

"We are human too. We wish for a time that we won't be humiliated like this," an Iranian told me one night, walking away from the food line holding a small plastic bag full of cooked macaroni.

"I feel like crying when I go to the food line. My heart aches. We were not like this before," a young Afghan told me.

"We stand like beggars in the food line," another Afghan said. "But we came here with dreams."

Protecting the fence is among Greece's roles in the European Union. There are many layers of fortification in the EU, and the fence is an inner wall. The Greeks treated Patras differently from the borders separating the country from neighbors in the north. Strict border control was implemented along all borders, but in Patras, border control took on new dimensions. Unusually for the Greeks, the use of violence was common. Leaving Greece for other countries in the EU was to be stopped by all means possible.

Driving or on foot, the Greek coast guard patrolled the harbor. They spotted the migrants, chased them, and ran them away from the harbor. One member of the coast guard was especially known for his brutality. The Iranians and Afghans nicknamed him Jabbar

Farman, *jabbar* meaning "dictator" and *farman* "order." Jabbar
Farman instilled fear in the heart of the migrants.

"This happened not long ago. Jabbar Farman found Madjid hiding under a truck. He pulled him out and punched him on the head.
Madjid fell down and became unconscious. They had to take him to
the hospital, but Jabbar Farman took him out at four in the morning. He took him to the sea and forced him in the water to his neck,"
an Iranian told me. Similar stories were told by Afghans and others.

Crossing the border to Italy, the migrants not only had to escape
the watchful eyes and the beatings of the coast guard but had to pay
off the human smugglers who practically controlled clandestine entry to the trucks. "Let me tell you something. There are some op-
portunists here called smugglers. Our main problem is with the
smugglers," an Afghan told me, refusing to tell me his name. Fearing
repercussions, he asked me to turn off my tape recorder and said, "All
they do is open and close the trucks, and charge the boys six hundred
or seven hundred dollars for it. They beat you up if you refuse to pay.
I don't have any money to pay the smugglers. So I have to stay here
or get beat up by them, even the Afghans."

There were seven gates to the fence, providing access to the harbor
for trucks, passenger cars, and the tourists. The smugglers controlled
the migrants' access to the fence. A well-established system divided
the fence and its gates between Kurdish and Afghan smugglers when
I visited Patras in March 2003. The Kurds had four gates, and the
Afghans had two. The seventh gate was a "free gate"—no nationality
controlled it.

"There was a war between the Afghans and the Kurds over the
control of the *fance*. The Kurds wanted the whole *fance*. The Afghans
demanded a share. So a fight broke out. The Afghans called people in
nearby towns. In less than a few hours, two hundred Afghans arrived
with knives and chains. A few people were stabbed, but in the end,
the Afghans took two gates. I wasn't here at that point, but I heard
this from a lot of people," an Afghan told me.

After the conflict, a truce was negotiated between the leaders of the two warring parties. Kurdish and Afghan zones were established. The Kurds did not enter the Afghan gates, and the Afghans stayed off Kurdish turf. But no one escaped without paying off the appropriate smugglers.

"Before the war on Iraq, the Kurds were the largest group in Patras. There were almost nine hundred Kurds, five hundred Afghans, and fifty Iranians. The Kurds wanted everything because they were bigger than the rest, but the Afghans were not very small either. In the end, the Kurds got more gates because they had more people," Arshan, an Iranian migrant, told me. "We got the 'free gate,' " he said, laughing.

Located a short walk from the bus station, and facing a large pedestrian area surrounded by shops and restaurants, the "free gate" was the main pedestrian entrance to the harbor. "This is called the free gate because there are always people going in and out. You see Greek lovers holding hands and strolling on the waterfront," an Iranian migrant told me. The waterfront had benches and an area for strolling and enjoying the Mediterranean air. The area behind the gate was often crowded with Greeks passing time, travelers, ship crews, and the coast guard. The smugglers avoided the gate. They used the six gates to its left and right.

Most Afghans and Kurds paid their smugglers to be put in trucks using the remaining six gates. The last two gates before reaching the Afghan *kheimeh,* or shantytown, were in the hands of the Afghans, and the area behind the fence was Afghan turf. The remaining four gates to the left and right of the free gate were Kurdish controlled.

"Our main problem here is not with the commandos. It is with the Kurdish and the Afghan smugglers. They think they own the *fance.* They demand a lot of money, sometimes a thousand dollars. They charge whatever they can. There is no rule. When we object, they say, 'We have given blood for the *fance.* It is our time to collect,' " Arshan told me.

"I spoke to a Kurdish smuggler today for one of my friends. He said, 'We charge fifteen hundred dollars for guaranteed delivery, and seven hundred dollars for normal delivery.' I asked what he meant by normal. 'We hide you under the chassis of the truck,' he said. I don't understand this, they talk as if they own the trucks.

"There is no guaranteed delivery anyway. No matter how much you pay, at the end everything depends on luck. The smugglers don't do anything special here. They don't get you a passport or a fake visa. All they do is open and close the trucks. Anybody can do that. They should not be called smugglers," Arshan told me.

"What will happen if you tried to do it yourself?" I asked.

"The trucks usually stay in the parking area for a few days before they board the ships. The smugglers send their passengers at certain times, usually two hours before the boarding time. In those times, nobody is allowed to use the six gates without paying. They would beat them up and even attack them with knives. They would loosen their control when there was no boarding.

"The Iranians usually don't pay. They use their brain and methods that the smugglers do not use. The Iranians know the exact schedule of all the ships and their loading and unloading time. The operation time is no longer than two hours. Sometimes the boys hide somewhere near the ships that are loading for the journey. They run inside and hide somewhere when nobody is watching. Then they hide under a truck until the ship leaves."

Climbing ropes was among the Iranian inventions. "The boys climb the ropes that are used to anchor the ships. This is a very hard job and requires a lot of courage and practice." Two ropes not too far apart were needed for the acrobatic act. There is no time to be wasted. The short pause between coast guard patrols was the time the rope climber could use to perform the toughest act of his life. "You should not look down. If you make a mistake, you either fall on the concrete and die right away, or fall into the sea and drown if you don't know how to swim," Arshan said.

The Afghan Kheimeh

The migrants arrived in Patras vulnerable, often penniless, and without any protection and support from the Greek government. They arrived looking for shelter and a roof over their heads. Renting a private space was beyond their means. Except for a handful of cases, all ended up living in squat homes or shanties. The Afghans lived in the *kheimeh*. I visited the *kheimeh* in the afternoon of my first visit to Patras. "You have to come to our *kheimeh* to see how we live," an Afghan boy said, standing by the fence.

Kheimeh is a word used by the Afghans for both "tent" and "makeshift camp." The term signifies life in transition, a nomadic life. All Afghans entering Patras lived in the *kheimeh,* their communal guest house. Apart from personal belongings, such as clothes and so forth, there was no private property in the *kheimeh*—everything was owned by all, the current residents as well as the migrants arriving in the future.

On a piece of land sparsely covered with shrubs and short trees, off the main road and away from the town center, there stood many shacks made of multiple layers of cardboard and plastic. The land was privately owned. The owner had consented to the building of the *kheimeh,* I was told. The municipal authorities had closed their eyes to the illegal wiring and the free use of electricity by the residents. There was no drinking water. The Afghans fetched water from nearby places in buckets.

A narrow creek separated the *kheimeh* from an adjacent plot of land. In summertime, the residents of the *kheimeh* washed their clothes and bathed in the creek. Bathing was always a concern. Some washed in the sea, even in winter, a resident told me. They waited for a sunny day and dipped in the sea. However, there was an open bath somewhere in the *kheimeh*. This was a small space with no roof and four walls made of plastic and cardboard. The Afghans

The Afghan kheimeh *in Patras*

boiled water in a barrel over a wood fire and sometimes bathed there in the winter.

The shacks were artfully put together. All corners were sealed to protect them from rain and wind. Some were bigger than others. Each housed between three and five migrants. They were tidy and clean, built on cleared but bumpy ground. There were old carpets and blankets covering their floors. All were equipped with numerous blankets and pillows. Some had televisions and refrigerators. A small shack served as a mosque.

When it rained, the *kheimeh* was a sea of mud; there were potholes full of rainwater. However, following the Afghan tradition, no one entered the shacks with their shoes. The mud stayed outside. Damp and wet at times, the interior still remained spotless, free of mud and dirt. Keeping the shacks clean was their culture, an unwritten rule that all followed.

The interior walls were cardboard. Some were decorated with

posters, pictures of religious shrines, or personal photos. The exteri-
ors had a common look: clear plastic over cardboard, with long ropes
wrapped around the plastic. Some shacks were partially covered with
white canvas or thicker plastic.

Among the shacks, one stood out for the large stuffed animal—a
black-and-white teddy bear—on the roof above the entrance. Standing in the doorway, a young man in his teens, dressed in a striped
soccer shirt with the emblem of the German automaker Opel, invited me to a cup of tea in the shack. I accepted the invitation. Leaving the shack, I noticed the writing on the wooden door. It was two
short lines in the Persian alphabet: "Patras, the open prison."

I was walking through the shacks chatting with a few residents
when I heard music. It was live music, a beautiful tune played by a
sole string instrument—one that sounded like the Iranian *tar* or the
Turkish *divan*. I asked about it, and they pointed to a shack nearby. I
followed the sound and stood by the window looking inside. Playing
his instrument, a smiling young man greeted me, asking me to enter
his home in the *kheimeh*.

This was a shack unlike others. Its interior walls were wallpapered
with old blankets. The musician, who looked to be in his late teens,
sat on a bed covered with a green army blanket. Two large blankets,
full of big red flowers against a black background, covered the wall
behind him, along with a third in dark gray. To his right was the wall
with the window. A ripped green blanket with white and red stripes
and one in light brown were nailed to the surface around and under
the window. The window was a hole on the wall with a piece of wood
nailed vertically in the middle. The curtain, a blanket too, was
pushed to the side. Two young men, one wearing a black T-shirt, the
other wearing white, stood outside the window, looking through the
hole, listening.

Immersed in the music, I sat before the young player. Following
his fingers moving up and down, touching the strings, I stared at the
instrument. No *tar* or *divan*, this was a homemade string instrument, a makeshift music box following the young Afghan on the

*Afghan refugee, on the
road with his
homemade string
instrument*

road to the West. He noticed my awe and stopped the music. Laughing, he handed me the instrument: a red plastic ball sealed by a piece of wood, and two strings attached to a long stick. Patiently sanded, the wood was smooth. Its discolored surface told stories of its repeated use under the artful fingers of the young Afghan, and of the melodies it created on the road.

A gentle smile on his boyish face, the Afghan took back the instrument and pounded the wood, striking the strings with his fingers. Music resumed.

It was a few minutes past noon. I said goodbye to the Afghans and returned to the fence.

The Truck: Farshad

The truck was a legend in Patras and beyond. In public parks and along the railroad tracks, in Paris and in Calais, I heard tales about the truck and the men who had once occupied it. This is the story of one such man. His name is Farshad. We met late in the afternoon on March 7, 2003.

An Iranian I met by the fence after leaving the Afghan *kheimeh* took me to the truck. "Have you been to the truck?" was the first question he asked after our initial introductions. He agreed to accompany me there to show me "how the [Iranian] boys lived in Europe." Walking on an isolated road parallel to the fence, we saw an abandoned truck covered by a thick discolored green tarpaulin. "This is the truck," he said.

A broken school bus stood across the street. A mild wind was blowing. There were no shops, no signs of life on the street.

"I am with an Iranian writing a book about migrants," he cried.

A hand appeared, pulling aside the tarpaulin on one corner. That was my first encounter with Farshad. "Please come in. Welcome.

Farshad

Welcome" were his first words. He was average height and a bit chubby. His thick, graying short hair and his unshaven face made him look older than his age. He was wearing his winter clothes--a turtleneck under a zipped-up fleece vest.

Farshad bent down and held my right arm, and I climbed up into the truck. The floor inside was covered by old blankets. There was a small portable gas burner in one corner, four plates, a small, beat-up pot for boiling water, a frying pan, three glasses, a few extra blankets and pillows, and a plastic water container. These were the truck's public property. They were left behind by those who succeeded in crossing the fence and escaping, and used by new migrants.

There were four other men, all in their twenties, in the truck. Rising to their feet, they greeted me. "Welcome," everyone repeated. I took off my shoes, leaving them among a dozen or so pairs of old shoes at the entrance of the truck. "Welcome," the men said again. Initial introductions followed. Shaking my hand, all said their names. Farshad directed me to a spot on the floor at the far end of the truck, away from the entrance. This was a special place for honored guests.

As is the custom in all Iranian homes, I was offered tea. Three glasses were brought to the fore. Waiting for the tea, we nodded and smiled. When the tea was ready, I was given the biggest glass. More water was boiled and more tea was prepared. Taking turns, the men drank from the shared glasses. Cigarettes were lit and soon grievances were told. Some told their stories with laughter. They joked and made light of their beatings by the coast guard and their repeated failures to flee to Italy. Farshad remained silent. Waiting for his time to tell stories, he merely smiled when others burst into laughter.

I took out my camera and began taking pictures. Some covered their faces, still laughing. I photographed Farshad pouring me tea. And when others stopped their laughter, he began to tell his tale. He spoke without pausing.

"The mullahs hurt us a lot. But the worst thing they did was to cause us to lose respect in the eyes of the rest of the world," Farshad said.

He spoke about a time not so long ago when the Iranians were given visas "with respect." "Now they beat us up in Europe. We are the very same Iranians," he said. The other men nodded.

I asked if they wished to return to Iran.

"There is no work in Iran for us. All the boys I grew up with do drugs. They stand on the street corner and waste time most of the day. They get high and sleep the rest of the time. This is what awaits me if I go back," one man said.

As if in the presence of a psychologist in a group therapy session, they took turns telling of their experiences and their fears. They complained of idleness and boredom in their place of birth.

"I blame Iran for all of this. I would have never come here if I had a car and my own small shop in Iran. I would have opened my store every day, worked, and returned home happy. I would have stayed in Iran. It is very hard here. I miss my family.

"I worked six years in Turkey before coming here. Look where I am now. I lie to my family when I talk to them on the phone. I say, 'Don't worry about me. I have a house here. I have a good job,' I tell them. They don't know I sleep in a truck. I swear on the Qur'an that I am blushing from embarrassment now."

"My parents keep on asking me to go back, but I have nothing there. I would be standing on the street corner getting harassed by the morality police, or doing drugs like most of the boys from my neighborhood. Why should I go back?"

A few minutes of silence followed. I turned to Farshad. He was staring at the floor, playing with his tea glass. "Why did you leave Iran, *agha* Farshad?" I asked.

Farshad was born into a military family during the time of the late shah. In 1979, shortly after the revolution, the new government executed his father, a member of the deposed shah's Royal Guard.

"They hanged my father in 1980 and confiscated our home. We moved to Karaj [a town some twenty miles north of Tehran] and rented a small house. It was my mother, my sister, and me," he said.

The killing of his father politicized Farshad. "I loved my father, and I couldn't forgive them for killing him. I wanted to do something for my father, so I began working with the monarchists." Not long after, at age twenty-two, Farshad was arrested and sent to the notorious Evin Prison. "I spent the next sixteen months in solitary in the Evin Prison. I had no visiting rights. They regularly tortured me. They hung me upside down from my testicles, and burnt my back with hot metal rods. That damaged my testicles; they hang very low after that. My kidneys don't function right," he said.

"After solitary, they gave me seventy-five lashes and then banished me to Bandar Abbas [a Persian Gulf port known for its heat, humidity, poverty, and unbearable living conditions]. I spent three years in Bandar Abbas.

"After finishing my years, I returned to Tehran, but I was under their surveillance. Once again, they arrested me and sent me to the Evin. This time, I was there one year."

Upon his release, they arrested Farshad once more, in Tehran at Nur Square. This time they sent him straight to the Dastgerd Prison in Isfahan. After nearly one year in jail, Farshad qualified for a weekend leave from prison. He did not return.

"I said to myself, 'Iran has had nothing for me but flogging and prison.' I was tired of spending time in jail. I decided to leave and look for a normal life somewhere else. Why should I have stayed?"

Escaping the country, he crossed the mountains to Turkey. "I did not want to stay in Turkey, and with a lot of difficulty I crossed the Turkish border with Greece. They arrested me right away and put me in a camp for ninety-three days."

A younger Iranian abruptly interrupted Farshad. "*Agha* Farshad, please explain how we cross these borders. It is not easy. Please explain." Turning to me, he said, "We put our lives in our hands and cross the sea in small floats. There are sometimes waves as big as this truck. There is a 100 percent chance of dying, but we take the risk and hope to find a better life somewhere." Farshad agreed, and continued to tell the story of his three-month detention in the camp.

"They fed us twice a day, once at eleven-thirty in the morning and then at six in the evening. We used a hose and bathed outdoors. They attacked us with electric batons anytime we complained. My foot became numb when they hit me after I complained about food. They gave me a piece of paper and asked me to go to Athens after ninety-three days. I arrived in Athens with no money, food, or a place to stay."

For three weeks, Farshad slept on a piece of cardboard in Alexandra Park not far from the office of Médecins du Monde Grèce in Athens. After working random jobs for three months, he left Athens for Patras in September 2002. "I have been living in this truck for seven months. I tried to leave a number of times, but I am still here. I hope to leave soon."

The White House

I t was in the truck that I first heard about the White House. Arshan, an Iranian in his mid-thirties, offered to show me the place, which he shared with three other Iranian migrants.

On a hilltop a long walk from the fence was an old Christian cemetery. Only two graves there were lacking headstones. Two Muslim migrants, a child and an adult, father and son, were buried in those graves. Near the cemetery, a small white church faced a trailer home. Four Iranian migrants lived in the trailer when I first visited Patras in March 2003. The trailer had a broken bed at one end, a round dining table and four chairs, an old television set, a radio, and a few pictures on the walls. A door at the far end opened to a small space with a shower and a toilet. The only residence with hot and cold running water throughout the year and heat during winter, the trailer was the envy of all migrants in Patras. They called it the White House.

Attached to the White House was another trailer with large sinks and stoves. It served as the port's sole soup kitchen for the migrants. Every night at half past seven, the hungry migrants queued before a truck to receive their daily food ration, prepared in the soup kitchen.

The church provided the space for the White House and the kitchen. The citizens of Patras—individuals, hospitals, schools, and others—donated the rice, macaroni, and other ingredients and implements used in the soup kitchen. In return for living in the White House, the Iranians helped a single cook prepare the food, and they cleaned the trailer. The cook was a lively, overweight Greek woman in her late forties with a charming, rosy-cheeked face and a good

Drowned in the sea, two migrants, a child and an adult,
were buried in this cemetery.

sense of humor. The boys and the cook frequently joked and
laughed. Hugging and kissing was common. To the boys of the
White House, the cook was a mother in exile. She gave them affection and the feeling of family love they were deprived of.

The cook was the only paid staff of the soup kitchen. She arrived
there every day at eleven. After preparing the food, she would distrib-
ute it with the help of the boys. Though she was usually loving and
kind, she became furious, a raging bull, when the boys slacked off
when cleaning the kitchen. Afraid of her fury, they kept the kitchen
tidy and shining at all times.

One among the boys was the cook's favorite. "He is my son," she
would say, kissing him on the cheek. His name was Kia. He was
twenty-three years old, charming and handsome, and had thick eyebrows and dyed hair.

Kia was the one designated to sleep on the bed. Many in the past had used that broken bed. An Afghan whose leg was broken by the commandos was the last person before Kia. As for Kia, he had tried leaving Patras once. His first attempt was his last, as the beating was too hard for him to bear. He gave up.

"The commandos got hold of me. They hit me hard. That was it for me. I won't try it again," he told me. Five years before our meeting, Kia had left Iran with the hope of applying for asylum and finding a new home somewhere in the West. He only made it to Greece. He had no hope of moving forward. Kia stayed in bed until late afternoon, joked with friends, roamed around the port, and repeated the same routine day in and day out. It was nearly five in the evening the first time I visited the White House. Kia was awake but still in bed under the covers.

He was entertaining and funny. The boys poked fun at his dyed hair and laughed when he told me of his failed attempt to leave Patras. Kia was the only migrant to give up after one failure. The rest had tried many times.

One night during the carnival, I saw Kia late in the evening. He had roamed around town drinking and enjoying himself like those traveling to the port from elsewhere in Europe. Mingling among the celebrating crowd, he forgot the fence and the coast guard. After hours of celebration, the tourists returned to their hotels. Kia walked along the fence and returned to the White House. "We are not like them. We are always strangers. I know my place in the world," he told me.

Of the Iranians living in the White House, Arshan was the oldest; he was the voice of reason, the guide, and the person who brought calm and sanity in times of crisis. He was an older brother taking care of the boys, correcting their mistakes. I remember how once, fearing the anger of the cook, Arshan made the boys wash the kitchen at half past four in the morning.

He was balding and short, less than five feet tall. From the outset, he became an invaluable assistant to me. He guided me through the back alleys of the port, the fence, different gates, and the coast guard booth. Holding my small tape recorder in his hand, he would describe the escape routes and speak about the gates and those who controlled them. Like an expert in the field of migration, he would interview the Afghans and Kurds and record their voices for me. He would ask questions about their border crossing, their life on the road, all the things that experienced sociologists or anthropologists would ask from their interviewees. In the few days we spent together, Arshan became a journalist wishing to tell the world the truth about the journey of migration. "You take pictures and leave the rest to me, *agha* Behzad," Arshan would say.

Arshan had been born to a large family in Tehran's oldest ghetto, Javadieh. Javadieh was an impoverished zone on the southern outskirts of Tehran, a place for the poorest of the poor, men and women who worked long hours and hardly survived. To many, the poor of Javadieh were signs of the corruption, neglect, and failure of the regime that was toppled by the revolution in 1979. Though it saw some noticeable improvements in the 1990s, Javadieh maintained its old characteristics, its social fabric, and its place on the margins of society.

Many boys and girls in Javadieh did not finish high school. Only a few entered universities. Most continued the life of destitution they inherited from their families. Arshan's family, he claimed, was an exception. His oldest brother had a doctorate and made a good deal of money working for a private firm, he told me. A younger sister and brother studied in the university. The family owned a large fruit garden. Arshan had remained in Javadieh, in the family's home, until he left Iran for Turkey. And despite the stories of money and relative comfort in Iran, he was penniless in Patras.

Like others in the port, he had been beaten up many times by the coast guard for getting near the ships leaving for Italy. The day I met Arshan, he had just returned on a ship from Italy. After weeks of planning, Arshan and five others had managed to hide inside a ship, but when they arrived at the port of Ancona, they were spotted by the Italian police and returned to Greece.

Like many his age, Arshan felt betrayed by the Islamic Republic. He had been thirteen when the new government came to power. In his adolescent years, he was dizzy with the rapid changes in his country. In his twenties, he resented the new government for having stolen from him the possibility of living like men his age in other parts of the world. The world he once knew had changed for the worse.

He was thirty-two when he left home, hoping not to return as long as the Islamic Republic remained. I met him in the fifth year of his journey. "Look at the men and women here. They walk together, hold hands in public, go to the bars, and nothing happens. Why can we not do that in Iran?" he asked me in Patras.

Arshan left Iran for Turkey in early 1998. He applied for asylum with the UNHCR and lived in Ağrı, in Turkey's southeast. After three and half years of waiting, a final rejection letter arrived from the UNHCR. He left Turkey hoping to try his chances elsewhere in Europe. Greece was the next country on the road. Avoiding the risky journey at sea, he crossed the Meriç River, but not long after setting foot on Greek soil he was arrested by the authorities. Disappointed, he expected to be deported to Turkey in the dark of the night. Instead, he was detained for three months and kept in a small room along with ten other migrants. The number of detainees in the room would increase to sixteen or seventeen some days, he recalled.

"There was not enough room even for stretching our legs," Arshan told me.

He was kept in the room for ninety-three days and taken out for a walk in the fresh air on only three or four occasions during that period, each time for about fifteen minutes. His voice shrill, he said, "In ninety-three days, I left the room no more than one hour altogether. This is how Europe treats us now."

Lice were a common complaint among the men who experienced

the Greek detention centers. Fighting lice was a losing battle. Getting disinfectants and cleaning materials in detention centers proved impossible in most cases.

"We fought hard and managed to wash our room three times a day," Arshan said.

After three months, Arshan was released and allowed to move on to Athens. Not long after, he was in Patras, living in the White House.

One among the boys, twenty-two-year-old Cyrus, was closest to Arshan. Like Arshan, he felt responsible for helping me with my project. On the night of March 12 he risked his life to show me one very common but hazardous escape method.

There were coast guard patrols all over the harbor. Trucks were lining up to enter ships leaving for Italy. Showing me a parked truck away from the line, Cyrus said abruptly, "Start taking pictures. This is how it's done."

Holding my camera, I followed him as he passed through the fence. Cyrus looked around, studying the situation, and suddenly started to run. I took pictures while he masterfully moved between the parked trucks and in an opportune moment ran under a long trailer to find his hiding place. Everything happened in a short few seconds. He was fast, artful. There was no hesitation in his demonstration. Standing behind the fence, the boys watched the show with awe. Hearing the noise, the truck driver came out of his cabin. I waved, showed him my camera. Confused by my gesture, he returned to his cabin. Grabbing Cyrus, who was laughing, I joined the boys outside the fence.

Cyrus was a child of the 1979 revolution. There were tanks rolling along the streets of Tehran the night his parents were pronounced husband and wife. A year later, in a country ruled by clerics, Cyrus opened his eyes on this world. Along with others in his generation, he was to be the future in a new Islamic society. He had no memories of the prerevolution Iran, no lived experience in an Iran that was not ruled by religion. Still, he grew up resenting the government, resenting all that made him different from people his age in other parts of the world. "I was not a political person. But I knew how other people lived in other countries. I knew what the young people in Iran were deprived of. That angered me. I developed hatred toward them [the government]. I left because I couldn't stand being in Iran anymore."

Arshan and Cyrus, two men from different generations, left Iran seeking respect and normality elsewhere in the world. Long after leaving home, they were fugitives living in a trailer in the European Union. The more they traveled, the more they felt the loss of respect that had made them leave their place of birth. Thousands of miles away from home, they could not escape the image of them created by the Islamic Republic. "I hate them even more now," Cyrus told me.

Like others in the White House, Cyrus joked about his misfortunes, amusing the others and making them forget their own situations. The boys could not stop laughing when he told us about his experiences in Istanbul.

"We called the Istanbul police beggars," he said. "Once the police stopped one of the boys [Cyrus's friends] and asked for his passport. He didn't have one. The police asked for money. He didn't have any. They searched his pockets and found a phone card. The card had only ten units [enough for less than five minutes of a local phone conversation]. They took the card, hit him on the head, and let him go."

His stories had a mix of laughter and sadness. At times he would nearly break down. He would then control his emotions, make a joke, and laugh with the boys. That was the coping mechanism he had acquired on the road.

After a year of idleness in Istanbul, Cyrus decided to go to Greece. Alone, he left for the Meriç River.

"It was winter and I was wearing gloves and a hat. I had to cross the river. I wrapped my passport and all my money—three hundred dollars, I remember—in a plastic bag and put the bag inside my shirt. For five hundred feet, there was nothing but dry thorny bushes, kind of like natural barbed wire. Walking was very difficult. I had just walked maybe three hundred feet when I realized that the plastic bag was missing. I started screaming, cursing the whole world. That was all the money I had.

"I was angry and scared. I could hear the barking of dogs. I could not even run if the dogs attacked me. The bushes were so dense. I started crying.

"It was dark. I couldn't go back looking for my passport and money. I took off my shirt and ripped it into pieces. I walked ahead. Every thirty feet or so, I tied a piece of my shirt to a tree. I wanted to be able to return to the same spot in the morning. I continued until I had tied all the pieces. I then saw a road and a tree. I could still hear the dogs. I thought perhaps the tree was the safest place for me during the night. So I climbed the tree and stayed there the whole night. It was cold and I didn't have another shirt. I was shivering out of control. I don't think I will ever forget that night.

"The next morning, I walked back the same way following the marked trees. Not far from the last tree I saw a black plastic bag on the ground. I was so happy. A number of times, I opened and closed the plastic. I couldn't believe that I found my money.

"I took the bag and walked back to the road. I was thirsty and hungry. My jacket was ripped. My face and hands were dirty. I was so tired. I wanted to sit somewhere and cry."

Not long after, walking along the road, Cyrus was spotted by the Greek police. He was taken to detention and brought back to the border the next night.

"That was the story of my first trip to Greece. I returned to Istanbul. The first thing I did was call home. When I heard my mother's voice, I started crying. I couldn't talk to her. I hung up."

Invited by Arshan and others, I stayed at the White House on the night of March 12. Arriving there an hour past midnight, I saw before me two men with shaved heads. After moments of hesitation, I recognized Arshan and Cyrus, their heads shining from the reflection of the ceiling light.

"We wanted to look like the tourists in the carnival," Cyrus explained, noticing the shock on my face.

"How do we look?" Arshan asked. They both broke into laughter.

Penniless, they could not purchase new outfits for the carnival. As they washed their old clothes and cleaned their shoes, hoping to shed their refugee appearance, they got the idea to shave their heads, a physical transformation that would make them look like some of the hip tourists from the West. Thin and tall, wearing denim pants and jacket, Cyrus touched his hairless head and said, "How do I look, *agha* Behzad?"

"Like many Americans your age," I replied.

Though poor, the boys were hospitable and generous. Preparing for my visit, they had planned a feast. Arshan was the master chef of the night. Cyrus cut the onions. Instructed by Arshan, Kia cleaned a chicken and cut it into very small pieces. Breading them one by one, Arshan put the pieces in a big frying pan. He fried the chicken in oil while stirring the rice in a big pot full of boiling water. By three in the morning, a delicious meal was ready. Newspapers were put on the floor of the White House. The pan full of chicken and the pot of rice were placed in the middle. Then came a family-size bottle of Coke, two glasses, and three loaves of bread. We began the feast amid jokes and laughter.

"Whenever we get bored, we go to the *fance* and laugh at the boys who are pulled from under the chassis and beaten by the commandos," Kia said.

"It first made us cry," Arshan continued. "Now it is all a comedy."

"The same thing happens to us," Cyrus said. "Our friends laugh when we get beat up. We take turns laughing."

"We laugh to lighten up the situation for our friends," Arshan said. "This is the reason we laugh. Otherwise we would attack the commandos with bottles of water or anything we have with us to stop them from beating up our friends." Hoping to correct the wrong image that perhaps the boys' comments had created, he gave an example.

Two and a half months before I arrived in Patras, a Greek truck driver who had found a young Kurd hiding inside his truck, hoping to reach Italy, struck him on the head with a metal bar, killing him instantly. Accompanied by a number of tough Kurdish smugglers, the boys of the White House had visited the hospital where the body was being held and asked to redeem it for special burial.

"We saw the dead body. He looked fine. There was a hole in his head," Kia said.

The authorities would not release the dead man. The boys returned a number of times. Finally, the body was removed from the hospital, and there was no further news. The dead Kurd soon became a legend. From Athens to Patras, everyone told me about his murder. This was the first death in Patras.

The story had left us feeling somber. Kia prepared another big pot of tea. Hoping to change our mood, Cyrus said, "Let me tell you a story to make you laugh."

This was a story about another failed escape. The boys had decided to swim around an anchored ship and enter the ship from an angle not seen by the guards. The plan was simple. They put their clothes in heavy plastic bags and sealed the bags to make them waterproof. On a cold winter night, ten men sat behind the bus station, waiting for the right time to escape the attention of the coast guard and enter the fence. Nearly naked and only in their underwear, each had a plastic bag hanging from his waist by a piece of rope. The time for action finally arrived. The boys ran and crossed the boulevard toward the fence. A coast guard car suddenly appeared before the running boys. The ten seminaked men were busted. The coast guard started laughing.

"What are you?" one asked.

"Please don't hit us," one boy said to the coast guard. "We're not humans. We're foxes."

The officers laughed. The foxes were free to go. Cyrus rolled on the floor laughing.

It was a few minutes past five in the morning. Blankets were laid out on the floor, and I was offered the blanket next to Kia's bed. That was the last time I visited the boys in the White House.

The Eagle's Fort

After my visit to the White House, I followed Arshan and Kia to the Eagle's Fort. Walking along the fence, and passing the bus station and the free gate, we were soon in front of a run-down two-story building that was the largest Iranian squat in Patras.

The Eagle's Fort came to life in the summer of 2002 through the efforts of an Iranian migrant nicknamed Ali Almani, or "German Ali." After living four years in Germany, Ali was deported to Greece, the country where he first entered the European Union. He arrived penniless. Staring at the fence, he looked for ways to hide in the ships leaving for Italy. But he failed time and again, and had to remain in Patras longer than he had anticipated upon arrival.

Along with a couple of other Iranians, he spent the nights sleeping on the shore somewhere far away from the city center. During the day he returned to the center and schemed for his next journey out of Greece. One day, killing time and strolling on the boulevard, Ali Almani noticed an abandoned building. The next morning, he returned with a few Iranians. Soon the Eagle's Fort was born.

The night I visited the Eagle's Fort was cold and damp. Standing by the wide-open door, we looked inside. As we entered, the nauseating odors of urine, human sweat, and burning wood put out by water overcame me. The air was heavy, and breathing was difficult. A few scattered candles partially lit the ground floor, a space the size of a small living room. In the middle was a big barrel full of burning wood, blackened by repeated use. Men had assembled around the barrel. Greeting me, they came forward, shook my hand, and welcomed me.

There was no bathroom in the Eagle's Fort. The squat did not have electricity and running water. Bathing was a luxury most could not afford. "I have not had a regular shower for three months," a man said. The barrel on the ground floor was used for heating the place and warming up water for the men to wash. Going to the bathroom was a problem. The men walked to the bus station to use its facilities. When the station closed at night, they used the streets or the ground floor.

A loose and rattling metal stairway led to the rooms on the second floor. As we walked up the stairs, the light from the candles diminished, and I grabbed on to Arshan, who was walking ahead of me. Reaching the second floor, I took off my shoes outside a room and entered. A single burning candle on a corner was the only light in the room. Getting up on their feet, four men welcomed me to the room. Following Iranian rules of hospitality, they offered me a spot on the floor away from the door.

My visit gave the men a chance to lament about their life in Patras, the beatings by the coast guard, and their failed attempts to leave. One showed me bruises on his back. "He was howling from pain when we brought him here," a friend said. The bruises were new. Two nights earlier, the man had unsuccessfully tried to enter a ship leaving for Italy. Spotted by the commandos, he was clubbed and kicked. His friends were called to take him out of the ship. He was still limping when he welcomed me to the room.

The stories of the beating by the coast guard had brought a somber mood to the room. With our heads down, we sat without talking. Some smoked cigarettes. Then, making a lot of noise, a man entered the room. "I brought candles," he said loudly. I looked up. He was a short and skinny Iranian, carrying plastic bags and three very long candles. Noisily he said hello to everyone. Seeing a stranger in the room, he came toward me. I shook his hand. "Welcome to the

Eagle's Fort," he said, sitting in the middle of the room, spreading the bags around him.

The arrival of new candles excited the men. Knives were brought out; the candles were cut into two pieces each and lit around the room. I could now see everyone's face. The man with the candles was unshaven. He was sickly pale, and his teeth were dark yellow. He had no socks and wore an old pair of black trousers, an unwashed sweater, and a thin blue jacket. His name was Farid.

All other stories stopped with his arrival. It was Farid's turn to tell his tale. The other men listened patiently, nodding and laughing at times. When he paused, others used the opportunity to say a word or two about themselves.

Farid was Patras's only panhandler. "This was a good day," he said soon after joining us in the room. After three hours of begging from passersby, shopkeepers, and even the police, he arrived with 20 euros in his pockets. He had worked out a routine. He stayed in bed during the morning—his bed was a sole blanket on the floor—and would leave for "work" at four o'clock in the afternoon, returning in the evening with money, food, and cigarettes. Farid had a logical explanation for his hustle. He collected "the interest on the oil money robbed from Iran by the Europeans." This made Farid not a beggar or panhandler, he thought. Rather, he was collecting public debt on behalf of a nation robbed by foreigners. The money he took was the money he was owed.

"I even take our oil money from their police."

So Farid turned his begging into a noble act. He boasted to others, joked, and made them laugh. But sometimes at night, in moments of reflection and honesty, he was riddled with humiliation and shame. He was a sophisticated beggar in a foreign country. Nothing could disguise that.

Four days after our first meeting, I spent an afternoon with Farid watching the ships from the free gate and telling stories. He knew all the ships in the harbor. Cadging cigarettes from passersby, he told me the details of the designs of every ship, their structure, their schedules of arrival and departure, their routs, and the difficulties of breaking into them for a run to Italy.

In Iran he had had money, a girlfriend, a loving family, and a business—an illegal business. I asked why he had left.

"I could not take the prison anymore," he replied.

Farid was a drug dealer from Javadieh, the neighborhood Arshan had lived in. "I had seven arrests and convictions," he boasted. In total, Farid had served six years of jail time. He left Iran after his seventh imprisonment. The tough boy of Javadieh had reached his limits. "I could not go to jail anymore," he repeated.

A young man accustomed to breaking the law and surviving through illegal activities in Iran, Farid had had a change of heart, he claimed. He would not steal, sell drugs, or break the law in any form, he told me. Instead, he collected oil money in Patras. Some were scared of him. Others paid him and quickly walked away.

"They think I'm dirty," he told me, shaking his head, staring at the dirt under his fingernails and the hands that had not been touched by soap for days.

There were two sides to Farid. He wanted people to respect him as a tough young man, a "crazy" man from the ghetto, someone with no fear of the law. That was his facade. Inside, he was an ordinary man with ordinary weaknesses. Twice during our meeting he broke down and cried.

Farid had a soft spot when it came to his parents: his ailing mother and his father, a retired garbage collector. Being away from his family was the hardest part of his indeterminate journey to the West. Fearing his mother's disappointment and sorrow, Farid lied about his whereabouts, like many others I met in Patras. "I told my family that I lived in Paris and had a comfortable life," he told me. His mother bragged to neighbors and relatives that her son lived in Europe. "My brother asked me for a pair of sneakers three months ago," he said;

nearly in tears, he told me of his shame at not fulfilling his brother's simple wish. Buying a pair of sneakers was an unachievable dream. His own shoes had many big holes.

Farid's mother suffered from a severe heart ailment. When I met him, she was in a hospital in Tehran. Breaking down, he told me his fear of never seeing her again. He carried her picture in his wallet; he stared at the woman's face and wept in moments of solitude. He showed me his mother's picture that day in the harbor. I could only see one eye. Everything else was hidden under a black *chador.*

"I come from a religious family," he said. "No one has seen my mother's face except for my father."

Around Patras he was known for snapping, getting wild, banging things around, and hurting himself. He showed me the scars on his right fist as proof of his passing insanity. Drunk and upset about life one evening, he punched the burning wood on the ground floor of the Eagle's Fort, holding his fist in the fire. The result was a serious skin burn and infection, and a scar that would perhaps last for the remainder of his life.

"I break bottles on my head when I get upset. Ask Arshan if you don't believe me," he said.

Arshan confirmed the claim. "He is crazy."

Once in Iran, Farid's younger brother had disrespected their father, he said. To Farid, this was a grave sin. He snapped and lost control. Pulling out his knife, he cut his brother's back from top to bottom.

"My father had done everything for us. He did not raise us to disrespect him," he explained to me.

I left Greece for Istanbul not long after my meeting with Farid. In June 2003, I took a ferry to Athens and prepared for another visit to Patras. Calling my contact numbers, I inquired about the boys of the White House and others I had met in March. Many had left Greece;

Kia was back in Athens selling T-shirts, saving money to pay a smuggler for the trip to Italy. I tracked him down, and early one evening we met in a restaurant in old Athens. He hardly smiled during our long meeting and nearly broke into tears at times.

"I knew you would come back someday. I had prepared a long story for you, rehearsed it, and memorized it. Many things happened since you left." He began with Farid.

Farid had been a drug dealer and an ex-convict in Iran. In Patras, he was "clean," as he had told me when we first met. He stayed away from drugs. Alcohol was his vice. But all that changed in the weeks after March 2003.

Drugs slowly penetrated the Iranian community. Like many others unable to leave the port, Farid took refuge in drugs. His old habits returned. Panhandling provided easy money for his drug habit. He worked longer hours, earned more money. He began with opium. Smoking heroin was next. Then came shooting heroin. The crazy beggar from Javadieh now worked to pay for his habit.

"When you came to Patras in March Farid had just started panhandling. He was learning the trade. That was the time of his practical training. Later, he taught his learned techniques to others. He started taking students. A long list of people wanted to be Farid's apprentice, but he would not accept them. He chose only a few," Kia said.

His first apprentice was Ali Almani. Farid collected a share from his daily earnings, and Ali Almani objected to this exploitation. New terms were negotiated, and the dispute was resolved. Slowly Farid trained more beggars. The port was divided up into zones and areas of work. He collected a small share from all zones. There were occasional disputes and fights between the beggars, but overall, the system functioned smoothly.

Farid's men begged not as Iranians but as Iraqi Kurds. Choosing a different identity was a smart move. In smaller cities, if not in Athens, there was a good deal of sympathy for the Kurds among the Greeks. The Kurds were victims of many wars and misfortunes, whereas the Iranians came from a relatively wealthy country. They were the descendants of a great civilization, the Greeks thought. The Greeks could not understand an Iranian begging for food.

Like their master, the panhandlers of Patras begged during the day and used drugs at night. As time passed, they became thinner, weaker, and frailer. More drugs came to the port from Athens. By May 2003, the Eagle's Fort had become a drug den, a distribution and consumption center in Patras.

In the beginning, many Eagle's Fort residents stayed away from drugs, but temptation was high. Some gave in to social pressure and boredom. Others saved themselves in time; they left the Eagle's Fort and Patras.

"The drug dealers started as users, but they needed money for their habit. Only a few were panhandling. The rest had to find other sources of money," Kia explained.

"Soon after you left, Patras became a different city. The Kurds declined in numbers; they became less than three hundred people, down from their nine hundred peak. The Iranians remained the same."

Many Kurds returned to northern Iraq, and no newcomers arrived from there. Kurdish smugglers lost their business, and with it their power. Having lost their customers and the source of their income, the smugglers approached some Iranians. Among them were the drug dealers of Eagle's Fort. "They offered to share one of the gates with them for a small commission." That is how the new relationship between the Kurds and the others started. The war in Iraq had changed the balance of power in the port. "The Iranians began spending more time with the Kurds, and visited the Kurdish teahouse."

The teahouse was an empty building lot some fifty feet or so to the right of the bus station. Squatted by the Kurds, there was a tent in the middle, a few tables and chairs, and scores of visitors going in and out. In the beginning, only the Kurds visited the teahouse. Respecting the turfs and zones of control in the port, the Afghans and other nationalities passed by the teahouse but did not enter. A few Iranians used the service of the Kurdish smugglers. To make deals, the Iranians were allowed to enter the teahouse. Outside the teahouse, men leaned against the wall, smoked cigarettes, and stared at the fence and the world behind it. Inside, they drank the usual sugar-saturated tea. Some chatted with friends, talked about the fence, made deals for their next great escape. They spoke to other migrants, negotiated with smugglers. Such was the case in March 2003.

Soon the leaders of the Kurds came to frequent the Eagle's Fort, and with that came a new source of income for the Iranian distributor. The temptation of smoking hashish brought the Kurds to the fort every night, and they stayed in the rooms for long hours, hallucinating and spending the money they earned from smuggling people.

"Iranians were the middlemen between the Albanians and the Kurds. They got the drugs from the Albanians and sold them to the Kurds at a much higher price. This is how they paid for their own addiction. In the beginning, the Iranians were only smoking heroin. Then they started shooting, and very quickly their consumption increased. They needed more money. Selling hashish to the Kurds wasn't enough anymore. So they went to the Afghans." Unlike the Kurds, the Afghans went all the way. Some of them were hooked on opium. Others did heroin.

"The distributors started with Afghan travelers first. Naturally, their big shots, the smugglers, came later. They [the Iranians] left the poor Afghan travelers alone. The smugglers would come to the fort with their bodyguards. The guards and the passengers would hang around outside the fort, but the leaders came up to the rooms. They brought all the money they had got from the passengers and smoked it there. These were famous Afghans, those who were known even in Athens. The famous Nassim was a regular visitor. He was making a lot of money those days, but whatever he made, he either lost it in gambling, or burned it in the fort," Kia said.

Late one night, a few days after my meeting with Kia in Athens, the police raided the Eagle's Fort. They asked everyone to leave the squat. Those who refused were escorted out, forced to leave their belongings behind. Many had seen this in the past: the police frequently raided the Eagle's Fort, and always the men had returned the next day. But this time the Eagle's Fort was shut down permanently. Its entrance and windows were closed with brick and cement. Breaking in was impossible.

Three days after its closure by the police, I returned to Patras for the last time and stood outside the Eagle's Fort, accompanied by one of the founders of the squat. "There was a window here before. We entered through that when the police padlocked the door," the young man said, pointing. There was old graffiti on some walls. The area was quiet and secluded once again.

I asked the man about Farid and his whereabouts. "You will see him at the Kurdish teahouse," he said.

Leaving the Eagle's Fort, I walked to the Kurdish teahouse. There were no men standing outside. Seeing a group of Iranians squatting against the wall inside, I entered, said hello, and introduced myself. "I am looking for Farid. He is my friend," I said.

"He will be back in a few minutes," one said.

I sat on the ground beside the Iranians. Some were the last residents of the Eagle's Fort. Their shoes were dirty and old, covered by dried mud and holes on the top. Some wore ripped T-shirts, and like Farid, they had dirt under their fingernails. Others had needle tracks on their arms.

"Look at these guys. They are all junkies. They shoot more than one hundred fifty euros a day, each one of them," an older Iranian said, laughing. Looking pale, the others smiled with indifference. No one said a word. Pointing at a young Iranian, the older man said sarcastically, "Look at him. He needs to get a fix now." The young man smiled, did not refute the claim. I asked if I could photograph an Iranian leaning against the wall. "My picture will bring you misery," he said.

The jokes continued. More men arrived and left the teahouse. An hour later, Farid arrived, sweating and looking frailer than before.

Embracing me, he offered me a cup of tea. Soon we left the teahouse and retreated to a quiet corner, a small patch of shade on a street corner a block away from the fence.

I was asking Farid about life in Patras after the closure of the Eagle's Fort when a man arrived on a bicycle. Stopping before us, he whispered into Farid's ear. "This is *agha* Behzad. He is a great friend," Farid said, introducing me to the man. To me he said, "This is Nassim. He is one of the biggest Afghan smugglers in Patras." Short and a bit chunky, with a head full of brushlike hair, Nassim was clean-shaven. He wore a sleeveless shirt and shorts. "I will be back in no time," Farid said, taking the man's bicycle and riding away. I sat in the shade with the Afghan smuggler.

We sat quietly, staring at the ground. At times we would look up, smile at each other, and then return our gazes to the ground. He played with a small tree branch he'd found on the ground. I tried to think of a way to break the silence. Finally I started talking abruptly and told him my story.

He listened attentively, and to my surprise, without any hesitation, he told me his secrets. With patience and in detail, Nassim explained his operation—the details, the risks, the complications, and the financial benefits of assisting people's journey to Italy.

"I was not always a smuggler," he said. Like many others, he had left Afghanistan because of war. He took refuge in Iran, living and working there for three years, until he "felt the urge for Europe." Crossing the borders to Turkey, he worked there for a number of months, then proceeded to Greece. After weeks of sleeping in city parks in Athens, Nassim moved to Patras, hoping to leave for Italy soon. Like others before him, he arrived in the *kheimeh*. He was poor and hungry, spending his days standing by the fence, hoping for the chance to move forward. Then one day a friend approached him with an offer for work. He agreed. He became an apprentice to an Afghan smuggler. Not long after, he became a smuggler himself, a big shot in the Afghan community.

A fast learner, quick and intelligent, he mastered the art of opening sealed trucks, loading them with passengers, and resealing them before the arrival of the coast guard and the driver. "I practiced in the *kheimeh* for a month. I would break and reattach seals until I became very good at it," he said. Like a teenager boasting about his mischievous deeds, Nassim smiled as he explained his work.

For a long time, the money was good. "Sometimes I made twenty thousand euros from each human cargo. I shared the money with my partner," he said. This was the heyday of smuggling in Patras. Nassim had had more money than he had ever imagined, more money than he could spend in Patras. "I started gambling." Using drugs was next. He was soon a regular visitor to the Eagle's Fort.

When we met in June, Nassim was nearly broke. There were not many migrants in the port. His consumption was high. He was an addict and a gambler. Looking me in the eye, he said, "I wish my parents had never met and I was not born. I cry anytime I touch opium."

Half an hour after he left us on the street corner, Farid returned, sweating and taking long breaths. "I had to go to a couple of places to get this," he said to Nassim. Then he turned to me. "Sorry, *agha* Behzad, this Afghan is a good person. He needed a small amount of opium, but he doesn't know anyone. I usually get it for him from an Iranian, but he wasn't there today. I had to go really far to get the opium from an Albanian. They charge a lot of money. I had to put fifteen euros of my own money," Farid said to me. Nassim remained silent. He was preparing to leave when Farid said, "I can go to Athens and get you a one-month supply. You will be saving money that way."

"I only have fifteen hundred euros. I need the money for work," Nassim replied.

"I can get you the drugs and you pay later. Just tell me when you can pay and I will make all the arrangements," Farid insisted.

"I'm not sure of the work in the weeks to come."

Saying farewell to us, Nassim rode his bicycle to the Afghan *kheimeh*.

I sat with Farid, hearing his complaints about life in the port. Many of his friends had saved themselves from Patras and its morass of drugs. Some were in Italy. Others had gone as far as France and Germany. Among them was Arshan. Farid was left behind.

"Arshan left without even telling me. I wouldn't have gone with him, but I expected him to tell me. He took others with him. I had to find out about it from strangers. What can I expect from strangers when someone from my neighborhood treats me this way?

"I could leave tomorrow if I want. The biggest Kurdish smuggler is my friend. He told me, time and again, that he would send me off for free. But I want to go with my own money. I don't want a Kurd to tell everyone that he helped me leave Patras."

PART FIVE

Paris

The Colony

It was June 27, 2003, and I had just arrived in Paris hoping to find Arshan and others from Patras. I had heard that they were sleeping in parks, and a story in the French paper *Libération* led me to one such park on Boulevard Magenta near the Gare de l'Est, one of the central train stations in the city.

The park was crowded with migrants from Iran, Iraq, and Afghanistan. Many were new arrivals. Having left Greece, they had spent a few days in Italy before boarding trains for Paris. There were no French in the park, not even the unfortunate homeless French, the alcoholics or addicts. An Iranian migrant called the park "our colony in Paris."

The migrants spent many hours a day in the Colony. There they met friends, exchanged news, and planned for the next leg of their journey. When not in the Colony, they moved between the charities and soup kitchens in different parts of the city. They ate two meals a day. Breakfast was served at eight-thirty in the morning. Dinner packets—a can of sardines, a small roll, an apple, and a small bottle of water—were handed out between five-thirty and six-thirty in the evening. Missing them meant hunger for the night.

The charities were far from the Colony, and walking was not possible. None had money to pay for Metro tickets. "We hide and wait for the right moment to follow someone who is entering the train and run and enter after them," Tufan, an Iranian migrant I befriended in Paris, told me. "I have to admit, I crossed many borders to come here. I spent time in jail and lived under very bad conditions. But taking the Metro this way feels worse than all of those experiences. I feel embarrassed. Everyone stares at us. They know we are breaking the law. Some people are afraid of us. I never felt so bad in my life."

At midnight, the police shut down the Colony and migrants moved to other city parks. Some slept on cardboard on the grass in an area outside the park. They hid under layers of cardboard, rested their eyes for a short few hours, and then began the next day of roaming between parks and places of charity.

While in France, migrants make their final decisions about the remainder of their journey. They contact friends, inquire about migration policies and government support in different states, and weigh the difficulties of traveling against the chances of receiving asylum. Some remain in France to reunite with family and friends who arrived there earlier. Others remain because they are tired of the journey, or discouraged by news from other countries; they register with the French authorities and apply for asylum.

Some applicants register with the police in border cities. Since the 1990s, the border control officers are given permission to summarily review asylum applications at France's borders and reject the ones that are viewed as "manifestly unfounded." As a result, thousands have been denied the right to present their cases for asylum through appropriate channels.

Registering with the police in Paris is a daunting task. For many, it takes weeks or even months; while waiting, they have no official identity. They do not exist. Most applicants are rejected in their initial try and are forced to try their chances with the Refugee Appeal Commission (CRR).

France has a restrictive interpretation of the 1951 refugee convention. It considers for asylum only those persecuted by governments,

*Arshan carrying a map of Europe and crossing
borders in search of a new home*

Iranian, Afghan, and Iraqi migrant children in Sofia

African migrant in Istanbul

Born in Istanbul to an African father and a Russian mother

African migrant in Istanbul

Sudanese and Eritrean migrants in an Istanbul safe house

Kurdish migrant spending the night at the Colony

and excludes the victims of violence by militias and antigovernment armed forces. In 1998, France invented "territorial asylum," a new category, to deal with the latter group of applications. The acceptance rate for territorial asylum is very low. In 2000, only 3 percent of twelve thousand applicants were accepted, while the acceptance rate for conventional refugees was 16 percent. In 2002, only 2 percent of the seventeen thousand applications for territorial asylum were accepted.

While waiting for an answer, asylum seekers are barred from working. Those considered for asylum under the laws of the 1951 Refugee Convention receive a one-time "waiting allowance" of about $271 when they arrive in France. Some are provided housing. For the most part, the number of applicants outweighs the number of available beds. Those not provided with housing receive a monthly allowance of about $244 for one year. Applicants for territorial asylum are not provided with housing, food, or pocket money.[8]

France's harsh asylum policy is the main reason for the relatively small number of migrants submitting applications there. In 1999, a total of 30,883 people submitted applications for asylum in France, whereas in England and Germany, the numbers were 91,200 and 95,113.[9]

For these reasons, remaining in France was of no use for many in the colony. Even worse, registering with the French authorities eliminated their chances elsewhere in the European Union. These were the post–Dublin Convention years. Having come into effect on September 1, 1997, the Dublin Convention allowed member states to deport migrants to "safe third countries," the first country they entered in the EU. The enactment of the new rule was to deter the migrants from "asylum shopping," applying for asylum in different countries until their cases were accepted.

The use of the Dublin Convention required fingerprinting and the collection of comprehensive data about the migrants' identity and the borders they crossed. On December 15, 2000, the European Documentation Centre on Nationality (EURODOC) was legislated into existence for the purpose of "determining which Member State is to be responsible pursuant to the Dublin Convention for examining an application for asylum lodged in a Member State."[10]

Once fingerprinted in any member state, the migrant (and the potential asylum seeker) had no chance for applying elsewhere within the EU. Knowing their bleak chance of acceptance in France, many migrants at the Colony chose not to register with the police and continued their journey to what they considered to be a more hospitable country. Most were dreaming of reaching England, despite the tightening restrictions in its asylum policy. Calais, a port in northern France, was their last stop in France.

Most of the migrants I met on that day in July 2003 were waiting in Paris for money from friends and family to pay human smugglers for the last leg of their journey.

First Day at the Colony: Farshad

I was on Boulevard Magenta, approaching the Gare de l'Est, when an unusual assembly of Middle Eastern–looking men outside a small park caught my attention. I crossed, walked toward the group, and introduced myself.

"Did you just arrive?" a man asked me.

"I am not a migrant," I said. I was writing about *their* journey, telling the world about their troubles and agonies, I told them.

"You see that man there? The Kurdish man there, he is from Sanandaj. He recently came from Patras. A guy who traveled with him died after reaching Italy." A young Iranian pointed at a short, unshaven man sitting alone on the curb of a green area outside the park. "That will be a good story for you," the young man said.

Walking to the Kurd, I said hello in Persian; introducing myself, I asked for his name. He said, "What difference does it make?" Sitting next to him on the curb, I talked about random topics, but the Kurd was reluctant to speak. "I am a loner," he said. Slowly, though, he began to talk about other migrants at the Colony.

"None of them has a real reason for leaving their country. They don't know why they are here. I don't respect the non-Kurds. I don't trust them," he said. I was a non-Kurd. I told him that I had been to Patras before and mentioned a few names, hoping to gain his trust. Finally, I inquired about the traveling friend who died in Italy, and the Kurd told me the story without any signs of emotion or pain on his face.

With three other men from Patras, the Kurd had managed to enter a truck carrying watermelons to Italy. "The truck was full of very big boxes of watermelon, laid tightly on the top and next to one another." Hiding from the surveillance of the coast guard and the human smugglers, "we entered the truck and removed two boxes from the middle." Two migrants positioned themselves in the empty space. Covering them with full boxes, the remaining two made other hideouts and sat for hours in the suffocating June heat, waiting for the truck to be loaded on a ship destined for Italy.

After nearly seven hours of waiting, the truck was finally moved. "We heard the loud whistle of the ship." It soon left Patras for Ancora. "It was hot and we were sweating." Eighteen hours after its departure, the ship arrived in Italy. The four migrants remained inside, waiting for the truck to be unloaded and on its way to its final destination in Italy. Coming out of the truck in the harbor was not advisable, as they heard noises outside, and knew from experience that the Italian coast guard patrolled the area.

I sat with the Kurd, thinking about the man who died in Italy, imagining his last moments, his wishes, and the agonizing hours he spent in the truck. Suddenly, the familiar face of a migrant walking toward me brought me back to my immediate surroundings. Hooshang, an Iranian I had met one night during the carnival in Patras, stood before me. We embraced. Hooshang had left Patras in late May and made it to Paris four weeks before my arrival. Happy to have seen me, he began telling me about his plans for the remainder of his journey. As with many, England was his next stop. He was on his way to Calais.

Seeing our engagement, the Kurd walked away, chose a corner, and sat alone, lost in his thoughts. Hooshang and I continued our conversation.

"Do you remember Farshad?" he said abruptly.

Farshad was the kind, chubby man I had met in the truck in Patras. Excited to hear about him, I said, "Yes, I was told he left Patras earlier this month."

"You did not hear the news," he said, becoming silent for a few seconds. "He died in Italy. He was on the truck with that man," he said casually, pointing out the Kurd.

My eyes traveled between the Kurd and Hooshang. Unable to utter a word, I sat down, holding my face in my hands.

"He had heart problems. I warned him before, but he did not listen to me. The watermelon truck killed him," he said.

Arshan

My search for Arshan and others from Patras brought me the news about Farshad's death. I was worried about Arshan, and in my first visit to the Colony I inquired about their whereabouts from Hooshang and many strangers. "I will see him tonight. We sleep in the same park," a young Iranian said. Delighted by the news, I asked the man to give Arshan a message to meet me at the Colony the following day at noon.

The next morning, Arshan and Cyrus arrived at the Colony.

"We came after breakfast," Arshan said, smiling and shaking my hand.

"Who would believe this?" Cyrus said.

The park was crowded, and we were surrounded by other migrants. I was full of questions about their journey, the place where they spent the night, and all that they had experienced since leaving Greece. We left the Colony for a café off Boulevard Magenta.

"*Agha* Behzad, you will not believe how we made it here" was the first thing Arshan said. Noticing the tape recorder in my hand, he smiled and said, "I will start when you press." For the next few minutes, he explained in detail how he escaped the scrutiny of the smugglers and the coast guard and left Patras. Arshan had invented a new method and was proud of his ingenuity. This is how it worked.

The smugglers of Patras only worked with loaded trailers. They hid their passengers between boxes of merchandise, covered them, and closed the trailers. Empty trailer trucks waiting to travel to Italy to bring back merchandise were not a part of their operation. Hiding travelers inside them seemed impossible, but to Arshan, this was a perfect opportunity to escape Patras without paying the smugglers.

"The boys would escape the attention of the commandos if they could hide between the rear end of the empty trailer and an artificial wall made with the same material and size. The commandos did not check the empty trailers with the same care. They did not believe anyone would escape with them," Arshan reasoned. All that was needed was to measure the trailers with precision, buy pieces of plywood, cut them in two or three pieces easy to carry to the parking area in the harbor, enter the trailers, put the wood together as a false wall, and hide behind it. Arshan had seen the escape method in a movie. "In the movie they did it in a train and it worked. I wanted to try that in a truck," he said.

They chose parked trailers ready to be picked up and connected to a truck, then boarded into ships. This was central to the scheme.

"Trailers connected to engines were not usable. The drivers checked them prior to being loaded into the ships. The drivers knew the rear end of their own trailers. They would know the difference between our wood and the real material in the trailer.

"We practiced every night." They hid behind the pieces of plywood, made new measurements, and perfected the device. "Some of our friends laughed at the idea." But Arshan was determined. They spent a number of weeks on planning and implementation. By June the job was complete. "We had to wait twenty-seven days to get the right trailers," Arshan explained.

Two migrants had left a few days before Arshan and Cyrus.

"They called us when they reached Italy. We knew the method works. It was our time to leave. We found an empty truck going to Venice. Five of us left with this truck." They positioned themselves behind the pieces of plywood hours before its departure and moved only when the ship left the port. The ship broke down on the way. "I know we were not moving for a few hours. Our trip took longer than the usual." After twenty-seven hours, the ship arrived in Venice, and the truck was taken out of the ship. When there was no noise out-side, the migrants left the truck and ran away from the harbor.

Venice was a bigger port than Patras. The men were broke and did not know their way around. "We slept in a park at night," Arshan said. Using a map of Europe, they planned the rest of their journey, and after a week of resting, they left Venice for Milan. "We had no money for the fare. We would get on the trains and move anytime we saw the conductors. We were thrown out twice. They were nice and did not hand us over to the police." Arriving in Milan, they waited a few days, then left for the border with France.

"We found the train going to France and boarded it right before it left the station, but we were caught in France when they came for tickets. They put us on the train back to Ventimiglia. We took the next train to Paris, at eight at night. We entered a car and hid under the long seats. We were five people. Again, we got caught, but this time, they did not send us back to Italy. They just dropped us off in the next station." The migrants waited in the station and took the next train to Lyon. "Fortunately, there was no ticket control this time." Arriving in Lyon, Arshan and the other migrants took the ex-press train to Paris.

Like most transit migrants in Paris, Arshan and Cyrus had not seen the Eiffel Tower, the Louvre, or any of the other famous tourist sites. Their life was confined to moving between parks and charities, and scheming their next border crossing. We were not far from the historic Montmartre district, and I offered to show them around. Leaving the café, we walked through the charming back streets, vis-ited souvenir shops, and took photos. And like in our meetings in Patras, Arshan held my tape recorder and began recording his report. My job was only to observe and enjoy the time with my friends.

"Your reporter is back to work," Cyrus said, laughing.

Excited and thrilled, Arshan spoke into the recorder: "This is Saturday. I am in Paris. The boys told me that *agha* Behzad is here. I rushed to see him. We are very happy to meet again. It is unbelievable—we met in Patras, crossed two countries, and now we meet again in Paris. Unbelievable!"

Arshan imagined the readers of the book, men and women he would never meet, strangers who would know the secrets of his life, his story, his words. That intrigued him. A strange feeling of loyalty to the unknown readers of the story was evident in Arshan's words. He spoke on behalf of the migrants, addressed his imagined readers, and wished them to understand the migrants' predicaments.

"I believe the readers will smile when they get to this part. They will be happy for our happiness. The readers have been with us throughout this long journey. They were saddened by our sadness. They understood our fears and felt our worries. Now they are sharing with us our happiness.

"I want to tell you something about Paris," he continued, still addressing the readers. "We have no money. We even take the Metro without paying. We enter from the door others exit. Of course, we feel embarrassed. Now we are strolling in Paris like real tourists. I wish you were all here, all of you who will read this story. I hope a day will come that all people in the world can come here to stroll and have a good time. We are happy from the bottom of our heart. I hope someday everyone else will be happy like us."

Tufan

June 28, 2003, was the last time I saw Arshan and Cyrus. Leaving Montmartre, I accompanied them to the charity that gave them their nightly meal. They took their dinner packets and we proceeded to a nearby square, where we joined a group of eight Iranians enjoying their last meal of the day. Among them was Tufan, a young Kurd from the city of Sanandaj. In his mid-twenties, he was soft-spoken, looked boyish, and had a small patch of facial hair under his lower lip.

There were men of different ages in the group. Mahmood, a thirty-year-old migrant from Mashhad, a city in Iran's northeast, had shoulder-length hair and a thick mustache. Daee, the uncle, was in his fifties, and Ebi, a short man with a beautiful voice, was twenty-nine. All were new arrivals from Greece. While the others had met on the journey, Tufan and Mahmood were friends from Iran.

"We are old friends from Mashhad," Tufan said about Mahmood. "I lived in the basement of his house for three years. I owe him a lot," he told me in the Parc du Luxembourg. Another time he said, "We traveled together from Iran. The first time we left Iran we made it all the way to Greece, but they deported us a month later. We didn't give up. We came out again. We traveled together all the way to here."

"We will travel the rest of the journey together," Mahmood said. Tufan remained quiet.

I left the group before dark, and they proceeded to the park, where they spent the night. Arshan and Cyrus would be on their way to Germany early next morning. We embraced and said farewell, and before leaving the square, Tufan and his friends and I planned to meet again.

Two days later, we met at the square at noon. Taking the train to the center, we began an afternoon of sightseeing, picnicking by the Seine, and strolling in the Parc du Luxembourg.

Tufan stayed by my side throughout the day, and when the others were not paying attention, he told me about his life. I asked how long he had been away from Iran.

"I left five years ago. But I have been wandering like a Gypsy from the age of fourteen," he said. In 1991 Tufan left Sanandaj for northern Iraq and joined the Kurdish resistance movement against the Islamic Republic. "That didn't work," he said. He was not a fighter, and soon he was back in Sanandaj, doing the mundane, studying, and passing time. Not long after returning from northern Iraq, Tufan's family moved to Mashhad, a city in Iran's northeast. A few years later, they returned to Sanandaj, but Tufan stayed behind.

His father was his favorite member of the family, but he died young of an unexpected heart attack. The last time they had spoken was two months before his death. "He was only forty-one. We never hugged or kissed. He was always closer to my older brother. I saw him two months before he died. He said he was going to die soon. I cried and told him not to talk like that. 'I am young. What will happen to me if you die?' I told him. But he knew his death was coming. For the first time, he cried in front of me. I saw death in his eyes.

"I had taken a week's break from my military service and returned to Mashhad. My father died two months later, but my family did not inform me. When I found out, he was already buried. I will never forgive them for that."

The time came for the migrants to return to the charity for the nightly dinner packets. It was nearly five, and we were walking to the gates when, in passing and without explaining further, Tufan mentioned his wife for the first time.

"We were neighbors. I was in the fourth grade in high school when my family moved there. She was a year younger. We grew up together.

"Contrary to me, she is calm and very patient. She has endured a lot of hardship since we married. I have been away for five years. She is tolerating all of this so I can realize my dreams. We have been married seven years. Many of the family girls who came to our wedding are now married with children, but she has nothing."

"What are your dreams?" I asked.

"Writing! That is the only thing that calms me. A piece of paper and a pen in my hand make me forget all my troubles. There were many difficulties in my life. My hope is to reach somewhere peaceful, begin a quiet life, and write the story of my life."

"Why did you not write in Iran?" I asked.

"It is not easy. There are many limitations there. You cannot write freely," he replied.

When we parted that day, we planned another meeting, again at dinnertime at the square. When I arrived, Tufan and the other men were already at the square. "Here, this is for you, *agha* Behzad," Tufan said, handing me a dinner pack. Clustering around a single bench, they ate their sardines and told stories, mainly of their journey. Then came the time for singing and reciting lines from their favorite prerevolution Iranian movies. Ebi was the star of the night; he had a voice like the famous Iranian singer Dariush. Closing his eyes and posing like a singer onstage, Ebi sang songs of love, exile, and the longing for home.

Unlike at our earlier meeting in the Parc du Luxembourg, Tufan was quiet this time. He sat silently, although he clapped at the end of each song. There was an unease about him. He looked nervous. When I left to buy cigarettes and wine, Tufan offered to go with me and show me the way. Walking to the store, he remained quiet. His uneasiness seemed heightened, and his legs moved slowly, as if he wished not to return to the square. Then, on our way back to the square, he suddenly stopped, looked around, and said:

"Do you want to tell the real stories of the refugees?"

I found the question strange. "Of course," I replied.

"Then you also need to talk about two forgotten groups in Iran. You should talk about gays and lesbians. Many have written about political refugees, but no one is interested in the stories of the gay people in Iran," he said.

His comment came as a surprise, and I was not ready for it. I had been on the road for nearly a year and had not even once considered writing about gay refugees. I knew about male prostitutes from Iran and northern Iraq in Athens, but I did not know men or women leaving Iran or elsewhere because of their sexual orientation. Now I was put on the spot. I told him of my ignorance and lack of interest until he had confronted me with the question.

"I can become interested in talking about that in my book, maybe. But I do not know where to start. I need help," I told Tufan.

He offered his help.

"Please, keep this between us. Don't tell the others about our conversation," he pleaded. I promised to keep it secret and did not ask about the reasons for his fear.

"Do you promise?" he asked again. I gave him my word. Standing on the sidewalk, his voice shaking, he told me a story. I turned on my tape recorder.

"Please make sure the others don't hear this," Tufan pleaded again.

Biting his lip, with tears in his eyes, he paused, looked around again, and began the story of Farid, "a beautiful boy from Sanandaj." They had been classmates in high school, and during that time Farid became aware of his liking for men. Women did not excite him. To him, they were like "sisters or good friends."

"Life in Sanandaj was very hard for a gay man." Farid eventually left his family and moved to Tehran. Not long after, Tufan and his family moved to Mashhad. They met a number of times in Tehran. "He had become even more beautiful in Tehran." Nearly a year went by before their next encounter, however, and when they met each other again, Tufan saw "the most beautiful boy turned into a miserable drug addict. I was horrified. I could not recognize my friend," he told me. Puzzled by Farid's transformation, Tufan stayed with him and comforted him. After days, Farid spoke, telling his friend about a threat by the authorities and making Tufan promise to keep it a secret till the day he died.

While Farid had been strolling in Park-e Daneshjoo in central Tehran one evening, the morality police arrested him. The park was a popular hangout for gay men in central Tehran. Brave and timid, out or in the closet, all types of gay men gathered in the park to meet their friends and find lovers. At times, the Islamic Republic's morality police assaulted them, but they returned to the park with more zeal, Tufan explained to me. As for Farid, he was taken away and "gang-raped for days, over and over," by many men each time.

They kept the young man in solitary confinement for two months. Bearded men visited him every night. First they violated him, then injected him with heroin before leaving his cell. Day after day, night after night, the door opened, and bearded men locked the door from inside. Farid closed his eyes. The same routine followed. Farid was soon begging the bearded men for heroin. His visitors taught him how to inject.

After two months, the men released Farid under the condition that he not speak about his imprisonment. He agreed. Tufan was the first he told his secret to. He was also the last.

Early one morning Farid's body was discovered in an abandoned lot in southern Tehran. The newspapers reported "suicide by shooting air in the vein" as the cause of his death. Tufan did not believe the report.

"My friends saw three men take Farid from his home." That was the last time he was seen alive.

Tufan and I met, time and again, always secretly. "My friends should not know I am meeting you. Please be careful. Make sure no one finds out about our meeting. Especially keep this from Mahmood," Tufan said the first time he told me about gay people in Iran. Tufan had beautiful Persian handwriting. "Tell Mahmood you want me to write a letter in Persian for you. This is what I will tell him too," he pleaded with me before our second secret meeting.

"Why are you so concerned?" I asked.

"It will be better for me. They are all very narrow-minded. They will not understand. Even your best friend would judge you and try to take advantage of you. Please make sure that he does not find out about what I tell you," he requested again.

The thought of Mahmood and his friends knowing about our meetings horrified Tufan, but the fear did not stop his longing to tell stories, his wish to bring me closer to a world unknown to and misunderstood by many.

"God bless his soul. He was very beautiful," he said one day about a gay friend whose name he wished me not to disclose.

Most called him by his nickname, a woman's name, Shahnaz. Shahnaz lived in Mashhad.

"He danced beautifully, like a woman," he said.

Talking about his friend, Tufan elegantly moved his hands to demonstrate the grace in Shahnaz's dance routines. His eyes radiated with the pleasure of telling the tale of a dear friend.

Shahnaz was a paid dancer. Like many gay men in his town, he was paid a good fee to dance at weddings. At times he was asked to wear women's clothes. One happy evening at a wedding in Mashhad, by mere chance, Shahnaz's brother saw him do his dance routine. Disgraced and humiliated, the brother assaulted Shahnaz, kicked him, stomped on his face, and left him with a broken leg. Two days later, Shahnaz took poison to end his life, but he did not succeed.

"Unfortunately he failed," Tufan said. He smoked silently. I looked away. Putting out his cigarette, he broke the silence.

"I also tried to kill myself many times. I was also saved unfortunately."

For days now, he had only told me stories of others, nothing about his life, nothing to bring me closer to his own secrets. This was the first hint. I wished to ask about the reasons for his suicide attempt, but, fearing I'd scare him off, I kept quiet. He continued with the story of Shahnaz.

Shahnaz was soon abandoned by his family and forced to leave home. At age fifteen, he left Mashhad for Isfahan and later Tehran. In Tehran, the young Shahnaz befriended other gay men. He spent many hours a day in Park-e Daneshjoo. It was in the park that he began shooting heroin, Tufan told me. He prostituted himself to make a living and pay for his habit. Soon he was going with anyone who was willing to pay. Among them were Afghan refugees illegally toiling in Tehran and married men who fancied sexual encounters with other men.

After a devastating stay in Tehran, Shahnaz returned to his hometown, Mashhad, which is home to the most important religious shrine in Iran, the tomb of Imam Reza, the eighth Shiite imam and a descendant of the Prophet Muhammad. It is a conservative religious city. The gays of Mashhad lived like "owls," Tufan said. They stayed in their rooms, "their jails," during the day, and left at night, seeking the cover of darkness. They strolled in Imam Reza's shrine, walked in parks, looked for mates, and returned to their homes at daybreak.

Shahnaz rented a room from an old woman in a poor ghetto of Mashhad, an enclave for "the most barbaric Afghans."

"Forgive me for calling the Afghans barbarians. I do not mean all the Afghans. But the ones in Mashhad were vicious. They were violent and wild," his gay friends had told him.

One night when he was walking home, Shahnaz was assaulted by a member of the morality police. His chest was cut open, his skull broken. Friends stayed at his bedside for one week to try to bring him back to life. He was near death. A month later, Shahnaz ended his life. "My only wish in life is to see my mother once more, embrace her, and feel her motherly love. That is all I wish. I will then be ready to die," Shahnaz told Tufan the last time they met.

"We bought fifty carnations and put them on the tombs of fifty strange men and women buried in the cemetery," Tufan said. The men gathered at a friend's home and spoke like warriors, members of a dissident group, and advocates of a common cause. One by one, they spoke in memory of their fallen friend.

"Shahnaz was taken away, but others will join," a friend said at his memorial. "Do not mourn when I die. Promise me one thing: stay together," he asked of his friends.

"We live like animals here, but we have one another. They kill us, but with each death, many more join us. We will prevail," another said.

I turned off my tape recorder. Tufan stared away. Minutes of silence followed. Then, lighting another cigarette, Tufan smiled again. The sadness brought on by thoughts of his friend's death had disappeared from his face. His smile revealed the pleasant thoughts now coursing through his head.

"What is it, Tufan?" I asked.

Speaking with a gentle voice, he began telling stories about the strong relationship and fraternity between gay men, their gatherings, and their "humble, spiritual" parties.

Friends gave a party when one among them found a new lover. They celebrated their friend's joy. The guests would arrive with gifts and flowers, and hugs and kisses abounded. The joyful men would put their meager resources together to help find a new home for the lovers. In their gatherings, they would embrace one another "like mothers embracing their loved ones." Some would talk about their saga. Others would weep. There would be consoling and sharing of pain. But one would always break the cycle. Jumping to the middle of the room, he would begin dancing.

"Get up, you miserable souls. Don't worry, one day the mullahs will go. There will be a new government and we can live like other normal people," the dancing man would say to his friends.

All would join the orgy of dancing and singing. They would clap and joyfully move their bodies.

"My words do not do justice to the sweetness you find in these gatherings," Tufan said.

The next time we met, he briefly returned to the story of his own life. At times, halfway through a story, he would hesitate and stop. There were times I did not know the protagonist of the story. He would start with himself, but as if changing his mind and not wishing to continue, he would stop, reorient, and tell a different story, the story of gay men in Iran. Wishing not to intrude, I would remain silent, not asking questions.

Now he frequently mentioned his wife. Though married for seven years, they had never made love. "Forgive me for speaking like this. My wife is still a girl [a virgin]," he said one day. "She is waiting for me. She thinks we will be real husband and wife when we have our own home someday," he continued. Following an old tradition in

Iran, married couples were barred from consummating their marriage until the husband found a home for the couple and they moved to their new space. Tufan's wife continued to live in her family home, waiting for Tufan to find a new nest for them. That had not yet materialized. She remained with her family, dreaming of sharing a home with her husband. He had lived in the basement of a friend's home until he left Mashhad and Iran in 1999.

Breaking my usual practice with Tufan, I began asking questions about his wife and their relationship. "Why did you marry and then leave her in Iran?" I asked.

"I was tricked by my family. I did not know I was getting married," he said.

One afternoon he had been asked to go along with his mother and brother for a visit to the neighbor's house. It was to be a casual visit, he thought. "I was wearing sweatpants and a T-shirt. My brother and mother were dressed up. I went along with them. I remember the television was on. I watched television and did not pay much attention to what was happening in the room." Then, suddenly, they called Tufan. Everyone smiled. They asked for his consent.

"I thought my older brother was getting married to the neighbor's older daughter."

That too was a tradition in Iran. Older sisters always had to be married off first. "I knew she liked my brother. He liked her too. Everyone was waiting for their marriage." Thinking so, Tufan gave his consent.

"Why should I not agree with my brother's marriage?" he thought.

Everyone cheered, clapped, embraced and kissed him, and congratulated him. "Everything was fast. For a few minutes, I still did not understand what had happened. Then they began calling me 'agha damad' [Mr. Bridegroom]. I realized what had just happened. I sat there not knowing what to do."

Two days later, he signed the marriage papers. He was a married man.

As we continued to meet, the tales he told me remained the tales of others, those he called "they," the gay men of his stories. "They cannot be free as long as they travel with other Iranians. Leaving Iran does not change that," he would say. But, slowly and without making direct references, he was becoming a part of his stories. The way he told the stories changed. At times he was a narrator and a participant, and it was not possible to distinguish him from the distant "they." His body language changed. A new speech pattern emerged. A feminine Tufan surfaced in the way he moved his hands, in the way he smiled and talked about the mischievousness of his friends, and in the way he sat before me and quietly remembered them. "Thank you for giving me the chance to tell you these stories," he would say. "I feel free with you."

On July 9, I left Paris for a visit to Calais and London. When I returned in two weeks, Tufan and I met at a café, once again in secret. There were clear signs of fatigue on Tufan's face. He asked for help.

"I want to run away from the Iranians here. I am tired. I wish to have a room somewhere, somewhere quiet, somewhere away from everyone. I want to live in peace."

England was his country of choice, but a journey there required money he did not possess. Staying in France was not easy. He was impatient. He had to prepare a case for asylum prior to registering with the police. "I don't know what to do," he repeated. "I can give them a political case." A political party in Iran's Kurdistan had promised to support him. "They will write a letter for me. Will this help me? I don't know. I don't know what to do. I want to bring my wife out of Iran. That is my first concern. But I need to get accepted as a refugee first."

I knew that Tufan trusted me. He had shared with me many secrets he kept from the friends traveling with him. I wished to use his trust and confidence to help him. I had heard many stories and testimonies from him. Though he never told me his sexual orientation, by now I was sure of his homosexuality. Hiding behind the stories of Shahnaz, Farid, and others, Tufan had told me his own life story. I wished to grab him and tell him to be free.

Filing a case as a gay man from the Islamic Republic of Iran was his only chance for receiving asylum in the West, I thought. He knew firsthand all the details of the persecution of gay people by the government. He had personal experience with the social discrimination against gays in his place of birth. His marriage, I thought, was a perfect example. He was deceived, forced to marry a woman by a brother and mother who, I thought, suspected his homosexuality. To cover their shame, they married him off. Being married, his "sins" were washed off. He was a "normal" man. I wanted to tell this to Tufan, but I dared not. What if he was not gay? I doubted myself while he sat before me asking for help. Was he waiting for me to take the last step, to hold his hand and pull him out of his jail? There was nothing else to reveal to me. All had been said. It was my turn to act. I sat in confusion, torn.

"I can get support letters from Iran. What do you suggest?" he said again. Somehow in that moment I found the courage to tell him my thoughts. Looking at him, I said: "Why don't you stay here and give them a gay case? You know so much about this community."

I waited for a reaction. He was thoughtful and reflective. Covering his face with his hands, he sat quietly. Then he removed his hands, looked up, lit a cigarette, and said, "Will people know what case I give? Will my friends find out?"

My agonies were gone. I felt free telling him my thoughts. "No one will know. No one should know. This is between you and your interviewing officer. The Europeans are very careful about the secrecy of asylum applications. You should not worry," I said.

"Will my wife find out about the case? I am doing this for her. I have to help her leave Iran. Will she know? Can I bring her here if I submit a gay case?"

I reassured him again about the way the system operated.

"I will give them a real case, a case based on my own life story. I hope they accept me. I am tired of living in fear, tired of hiding things. I want to be away from everyone I know, especially Mahmood. I don't want him to know about my asylum case. He is always with me. Maybe I can get help and find a place for myself, somewhere quiet where I can breathe freely without worrying," he said.

Tufan registered with the police and applied for asylum. He was given a monthly stipend and a bed in a hotel room with two other migrants. Helped by a kind Iranian-born dentist, he worked irregular jobs for extra money. An Iranian psychologist saw him free of charge. He smiled more often and regained his hope, he told me on the phone.

Six months after filing for asylum, Tufan received a letter from the authorities. His case had been rejected.

A rejection on the first try was common in asylum cases in France. "I will appeal my court decision," Tufan told me on the phone. I had since returned to Istanbul, but a lawyer was helping Tufan prepare documents for his appeal. Then in August 2004 I returned to France and once again met Tufan in secret, in a café in a suburb of Paris.

"Show me your original application. Let me see why they rejected your case. This is important in writing a convincing appeal. I thought you had a very strong case. Your insider knowledge of the gay community in Iran should have helped you."

Smiling timidly, as if feeling guilty for having disappointed me, he said, "I submitted a political case. They interviewed me for almost two hours and asked many questions. I answered all of them, but I guess they were not convinced. I was afraid I would not be able to bring my wife here if I gave them a gay case."

For several minutes, Tufan talked about his wife and his commitment to her. "She has been waiting for me all these years. I cannot abandon her. I don't care about myself anymore. I will do anything to get her out of Iran."

I was frustrated and could not understand his loyalty to a wife he had abandoned in Iran. He escaped Iran pursuing a different dream. I questioned him, and for the first time I crossed the line and brought his homosexuality into the open in our conversation.

"Does she know you are gay? Why don't you tell her? You have no other way. How long do you think you can keep going like this? Free her. Free yourself."

Opening up his briefcase, he took out an envelope. "This is her last letter," he said, and began reading.

Greetings to my love,

From the beginning of our relationship, if you remember, I was never able to tell you my thoughts in person. Anytime I wanted to be serious with you, the minute I saw you, I forgot all my problems. I could not say a word. So I wrote to you. This was the only way I could talk to you. My unkind love, you have not yet realized how much I love you, how much I long for you. . . .

I shiver anytime I think about the past. I have nightmares. I do not wish the past to repeat even for a second. You do not know what I went through. Some nights I dream that you are back. I see all my hopes destroyed. Even in my dream, the thought of the return of the past horrifies me. But, God willing, the past will never be repeated. I hope for us to be together when you come back. Then things will be different. . . .

You do not know how hurtful other people's—the neighbors' and relatives'—comments are about you. Their humiliating looks are like a hammer striking my head. . . . I ask of God to send you back full of achievements. I can then tell all these people that someone loves me. I can tell them that you love me, my dear, and that you did not abandon me. . . .

Their looks have become more hurtful ever since they found out that you are living in Paris. They pity me. . . . They say, "Oh, he is having so much fun in Paris." Another would say, "Lucky you. You will be going to Paris soon."

I want to prove them wrong, to show them that everything they said about you was wrong. I want you to pray that I can successfully go through the remainder of this journey. . . . I want them to know that you are very kind. I want them to know that you are not what they think of you.

Perhaps you think I am complaining, but to me, these are my secrets, secrets known only by my God and me. I swear to God I do not want to trouble you.

I hope to be together for our next anniversary. I hope for the day that we would walk freely under the drizzle at night. We would walk to our small home. I would make tea and you would read me books.

It is 1:30 in the morning now and I am drinking tea alone. I wish you were with me.

Folding the letter, Tufan sighed, lit a cigarette, and said, "How can I tell her that I am not with her because I am gay? How could she live in her community? She would have to die. She would never be able to hold her head up. How can I do that to her? Sometimes I wish to die. I wish to go to sleep and never wake up. That way she can tell everyone that her husband died of some illness. She would not be the subject of rumors and laughter by others," he said. Tears rolled down his face.

Reading the letter from his wife, for the first time, Tufan openly referred to himself as a gay man. I saw the ease on his face. From that point on, our conversations changed. Many untold secrets were revealed.

We were in central Paris in a small park one early evening. No longer referring to the anonymous "they," Tufan spoke about his life as a gay man in Mashhad.

"I was very beautiful when I was younger. I had no hair on my face. I don't wish to brag, but everybody who came across me fell in love with me. They chose me right away," he said.

He told me of dancing in weddings and private parties for money. "Gay people are good dancers," he said. "We all had our specialties. Mine was Iranian dancing. Shahnaz was a perfect belly dancer," he said, elegantly moving his hands, remembering a pleasant memory. "Sometimes I dressed as a woman. They could not tell if I was a man or a woman."

Tufan and the dancers were rewarded with decent pay by the bridegroom. At most parties, the guests tucked money in their clothes. "You would think this is a religious city. [In Mashhad] they are worse than anywhere else. After my dance routines, I was often followed by the men at the party. Sometimes I had to fight to get away." A time or two, the men came to him with blades in their hands. Violence was not uncommon. They would demand sexual favors. "These were family men. Some of them were very religious." They were married men who violently opposed homosexuality but took pleasure in sleeping with Tufan and other male dancers.

"They called us filthy, but they would do anything to sleep with us. That's how it was."

We were sitting on a park bench talking about men who fancied Tufan and his gay friends when, casually and abruptly, he looked straight ahead and said, "I introduced Mahmood to all my gay friends after a week of going out with him. I was always very mischievous and flirted a lot, but Mahmood was the first man I really dated, the very first man I ever loved."

I looked at Tufan. Seeing the shock on my face, he ignored me, avoided eye contact, and continued to speak about Mahmood and other stories. That was Tufan's way of becoming free. Things were moving too fast. While he continued to talk, I remained trapped in his first few sentences about Mahmood. As if wishing to become sure of what I had just heard, and pretending not to be shocked, I asked:

"Does Mahmood know about your wife?"

"He knows everything about my life. I could not keep anything from him. I told him all my secrets. . . . I was very young, only twenty-two years old, when I met Mahmood. He was the first man I fell in love with.

"I used to be a pretty boy. Men would beg me to be with them. They would fall on their knees. But Mahmood was different. He would not beg. That was his weapon. He ignored me, lied to me, and broke his promises. And I loved him even more. I was crazy about him."

As their relationship continued, Tufan became more attached to Mahmood. Soon he deserted his friends. The frequency of his visits to his wife declined. He lived to be near Mahmood, to look him in the eye, to please him.

When they met, Mahmood was an opium addict. Wishing to be with him all the time, Tufan began consuming opium. Soon he was smoking four times a day. Mahmood supplied him; sometimes he kept Tufan waiting for a daily dose for hours, even two days, in his basement.

"I would wait shivering, crouched in a corner with my eyes fixed on the door. I hated my life and what I was doing, but I could not escape. I was unable to move. Killing myself was the only solution, but I even failed in that."

Rolling up his sleeve, Tufan showed me the big scar on his left arm.

"I cut myself with a blade. I wanted to die. I took pills. Again they saved me. I once tried to hang myself in the basement. Mahmood saved my life."

He was too weak to work, too tormented to focus on anything but his obsession with Mahmood. Day in and day out, he stayed in the basement.

"I did not see the sun for days at times."

A courtyard separated the basement from the house where Mahmood's family—his mother and siblings—lived. The family knew about Tufan; they were suspicious of his relationship with Mahmood.

"His mother was disgusted with me. I had to hide from all of them. Sometimes Mahmood would disappear for a couple of days. I was afraid of leaving and being seen by his mother and his family. So I stayed in the basement waiting, with no food."

While Tufan remained enslaved by Mahmood, his wife desperately waited for him in her room on the top floor of the building she lived in with her mother and older sister. Cooking him dinner, making sweets and preparing tea, she would wait for his arrival at night. Night after night, she would sit alone in the room, falling asleep, then waking up to see the food untouched. She would wait with patience, never uttering a word of complaint.

"I had become sick. I was afraid of people, but I felt secure in Mahmood's basement. My only friends were my books. I was scared of everything else. Even Mahmood frightened me. But I was addicted to him. At night, I was afraid to sleep. I had nightmares when I fell asleep. I would see Mahmood's mother screaming at me in the basement. My wife would be standing in a corner crying.

"Anytime I went to see her, I would be either sick or sleepy. I could not talk to her. She would sit by me and watch me sleep. Seeing me frail and becoming so thin, she worried about my health. She probably thought I was tired from working too much. She never suspected anything.

"Whatever my wife did for me, I did for Mahmood. I cooked for him, cleaned his room. I was there anytime he wanted me, but he ignored me. Meanwhile, I knew that my wife was waiting for me. I was becoming mad.

"I am sure my wife was suffering too. She was losing weight. At one point, her weight dropped to a hundred and twenty pounds, but she never complained. She gave me unlimited love. I cannot leave her alone now. I have to bring her here. That is all I want to do.

"I have told Mahmood that I will leave him soon. I know he needs me, but I don't care anymore. Things have a way of coming around. In Mashhad, I could not live without him. I was unable to think or do anything. Now everything is the opposite. He depends on me for everything. He cries and begs me, but I will leave him."

Ferial

"Have you seen how animals make their territories by pissing around themselves? Humans are like that too; they piss and make a circle around a part of nature and make it their private territory. That is how borders are created. 'This is mine because it smells like my urine,' the governments tell you."

This was in July 2003. We met on a hot summer day in Paris, and those words were how Ferial introduced herself to me. Hers is an unusual name for an Iranian, and I asked about its origin. "An old Armenian name," she replied.

Ferial had just arrived from Italy with all the appearances of a migrant. She wore men's shoes, white pants, a blue T-shirt, and a white short-sleeved shirt on top. She had a very short haircut—a man's haircut—and walked like a man. She said she was Iranian, but her skin was darker than that of most Iranians. "I am twenty-seven years old," she told me. She looked like she was in her early thirties.

A young friend of mine had met her accidentally in the Metro a couple of days earlier, and she had briefly told him about her voyage. Knowing about my work, my friend made arrangements for our meeting. The meeting was to be at noon in Place de la Sorbonne.

Sometime during our first meeting, I mentioned Tufan and the others who had recently arrived from Rome. Hearing Tufan's name, she rejoiced. They had met sleeping in parks, recovering from their long sea voyage. Like Tufan and the other boys, she too slept on a piece of cardboard, and crossed borders hiding from train conductors and the police. She was the sole woman sleeping in the park with the traveling men.

"You see this shirt?" She opened her bag and pulled out a long-sleeved shirt. "This is Tufan's. I was cold one night in Rome. He insisted on giving me his shirt. I did not want to accept. He was cold too, but he would not let go. I took it in the end."

Days later, I told Tufan about Ferial. "You mean Nasrin?" he said
with surprise. Ferial had used the name Nasrin in Rome. Spending
day and night with the men and not being intimidated by them, she
won their respect. They were intrigued by her. "She is a man," Tufan
told me. In the male-dominated culture of Iran, courageous, strong,
and independent-minded women were given respect by being
equated with men. Ferial was worthy of that respect.

She was the oldest daughter of a family of four from Khaniabad, a
ghetto in Tehran, she told me. Ferial had studied literature and completed a bachelor's degree in law from Tehran University. Traveling
was her love in life. She had made many journeys before leaving
home and her family for a trip around the world. This was the profile
she gave me in Paris. I told that to Tufan.

"She never attended university," Tufan said. She had never even
finished high school, Nasrin had told Tufan and the others in Rome.

Reza, an Iranian who had housed Ferial for a few days in Calais in
late July, told me, "She is not Iranian. Her name is not Nasrin. I saw
her birth certificate. Her name is Gonabin. She is from Kandahar."

"I don't believe she is Iranian. She does not even look Iranian,"
Hooshang said. He was in Calais waiting for the right time to leave
for England when he met Ferial.

"She may be a runaway girl. I suspected that early on. She had
been to Mashhad and is acquainted with some of the city's known
runaways. We have mutual friends among the runaway girls in
Mashhad. Who knows? She says she knows Shirin Ebadi [the Iranian
lawyer and law professor who won the Nobel Peace Prize in 2003].
She was her teacher at Tehran University," Tufan told me a year later,
in August 2004.

I will never know her real name or nationality, or her real life story.
Iranian or Afghan, runaway or a college graduate, Nasrin or Golabin,
Ferial intrigued me. She was a woman from the Islamic Republic on
the road alone, journeying like the men I had met earlier in Greece
and elsewhere. She crossed borders illegally, traveled in sealed containers, and slept in parks. With Tufan and the other men, she was a

street girl, a tough girl. In my presence, she had the language and demeanor of a disillusioned intellectual.

She told me that she had once been a photographer, a social worker, and a "believer in women's rights." After finishing high school, she said, she had moved to a village sixty miles north of Tehran in order to live with and help the poor. She wanted to "make a difference." But that was all in the past. By the time we met, her interest in helping the poor and fighting for gender equality had died.

"You cannot fight nature" was her new attitude toward the issues. Poverty was part of the natural order of things.

"I cannot turn a cat into a lion," she would say.

I challenged Ferial's views on poverty and wealth, told her how I saw both as the results of inequality embedded in the free market system. Wealth and poverty were not natural, I told her. "The unnatural borders lead to poverty. They keep people in deprived zones, and limit their mobility and their ability to benefit from the fruits of nature. Like borders, poverty is manufactured," I told her.

She laughed. "You are naive," she said, and explained that she had once had the same beliefs. "I cried when I saw hungry children, but I changed. I think this is all natural. Poverty is also beautiful, like anything else in nature. I don't know why I feel this way. Perhaps I saw too much poverty, or I saw laziness, saw the poor do nothing to change their condition."

Ferial had a subdued smile. Staring at me, she would pay close attention to my words, always maintaining her smile. Her language fascinated me. It was unique, unlike any other I had encountered on the road, and in some ways unlike any other I had encountered in Iran. Her words were sharp. Cutting through the surface, they were frank and learned. I wished to tape her words from the start. She did not welcome the idea.

"You can do that later. Anyway, it does not matter. You are not my friend. You are only interested in my story," she said, making me feel defensive and guilty for not being her friend.

"Did you come here illegally?" That was the first question I asked her.

"I did not cross illegally. Borders are illegal. They are not natural. Crossing them is my right. Doing what is my right is not illegal," she replied.

I had spoken to many migrants. None had given me that response. They disrespected the sanctity of the borders, broke the border laws, crossed them clandestinely, but not once did they challenge the very concept of borders. They wished to be the good citizens of another nation-state.

Ferial did not wish to be the citizen of another state.

"My understanding of borders is different from that of other people. In a classroom, you need to get permission from the teacher to leave the room. Nature is different. You can freely move from one place to another. I have not chosen anyplace as my home. I am free. I live in nature, like the birds," she said. Seeing the intrigued expression on my face, she started laughing.

I asked at what age she had begun thinking like a bird living in nature.

"I don't remember having ever believed differently. This is how I felt from my childhood. The earth equally belongs to everybody. It is not for the French, or the Iranians. Borders are created by power. Wealthy and powerful countries draw a line around them and declare their own that part of nature. That is against nature."

Migrants leave home in search of a new home. Ferial was not on the road for a new home. The very concept of a home frightened her. She found that limiting, enslaving, suffocating. For Ferial, the journey was the beginning and the end.

She had left Iran in the winter of 2002. "I tried to persuade my younger sister to go with me," but the sister was scared.

Next Ferial talked to two friends.

"You must be insane," they said.

Her travel plan included a voyage across Europe, North America,

Mexico, Africa, China, Russia, India, and an eventual return to Iran. One evening, Ferial took a world map and showed her family the countries she planned to visit. They laughed.

"Two days later I asked permission to go to a party. I never returned."

She shaved her head, dressed like a man, and took a bus to the border with Turkey.

"I don't regret any part of this trip. The only part I would not repeat is crossing the mountains between Iran and Turkey in winter."

The mountains were covered with snow. The deadly cold and the winds made the short crossing unbearable. She arrived in Van nearly dead.

She then moved to Aksaray in Istanbul. Unlike other migrants from Iran, Ferial had good memories of her short visit there. She visited the famous tourist sites, frequented Persian nightclubs, and enjoyed her life away from the Islamic Republic. Once bored with Istanbul, she was on the road again. Perhaps helped by luck, she made it to Greece on her first attempt.

Three months after leaving Iran, Ferial was in Omonia Square in Athens. "I had a great time there," she said. "I smoked cocaine all night long. There were cool people from around the world." When the time came to move on, she left Athens for Patras.

Walking around by the fence on her first day in the port, she met one of the last occupants of the truck. By then, Farshad and others had left the port. She was invited to stay in the truck, and shared it with two men for a week; she had no plans for staying longer in Greece. Soon she made all the necessary arrangements for her departure with a Kurdish smuggler. On the seventh day of her visit, accompanied by the first man she had met in Patras, Ferial was in a truck full of watermelons waiting to be boarded on a ship to Italy. In two days, she was in a city park in Rome, chatting with Tufan and others.

"You are the nightmare of the Islamic Republic," I told her in one of our meetings.

The Islamic Republic wished to mold a generation of obedient and virtuous Muslim women, clad head to toe in dark cloth, homebound, existing in the shadow of their men. Ferial was the personification of the Islamic Republic's defeat. Rebellious, restless, disobedient, independent, and courageous, she was the republic's antithesis.

Entertained by my statement, she nodded in agreement. Perhaps this was the first time in her life someone, a stranger, had admired her for precisely the attributes her native society scorned and condemned.

More than the experience of the journey, I was interested in Ferial the person. Something made her different from all the migrants I met in the past. She was challenging and had a story that puzzled me, one I am writing now with ambiguity and many unresolved questions. She caused commotion, controversies, envy, shame, anger, and excitement for the people she encountered.

"I used to look at men as the opposite sex. That is how they looked at me. We had no other way in Iran. I changed during the journey. I now see them as people first. I have a much better relationship with them."

Many of the men she encountered did not share her point of view. She was a woman on the road. To many, that meant a loose woman. Nothing could change that. Most men did not understand her. Many were afraid of her. They called her a "slut," "shameless," and a "liar."

She was aware of what people said about her. That did not stop her from meeting new men, spending time with them, and creating turmoil. In Paris, she lived with an Iranian man she had accidentally met at a hotel. He was a night receptionist, and a graduate student of French literature. I met him the day he gave Ferial the keys to his flat. That was two days after their meeting at the hotel. When other migrants slept in city parks, Ferial slept in a clean private home.

Unlike the others, she had French friends and attended French parties. She had a normal life. Her mobile phone rang frequently during our meetings. At times she spoke broken English. "I am invited to a big party outside Paris," she would say in English.

In less than three weeks of being in France, Ferial had become a known figure among the new arrivals and migrants in Paris and Calais. Hoping to move to Britain, she visited Calais. That was not as easy as she had earlier thought. Ferial mingled with the Kurds and became close to a Kurdish smuggler. The smuggler promised to help her to move forward. "I realized he was not going to do that. He wanted to keep me there for himself. I left," she told me. She left Calais when she saw there was no hope of crossing the water.

In July 2003 there were less than a hundred Kurds, Iranians, Sudanese, and Afghans in Calais, sleeping outdoors, hoping to leave for Britain. There were no women migrants except for Ferial. She was friendly and outgoing. Ferial was not afraid of being alone among men who had had no contact with women for months or perhaps years. She tamed the men around her. In Calais, the Iranians and the Kurds competed over her. The Kurds won the battle. She spent time with the Kurds. The Iranians were jealous and angry.

"She was shameless. You should have seen how she was dancing with the Kurds. This is not suitable for an Iranian woman. I am telling you, she is not Iranian," Reza told me.

"She is a junkie," he said later. Reza had housed Ferial for three days and offered to help her kick the habit, he told me.

One day he had found her birth certificate in her purse. "She is a liar, a disgrace. She is not Iranian," he told me over and over. "She is Afghan." The pronouncement perhaps helped him deal with the shame he felt at seeing an Iranian woman dance in public with a Kurd from Iraq.

"I had a great time. I love dancing," Ferial told me after she returned to Paris from her visit to Calais. "One day I was dancing with a few men. An Iranian man, Reza, became very upset seeing me dance with the Kurds. Next day, I saw him get out of the car of a *baba*—a sugar daddy. I looked him in the eye and he did not say a word. He understood. He held his head down and walked away."

It was raining lightly the last time we met in Paris. Standing on the Pont des Arts on the river Seine, watching the rain gently touch the water, she turned toward me and said, "I was happier before I met you. I now realize what I had missed in my life. You have seen more than me. You left a job and a good life in New York and started living with migrants." Evidently I intrigued her. "Why are you doing this?" she asked.

I told her that I thought there was a need to tell the world the stories of the migrants on the road, and to bring out the real identities of the migrants, which were buried under many layers of misunderstanding and false assumption. She was not convinced of my explanation.

"You have a secret," she said.

Was this my real identity, a writer traveling with migrants? She questioned that.

"You are hiding something from me. What is your real story?" she said again.

I did not see Ferial after that day. We spoke on the phone a number of times. She called frequently. At times she would send me text messages with pictures. "I was thinking about you," she wrote when she sent me a picture of a river and a bridge.

My time in Paris was nearly over, and I was preparing for my return to Istanbul. Having found some free time, I planned to see Ferial one last time. Then a call came from Tufan. "I am sorry to bother you, *agha* Behzad. Forgive me for this intrusion, but I have to tell you something. Please do not see Ferial or Mahmood. I know she has been calling you a lot lately. Mahmood will call you today. He will ask to meet you. Please do not meet with either of them. They know you are leaving. They want to borrow money from you and disappear. They planned this in my presence. I did not say anything. If they call you, tell them that you are busy. Do not give them any money."

I followed Tufan's advice. The next day, Ferial phoned me twice, but I did not answer her calls.

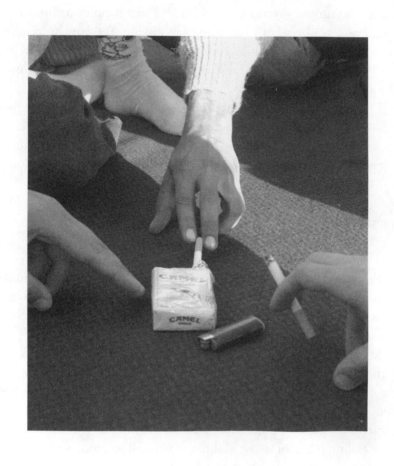

PART SIX

Calais

Calais

For many migrants at the colony in Paris, Calais was the last border they had to cross before reaching England, what they considered their Eden on earth. Many times a day French and English ferryboats left Calais for Dover. The journey took just an hour and fifteen minutes. The train ride through the Eurotunnel was only half an hour.

The construction of the Eurotunnel and the start of the operation of fast trains in mid-1995 increased the area's attractiveness to those wishing to reach England from places across the world. The tunnel opened a new opportunity to escape England's newly tightened immigration and visa policies.

The migrants came in large numbers. They camped out in the cold and under unbearable conditions, hoping to break into the Eurotunnel site and hold on to the superfast trains leaving for Britain. Others camped around Calais, hoping to board a truck on a Calais-Dover ferry. To shelter the migrants sleeping in the streets and parks, the French Red Cross built a camp with the capacity to house six hundred residents on the site of an abandoned warehouse owned by the Eurotunnel Company in Sangatte, a village a little over a mile from the tunnel.

The camp opened its doors to traveling migrants in 1999. Originally designed to house refugees from the war in Kosovo, it was soon a magnet for Iranians, Iraqi Kurds, Afghans, and some Africans on the last leg of their long journey. At its peak, an average of fifteen hundred men, women, and children slept in the camp.

Sangatte was soon a legend. From Kandahar to Kirkuk, thousands of migrants took to the road with one goal: arriving at the camp and preparing for the next stage of their journey. During its short life, some sixty-eight thousand migrants passed through the camp. Between August 1999 and December 2000, Eurotunnel security intercepted around twenty-nine thousand people trying to leave for England at the Coquelles terminal. The migrants were handed over to the French police. Nearly three thousand were deported. The rest were set free.[11]

The French authorities conveniently closed their eyes to the activities in Sangatte, inasmuch as it served as a voluntary deportation center: the asylum seekers left France on their own after a short stay. The English protested, and demanded the closure of Sangatte. The French resisted, and the quarrel continued. After months of negotiation and disagreement between the two countries, an agreement was reached. Sangatte was closed in November 2002. A month later the camp was demolished.

As a part of the deal to close the camp, the English accepted for asylum one thousand Kurds and two hundred Afghans with family already in England. The rest of the thirty-six hundred migrants registered with the camp were offered money for their "voluntary repatriation" home or were asked to apply for asylum in France. The closure, however, failed to stop the flow of migrants who continued to arrive, albeit in smaller numbers. Now they were dispersed in Sangatte and elsewhere.

The number of homeless migrants sleeping in public parks in Paris swelled overnight. Newspapers wrote about the potential for a human catastrophe. In a January 12, 2003, article, the *Observer* warned: "Hundreds of asylum-seekers, including families with small children, are now sleeping rough under the elegant bridges and in the doorways of Paris as the worst winter spell for years threatens to create a humanitarian 'crisis.' "[12] In Calais, the migrants were sleeping in public parks or makeshift shelters in below-zero temperatures. Soon many smaller Sangattes emerged, scattered in and around Calais. These were makeshift encampments created by the migrants. They slept on muddy ground and rough gravel, under abandoned tractors and construction machines, and out in the open without protection from the cold and harsh weather. The camp at Sangatte had provided temporary accommodation to many women and children. With its closure, Calais became a temporary male encampment for the transit migrants. Men from Iran, Afghanistan, northern Iraq, and Sudan assembled along the railroad tracks near the dock and camped at the border. Calais's harsh living conditions were not suitable for families.

On July 9, 2003, I took a train to Calais from Paris. Arriving at noon, I left the station and found myself on a wide boulevard. There was a near-empty café on my left, taxis waiting for passengers, and a few passersby. A short walk from the station, just a few feet off the main boulevard, was the nearest hotel. Checking in, I took my tape recorder and camera and returned to the boulevard, facing a water canal, railroad tracks, and a fence, standing between the street and the tracks. I strolled along the fence and away from the main thoroughfare.

Walking on the tracks behind the fence, keeping his balance by stretching his arms, a young African passed time. Four men who looked Middle Eastern sat silently on the gravel behind the fence. Passing me along the tracks, a young man cried: "Hello, when did you arrive?"

I turned around.

"Wait, I will come out," he said. Running fast to a small opening in the fence, he came out on the street, waving and calling me by name. Seeing my confusion, he said, "We met in Eagle's Fort, *agha* Behzad."

Area near the Iranian encampment in Calais

His name was Hussein. In his twenties, he had been on the road for four years, three weeks of that in Calais. He had no money, no plans, and no understanding of the exit routes but was happy to have clean clothes and a meager meal twice a day.

"We never have to wash our clothes here. Once a week we go to a church—I will take you there if you want—and they give us new clothes. We just throw away our dirty clothes," he said with a big smile. "We don't have to look for food. They feed us twice a day here. This is a lot better than Paris." Knowing I had just arrived, Hussein offered to give me a tour of the port. "I am not doing anything now. I just have to be back for lunch before two o'clock. I can show you the *fance*."

Walking away from the railroad tracks into quiet and deserted streets, Hussein showed me the world of migrants in Calais: the sites where they were fed, the church they got clean clothes from, and the boarded-up, abandoned boat he and a few others squatted in at night. "You see this boat. I sleep there at nights. All of its windows are boarded up. There is no air in the boat and it smells very bad. I really don't like it, but it is better than sleeping outside."

Passing by large lifts and gigantic machines, warehouses, and high fences with barbed wire, we reached the harbor. I stood across from a large sign that read "Calais 5," designating one of the eight exits from Calais.

"This is *fance* number five," Hussein said. A very tall fence separated the harbor and the sea from the town. The large gate, the entrance to Calais 5, was closed, and big passenger ships and trailer trucks were parked behind the fence. "There is no way to get to the other side," Hussein said with awe.

It was nearly two in the afternoon, time for Hussein's first meal of the day. "Let's go back to where we met. You can see others from Patras. They all go there to get their lunches."

The eating site was a large open space between the railroad tracks and the canal. There was garbage, broken glass, plastic bags and bottles, and a tree or two creating the badly desired shade on this hot summer day. An old, beat-up van was parked on a far corner near the canal. Blankets and towels covered the windows. Pants and shirts hung on a rope attached to the van. This was home to the men from Sudan, waiting at the border to move forward. Sitting on the ground, they waited to be fed. A deranged, unwashed, and shabbily clothed French man threw a beer bottle at a migrant. Picking up a small rock, the migrant chased him. When the migrant caught up with the French man, they hugged and laughed.

Across from the Sudanese van was a canteen, a trailer that served lunch. A private Catholic charity fed the migrants their first meal of the day. There were twenty or so men sitting on the ground in the shade, waiting. Some men clustered in groups of five or six, smoking cigarettes, chatting.

At fifteen minutes past two a station wagon pulled into the site and slowly moved toward the canteen in the middle of the site. Suddenly men rose to their feet and ran toward the vehicle. Others lined up behind them, pushing and shoving, hoping to get ahead. There was a scuffle, yelling, laughing, and madness on the food line, chaos and disorder, noise, and a sense of panic. Two French volunteers tried to maintain order. Men were sandwiched between the station wagon and the canteen. The woman inside the canteen shut the window. The noise escalated, and the window was reopened. The pushing and shoving increased. The first man on line emerged with a plastic bag in his hands. Happy and triumphant, he moved away, sat on the ground, and opened his treasured bag.

More men followed. Clusters of two or three assembled on the rough unpaved ground. Some sat alone and ate their food with their heads down. There was silence. Half an hour later, empty plastic bottles of water, wraps, and paper were tossed on the ground, and the men had disappeared. Some were lying down on the gravel, while others had moved to a nearby green space by the canal. The volunteers arrived with large black plastic bags; they patiently collected the garbage, packed, and drove away.

After lunch was served, I left the site to stroll in the port. Later that evening I met with Hussein and other Iranians, and visited their sleeping area for the night.

In the summer of 2003, Iranian migrants slept outside by a large abandoned warehouse surrounded by tall piles of sand, cranes, a cement-making machine, and scattered pieces of scrap metal. The warehouse was behind the boarded-up boat Hussein slept in at night. Months earlier, the boat had been confiscated from its owner by the French authorities, I was told. The deranged Frenchman I had seen earlier that day was the self-designated custodian of the boat. "He is crazy. He would let you sleep there if you have sex with him. I would rather die than do that," an Iranian said. The French man was thin, unshaven, and dirty. His hair was mostly gone. His movements were abrupt and unpredictable. "He throws stones at us when we are asleep at night," a young Iranian who slept in the open space by the warehouse told me. "He gets pissed off when nobody sleeps in the boat."

A very large trailer tire was hung on a chain in the space between the warehouse and the boat. "Come, let me show you my bedroom," a pleasant and friendly young Iranian told me. There was an old blanket inside the tire. Jumping inside and lying down, he demonstrated how he spent his nights at the border in Calais. "I prefer this to there [the warehouse]. You can sleep here tonight. You will have privacy here. We will get you a clean sleeping bag," he said.

"Can I photograph you inside the tire?" I asked.

"Take a picture of the tire alone if you want." He covered his face and moved away.

In Calais, most migrants did not wish to be photographed. Close to the final destination, they protected themselves by remaining anonymous. But earlier, in Sangatte, they had sought out foreign journalists and photographers. They wished to have a public profile. Publicity was protection. It was a way out. The international news coverage brought attention to their cases, made others aware of their plight, and helped them move forward. The men and women of the Red Cross camp were under the watchful eyes of the world.

But with its closure, a new world emerged for the migrants. The dark-skinned aliens roamed around Calais and nearby places. The locals resented them. Frightened and distrustful, they protested and wished them to disappear. Some locals defied their neighbors' wishes and took the homeless migrants into their homes to shelter and feed them, giving them the protection they were denied by the government. The migrants welcomed the assistance. The government accused these French citizens of assisting clandestine border crossings and threatened them with long-term jail sentences. Many continued to help. In 2003 Charles Frammezelle, who had sheltered two Afghans, was charged with "aiding irregular residence in an organized group." A crime normally attributed to human smugglers, the charge carried a five-year jail penalty.[13]

Occasionally, the police clamped down and harassed those who helped. They rounded up the migrants routinely, took them to places far away from the town, and released them by the highway. The migrants had to walk for hours along the highway to return to their "homes" at the border.

Some migrants withdrew from public sight. They hid in the woods and became ghostly figures. They avoided the occasional journalists and camerapeople who tried to pay them a visit. Some covered their faces. Others took shelter in their hideouts in order not to be filmed. Trust was rare. Unnecessary information could damage their newly constructed identities and reveal their false stories to the immigration officers beyond the waters. In Sangatte, silence was protection, and invisibility was the migrants' last weapon.

There are eight gates to the harbor in Calais. The fifth gate, Calais 5, was a short walk from the warehouse and the abandoned boat. Earlier, when the Sangatte camp was operating, a war broke out between the Afghans and the Kurds over the control of the exit routes and access to the Eurotunnel. The Afghans lost the battle, and like other temporary residents of the camp, they became traveling migrants, at the mercy of the Kurdish smugglers. With the closure of Sangatte, the Kurds consolidated their control, bringing their operations to the parking areas around the port. The trucks destined for England boarded the ships through the eight gates.

The harbor is state property, accessible to migrants with documents and to the trucks moving legally traded merchandise in and out of France. The gatekeepers were not only the state officials; they were also the smugglers making a fortune at the border. To enter and hide in the trucks leaving France, migrants had to pay off the Kurdish smugglers. Access and entry to the trucks and trailers were free of the watchful eyes of the authorities. But the parking areas were the smuggler's turf. Entering them had a price. The smugglers opened the trailers, let the migrants in, closed the door, and collected their fees.

"Sometimes I see them bloodied. I ask no question. I know the story," Pierre, a Frenchman helping the migrants, told me. He helped the Kurdish migrants camped in the woods by a highway near Calais, bringing them food and other necessities.

He had come upon them accidentally. One day Pierre saw dark-skinned men in the woods. That was the beginning of his quiet volunteer work. For more than a year, Pierre had been the lone provider to the Kurds hiding in the woods. His wife had left him twenty days before we met in July 2003. His children felt betrayed by a father who helped strangers and spent most of his free time in hideouts with men living clandestinely.

At times, he saw men bleeding, men whom he'd seen in perfect condition the night before when he visited the hideout to bring them food.

"I knew what was going on," he said.

The assaulted men were migrants daring to bypass the smugglers. They were stopped, punished, and made to respect the rules of border crossing in northern France.

Complaining to the police would have brought attention to the hideout, he feared. The Kurds trusted him. They felt safe in their

*Makeshift homes in the woods near Calais,
housing Kurds from northern Iraq*

secret arrangement. They succumbed to the violence of the smugglers, lived in subhuman conditions, but wished to remain invisible.

Accompanied by an Iranian and two French documentary makers, one afternoon in late July I visited the men in their hideout in the woods off a local highway, a short few minutes' drive from a trailer park. Walking through a narrow path, I reached a small open area. Three men stood by a shack made of plastic and cardboard. I introduced myself as an Iranian interested in their cause, and they embraced me. Telling their names, they smiled, came forward, and shook my hand. Others arrived. "He is Iranian," one said about me. The newcomers welcomed me to their encampment.

Asking for permission, I went inside the shack with my camera. "Three people sleep here," a man said. Three sleeping bags, a blanket or two, shirts, and pants were scattered on rough ground. "When it rains, everything gets wet and muddy."

Leaving the shack, I moved further into the woods. Clothes hung on tree branches. Pots and pans, a blackened teapot, and a number of empty jelly jars used as teacups and drinking glasses lay under a tree, with insects crawling in and out. The migrants carried water in buckets and plastic containers, and they cooked on an open fire.

"Please take a picture of this," a man told me. Following him, I found myself in a wide and open space. A long, thick blue plastic sheet covered a broken and rusted heavy machine. "This is my home," he said. There were blankets on the ground and under the machine. "Take a picture of this. We live like animals," he said, and I photographed his home. He moved away in shame.

"I once had a life," he said.

When I prepared to leave, the men surrounded me again, apologizing for not being able to show me a taste of Kurdish hospitality, offering me tea or lunch.

Like other stops on the journey, the smugglers' control of the gates in Calais often led to the invention of alternative methods of escape by the migrants. Hooshang, the Iranian I met in Patras, Paris, and later Calais, was among the inventors.

"Keep this a secret. I do not want others to find out about this now," he told me when he took me to the site of his escape, four hours before the operation. Looking around suspiciously, watching the surroundings for passersby, he hid a large black plastic bag in the bushes near one of the gates.

The smugglers began patrolling the gates an hour or two past midnight, he explained to me. High fences and barbed wire protected the gate. A narrow waterway stood between the deck and the area outside the gate. Swimming across the waterway and climbing up to the deck was the only way to bypass the gate and its fences. Quietly and without being noticed by the guards, the men would cross the waterway in the dark of night. To protect themselves from possible drowning, the men needed life jackets. With no money to buy them, Hooshang had designed a crude life jacket for each of the fleeing men: six empty plastic Coke bottles tied together with a rope, to help them float on the water. Wearing their underwear, they would put their dry clothes in airtight plastic bags tied to their waist. Once on the deck, they would change into dry clothes, choose a ferry awaiting departure the next morning, and hide on it.

All preparations made, the men met on the site for their escape. They had planned and practiced many times before the date of the operation, but a few meters into the water, a young migrant panicked. Shaking with fear, he could not move, and watched his friends swim away. The men returned for their friend, pulled him through the waterway, and took him ashore.

Dried and dressed, the escapees approached the anchored ferries, one after the other. All doors, windows, and entrances were locked; entry was not possible. Desperate, the men knocked on the doors, hoping to get the attention of a caring custodian or ferry guard. None responded. They stood on the deck touching the ferries, unable to enter. No security, no guards. They had to return before the smugglers began their patrol. Packing their clothes in their bags, they wore their vests and swam back to the familiar warehouse where they slept.

I left Calais the day after and never saw Hooshang again. Nearly half a year later, though, I received an e-mail from an unknown address letting me know that Hooshang had finally made it to England.

The men in Calais and the woods around it were on the road for months. Some had left their homes and loved ones three or four years before arriving at the last border. They lived in all-male enclaves, spoke to men, ate with men, cried with men, and laughed with men. Except for a few who could buy the sexual service of prostitutes, the migrants lived dreaming of women, longing for female warmth, touch, and love.

A few fared better than the rest. In their teens or early twenties, some found love in the arms of older French women, some in their sixties. The women had kind and motherly looks, gave the men love and attention, tucked them in their beds, and slept with them. The young men had the comfort of a home and all that came with it. Sex was the central part of the agreement. There was no shower or clean bed for those failing to deliver. This was a strict business deal, with its own rules and codes of conduct.

There were those who had sex with older men, the *babas*, in return for a shower and sleeping on a real bed. The men came in their cars, chose one they favored, and drove away.

Then there were the five or six young French girls who appeared to be in their teens. They dressed casually, jeans and T-shirts for the most part, and spent their days roaming around the small park by the railroad tracks, mingling with the Kurds. They joked and laughed, smoked cigarettes, and passed time.

"They met the Kurds, their big shots, in Sangatte," Reza, the Iranian migrant I met by the railroad tracks told me with jealousy. The powerful Kurds had befriended the girls and courted them. Now Sangatte was closed, but the girls had followed the Kurdish patrons to their new site. The old habits were maintained. The Kurds were happy around them. The scent of women, their laughter, their cries, and their female attributes made the Kurds feel human again. They joked with the girls—rough jokes, physical jokes, jokes without tenderness—touched them, embraced and squeezed them, and some slept with them. They had sex on the rough ground of their sleeping site at night.

"They take turns, go to the girls one at a time," Reza said.

The Kurdish big shots controlled the exit routes. Power gave them the right to control not only the gates but access to the young and badly desired women of the site.

Earlier, a war had broken out over the girls. A number of Iranian men had crossed the line by mingling with the girls. The Kurds objected. There were scuffles and arguments. A few Iranians moved out of the site and camped in a park on the opposite side of the canal; some of the girls followed the Iranians. The Kurds arrived with knives and chains. The outnumbered Iranians were assaulted and bloodied. The girls cheered their Kurdish heroes—this was perhaps the very first time that a man had fought for them, and they were proud.

After that the Iranians, Afghans, and others stayed away from the girls. All returned to the old rules. Peace prevailed. The Iranians stared at the girls, watching with envy as the Kurds roughed up the girls, kissed them, slapped them—jokingly of course—and touched them.

It was the afternoon of my last day in Calais. The migrants had had their first ration of the day, and now it was time for relaxation, contemplation, and flirtation. The Sudanese clustered around the van. There were some twenty of them. They rarely mingled with the other men on the road. The only two Romanians on the site

shopped around for a smuggler to take them to Dover for less than
two hundred euros apiece. Moving up and down, they talked to different Kurds, whispered, consulted, and schemed. An Iranian was
the dealmaker, the middleman between the Romanians and the
Kurds.

Two newly arrived Sudanese rested on a sloping bed of gravel
around the railroad tracks. A tall and fit African with long dreadlocks
moved up and down around the Sudanese van. He was known as the
"African of Calais." He had lived in Sangatte for months and now
worked with the NGOs "for refugee rights," he told me. When the
authorities closed Sangatte, he had moved in with a young French
couple, and was enjoying his life in Calais.

Some two hundred feet away from the van, on the grass of the
small parklike space by the canal, the Kurds assembled in groups.
Some rested on the grass. Others conversed. The French girls moved
back and forth between the groups. Bald and somewhat chubby,
dressed in clean white pants and shirt, a Kurdish man charmed the
girls. He smiled, hugged and wrestled with the girls, and moved on.

"He is a smuggler," an Iranian told me, looking at the man with
envy.

An overweight French girl, already drunk at midday, passed out
on the ground. A friend slapped her on the face. Half conscious, the
drunk girl took a few steps and collapsed again on the steps connecting the two levels of the park. The Kurds arrived. A man shook the
girl, slapped her hard, left her on the steps, and walked away. Others
poked the girl, yelled at her, and brought her to her feet. Minutes
later, she was allowed to sleep in peace on a corner by the canal.

On the park's upper level, four young Kurds sat on a bench. This
was the "beauty salon" for the penniless men excited by the presence
of the girls, or for men preparing for their older patrons. Using two
pieces of short string, one young Kurd pulled the extra hair from the
face of his smiling friend. Watching with enthusiasm, the other two
waited for their turn. The first young man removed himself from the
bench, tickled one of the boys, and showed off his reddened but

smooth face. Then the next Kurd sat on a park bench by the railroad tracks and beautified his young face.

Moving to the upper level of the park, the girls walked around, talked among themselves, and joked with the men. Some stayed by the canal. The boys clustered around them. On another bench near the gate, a group of Iranians conversed and stared at the Kurds and their girls.

Two older French women arrived, perhaps in their late fifties. One had short hair and wore jeans and a flowery short-sleeved shirt. The other, a bit taller and in brown trousers, had curly blond hair. Standing on the upper level of the park near its entrance, they were like a magnet, gathering the Kurds and the girls around them. There were jokes and laughter. A bold Kurd in his twenties moved between the women and the girls, hugging some, roughing up others. Many smoked cigarettes.

I asked Reza about the women. Pointing at one of the older women, he said, "She is the foster mother of one of the girls. She comes here a lot and usually takes one of the Kurds with her."

PART SEVEN

London

Zia

Despite the heightened security and stricter migration policy of the past decade, reaching England remained the dream of many migrants. In 2000, with eighty-one thousand applications, England topped the list of registered asylum seekers in the EU. Germany ranked second with sixty-five thousand applications, Belgium third with thirty-eight thousand, and France fourth with thirty-seven thousand.[14]

Although no work permit was issued, in London and some other big cities the migrants easily found jobs, even saved money. Entering the country, they registered for asylum, found housing in hostels and shared apartments, and received a monthly allotment of a little less than $300. Rejected asylum seekers freely moved around, looked for employment, and disappeared in the multiracial and multiethnic population of London. There were no random police checks. The government had made many attempts to issue identification cards with a traceable chip for asylum seekers in the past, but all failed politically, and England remained a relatively free country for clandestine migrants. However, many changes were occurring in the country's attitude toward migrants.

Facing unemployment and the loss of social services since the 1980s, many saw the migrants as free riders who took scarce and badly needed resources from British citizens. The National Front and other anti-immigrant parties were gaining more popularity. Hoping to get votes, the Labor Party also championed anti-immigrant policies. "We need to be able to show our citizens at home that European asylum policy is not simply a gateway for uncontrolled migration," David Blunkett, the British home secretary, declared.[15]

To deter them from working, the Labour government dispersed registered asylum seekers across the country, housing them in small towns far from London. A proposal was made to build separate schools for the children of asylum seekers. As a policy recommendation to the 2003 European Union meeting in Thessaloniki, England proposed the establishment of "protected zones" in non-EU countries and the regionalization of asylum procedure. The asylum seekers were to be kept in wards outside the continent while their requests for protection were evaluated.

Discussions were even under way to militarize the fight against illegal migration. In violation of Article 33 of the 1951 refugee convention, which forbids the contracting states from returning "a refugee in any manner whatsoever to the frontiers of territories where his life or freedom would be threatened on account of his race, religion, nationality, membership of a particular social group or political opinion," Prime Minister Tony Blair proposed using warships to intercept and return ships carrying would-be asylum seekers on their way to England.[16] England has also been considering the use of air force planes to deport the rejected asylum seekers en masse. Immediately after September 11, 2001, Afghans became a target of immigration control. "There is already a major problem on the Afghan border. The main aim is to stop people coming from that region and spreading across the world. That is also necessary for reasons of terrorism," Blunkett said.[17] Discussing the need to control Afghan refugees, he said, "We are freeing countries of different religions and cultural backgrounds and making it possible for them to get back home and rebuild their countries. . . . I have no sympathy whatsoever with young people in their twenties who do not get back home and rebuild their country and their families."[18]

Zia, a young Afghan working as a delivery boy for a Domino's

Pizza in central London, was among the Afghan migrants facing potential deportation. We met in the pizza shop one rainy evening in July. He was short, slim, and soft-mannered. Returning from his last delivery on a company scooter, Zia came in his full Domino Pizza outfit, wearing a baggy raincoat with a big hood, and dripping water.

Bahman, Zia's manager and the man who introduced me to him, was a forty-six-year-old refugee from Iran who was Zia's best friend—perhaps his only friend in London. All Zia owned in the world was an old Yamaha motorbike. He used the bike to commute between home and his place of work. He wore a windbreaker, pads of all types, and a helmet, even on hot summer days. The bike broke down frequently. When we met that summer, the brake pads were gone. There were other problems with the engine, he explained to me. He spent his free time—one day a week—fixing his bike or visiting the Iranian manager. While working, he used a Vespa to deliver the pizza. The shop was near a major university in London, and there were many delivery orders from the students, who often harassed Zia and the others. At times they refused to pay, and the owner took the money out of Zia's salary, which made the manager furious.

An Iraqi citizen of England was the owner of the pizza shop. He was "filthy rich," Zia told me. The employees, pizza makers and delivery boys, were mostly Afghans, Pakistanis, Poles, and Iranians. There were one or two British workers. The British worked for pocket money, but most of the migrants worked to survive. Some, including Zia, sent home a part of their earnings. Most were illegal. Many complained about the boss. "All he cares about is money," Zia told me.

The manager was a kind and supportive young man. He worked along with the employees, made pizza, took orders, and managed the finances of the shop. The delivery boys rushed in, took their orders, ran out, got on their motorbikes, and disappeared. The pizza makers put fresh dough in the oven, took the cooked dough out, cut the pizzas without looking, put them in boxes, and repeated the job, day in and day out. None stopped to take breaks. The flow was continuous.

Like other Afghans in the country, Zia had arrived in London fleeing war. Applying for asylum, he told the authorities his recollection of the war.

He was a Hazari, a Shiite minority in a country of mostly Sunni Tajiks, Uzbeks, and Pashtuns. He remembered how his life had been changed by the rivalries and shifting alliances between different warlords and political parties, each aligned with a different ethnic group.

Zia was a young boy when the Soviets invaded, only thirteen when they withdrew. He lived with his family in Kabul during the occupation. There life was normal for young Zia and others who did not oppose the Soviets and the government. Far from the war raging in the mountains, "food was plenty. There was gasoline, electricity. We could listen to music and go to the movies. These were my best years in Afghanistan." In Kabul, women were free to choose the way they dressed. "Some wore skirts and showed their legs. There were those who wore the *chador,*" covering themselves from head to toe.

But all that changed when the Soviets left Afghanistan in 1989. Old allies became new enemies. In the four years between 1992 and the capture of Kabul by the Taliban in 1996, Afghanistan experienced one of the most devastating periods of its modern history. "[The Pashtuns] abducted and raped the [Hazari] women; they cut off their breasts. They threw men and women into deep wells and attacked people's homes and ransacked them. They took doors and windows, pulled flowers and plants out of the ground. They took everything they could. We were horrified."

With the rise in violence, people began arming themselves. "I saw my neighbors taking arms to protect their homes," Zia remembered. A rocket came from the nearby hills and landed near Zia's school in Kabul. For months the school was shut down. "Our fears increased after that," he said.

Soon after, a rocket fell on Zia's house. The house was destroyed. The family was saved because they had earlier taken shelter in a basement. Weeks later, a second rocket landed on the ruins of the house. Zia's family crossed the border to Pakistan.

But Pakistan was too close to home for Zia. Living among other Afghans, he was constantly reminded of the violence and the killings that had changed his life. Wishing to escape the maddening violence, Zia decided to move far away. "I wanted to start a new life, live in peace. That is all I wished." Zia left his family in Pakistan and fled to Iran. Months later he was in London applying for political asylum.

The authorities reviewed his case expediently. He was not a refugee, they told him. His life story did not merit him protection under the 1951 refugee convention. There was no fear of persecution in his case. However, the British immigration authorities did not wish to return Zia to Afghanistan. He was a victim of war and deserved humanitarian assistance, they thought. He was allowed to remain in England for four years. At the end of the fourth year, his case was to be reevaluated. Living in London now, Zia was still longing for a life in peace.

"I have lived twenty-seven years without a day in peace. My dream is to have a quiet life somewhere in the world. But I am not hopeful. I am not very happy. I am far from my family. I don't have any English friends. People are not very friendly here. London is better than smaller towns, but still, it is hard to make friends with English people. The best situation for me is to have a quiet life somewhere. I just want to work, make enough money, and live in peace. It doesn't matter where, but I don't know if I can have that. I don't know what my future is. I don't know."

When I met Zia in London, he had had his temporary residence permit for two years. Deportation would be the most likely outcome when his case was reviewed. Afghanistan was a free country, the government of England thought. There was no more sympathy for Afghans traveling the world and looking for a home. Zia feared being asked to return to that home. The Taliban were gone, but many old problems prevailed. There was new violence and the feeling of insecurity. Theft and burglary were on the rise. Abduction and kidnapping were common.

"I can have enough money in Afghanistan. But your future is very unclear there. Afghanistan is not a safe place. You can make money. But you live in fear all the time. Somebody may come and kidnap you for money." He told me the story of an Afghan who returned home with his family from Canada. Wishing to start a new life in his place of birth, he opened a small supermarket in Kabul. Soon after, armed men attacked his home and kidnapped his youngest son. They asked for $1 million for his release. The Afghan could not deliver, Zia told me.

One evening a phone call came from Kabul. The call was from Zia's mother, who had returned to Afghanistan after the fall of the Taliban. Other calls followed in the coming days. For days, his mobile phone did not stop ringing. The callers spoke with joy. They called to congratulate Zia and wish him many happy years ahead. He had left Afghanistan a single man, but he was a "married man" the day he received the first call from Kabul. His mother wished to congratulate him on his engagement to a girl he had never met or spoken to, a young girl still trapped under the suffocating *burqa*. Though not yet married officially, she was to be his wife and he her husband. Nothing could change that. None dared disrespect and defy the old traditions. The neighbors and distant relatives were told of the engagement. The girl waited in her *burqa* for her absentee fiancé to free her from her life of agony and cultural imprisonment. Her freedom was Zia's entry to a new cage.

His family had engaged him to the girl without notifying him of their plans and intentions. That was an ordinary practice, he told me. His consent was not a requirement. "The time has come for you to have a family. You have a good job. Save money and come back home. You can open a shop and have a good life," his mother told him.

Zia's family had found him a "good girl" from the neighborhood.

She was humble and pure, and came from a good family. Negotiations were made between the two families. In Zia's absence, a large engagement party was given. Zia was called the day after the party. His consent was assumed. As for the girl, the idea that she would need to consent was laughable. She made no decisions. That too was their tradition. She was now married to a man in the West, a man who would soon return with open arms and a caravan of gifts to take her. The girl's parents were proud. Zia was grieved. No one knew how the girl felt. No one asked.

Zia's family wished him to return and take ownership of his wife. He wished to escape. But leaving the girl was not possible.

"She will be destroyed," he said. Not yet touched by a man, she was now considered a taken woman. To not marry her would be a sign of her undesirability. There was no future for her without Zia. She now belonged to him. Her family had in essence sold her to the pizza deliveryman in London, and Zia felt obliged to save the girl's reputation.

"I am a married man," he said with a bitter and painful smile.

"How old is she?" I asked Zia.

"I do not know for sure—twenty or twenty-one, I think."

"Have you talked to her?"

"They don't have a phone. It is not considered right in Afghanistan, anyway. I don't have a home for us yet. So I shouldn't see her. I cannot talk to her. That's how it is."

The girl's father was a sheik, a man of religion, Zia told me, now laughing bitterly.

"This is my luck. I have to live with the daughter of a sheik for the rest of my life." There was anger in his voice.

PART EIGHT

New York

Zahra

Traveling in different countries, I met many Afghans who risked their lives to touch the soil of the United States. In refugee camps and safe houses, they asked me about life in America. Many chose England and other countries within the EU only because of the seeming impossibility of reaching America. A vast ocean had to be crossed, and the smugglers charged prices beyond most migrants' means. However, there were those who received asylum after applying directly to a U.S. consulate overseas. Some were granted asylum by the UNHCR and resettled in the United States. In the year 2001, a total of 2,964 Afghan refugees were admitted to the United States.[19] Among them was Zahra.

I first met Zahra during a brief return to New York City in May 2003. She had agreed to meet me near her high school on the corner of Fourteenth Street and Second Avenue in Manhattan.

Approaching the intersection, I noticed the colorful head scarf concealing her hair and her neck. She was clad in tight blue jeans and a dark fuchsia-colored jacket, and wore modest makeup. She carried a knapsack on the right shoulder. I greeted her.

In the past, I had met Iranian and Afghan women who covered themselves and wished not to shake hands with men. Not knowing her, I introduced myself but did not shake her hand. She noticed my uneasiness.

To gain her trust, and to introduce my work to her, I had sent her the story of Shahrokh Khan, the young Afghan I met in Istanbul. "I stayed up the whole night crying," she told me in a café we chose for talking. I asked if she trusted me to tell her story. She nodded and smiled.

I came to see her without a notepad or my small tape recorder. Sitting silently, I watched her navigate through her memories. She spoke without stopping, only pausing to laugh or to wipe away her tears. Before leaving, I asked for another meeting. She agreed.

Two days later we met on the same corner. This time, walking to her, I offered my hand. A warm handshake followed. A big smile appeared on her face. We went to the same café. I opened my laptop and asked her to tell once again about the journey that had brought her to Fourteenth Street in New York City.

Zahra was born three years after the Soviets invaded Afghanistan. Her father was a humble man, supporting his wife and two daughters by working in a small grocery store he owned in Kabul. Life was good. There was food on the table. The girls were happy. "I had a few toys. Sometimes I played alone, sometimes with my sister or neighbors. I always played with Father when he came home at night. I loved that. I always waited for him."

But the good times came to an end with war looming in Afghanistan. Zahra and her family could not escape. The Soviet-backed government was recruiting soldiers to fight the enemies of communism, and the American-backed warlords were pressuring the Afghan men to join their jihad against the infidel. There were two choices for Zahra's father: he could be a holy warrior fighting in the jihad, or a member of the Afghan "people's army." He chose neither and left his home to take refuge in Iran. That was 1988, near the end of Soviet rule in Afghanistan.

Escaping was hard, especially for men. Soldiers from different armies were in search of new recruits. They stopped men and boys on the road, taking them away as soldiers. Zahra's father had to keep away from the recruiters. The family hid during the day and walked at night or in the very early hours of the morning. Some fleeing men disguised themselves under the *burqa*; they held babies in their arms and pretended to be mothers moving about with their children. Zahra's father was one of them. "He looked very funny," she remembered.

"We could hear gunshots everywhere." Bullets hit the safe house Zahra stayed at along the way. They were saved by chance.

The family traveled with a large convoy of men and women. The convoy crossed mountains and rivers. Finally, forty days later, they arrived at a camp in Iran.

Not long after their escape, the Soviet forces withdrew from Afghanistan. Rejoicing, many displaced Afghans returned to their homes. Among them were Zahra and her family. This was a chance to begin a new life without war and violence. Having lost the grocery store, Zahra's father took a civil service job under the first postoccupation government of Mohammed Najibullah, a Soviet appointee and former head of the Afghan secret police. The pay was relatively good. A sense of normality returned to Zahra's life.

Once again, though, the happy times did not last long. The holy war that began in the early 1980s reemerged with a new ferocity. From the mountains, the mujahedeen attacked Kabul. On April 15, 1992, the Najibullah government collapsed and several holy war groups formed a governing coalition, the Islamic Council of Mujahedeen.

Like Zia, Zahra is a Hazari. In 1994, Zahra's father sent his wife and two daughters back to Iran, not as an escape from the war and its violence but because he wished his girls to be more acquainted with Shiite Islam, a set of beliefs not taught in schools in Afghanistan under the government of the mujahedeen. He remained behind in Afghanistan, sent money to Iran, and wished for his girls to get a good education in Islam, sciences, and other matters.

"We went to Iran illegally. At first, they kept us in a camp in Sabzevar [a town in eastern Iran]."

After two months, the refugees were dispersed to other parts. Zahra and her family were to be transferred to Isfahan.

A year earlier, Zahra's uncle had migrated to Iran and resettled in Mashhad. On the day Zahra and her family were put in a convoy headed for Isfahan, he rented a car and followed them on the road.

"We stopped somewhere on the road to go to the bathroom, but we didn't go back to the bus. My uncle was waiting for us with a car. We got in the car with him and drove to Mashhad," Zahra said, laughing.

Not long after, Zahra's uncle took the family to Tehran, where they rented an apartment in a lower-middle-class neighborhood near Azadi Square.

"There were not many Afghans in our neighborhood. Our neighbors were good people. At first they did not know we were Afghans. They did not bother us when they found out. Some of them were our friends and even visited our home. One was an Azari family. They visited us frequently and left their children with us when they had to go somewhere. The husband's mother did not like Afghans. She would tell him, 'Afghans are killers. Why did you leave the children with them? They could kill them.' I don't know who the Afghans had killed," she said with a chuckle.

In the 1980s and 1990s, more than two million Afghan refugees lived in Iran. The government issued temporary residence permits, but the refugees had to remain in their designated cities and obtain special travel documents for leaving.

The residence permits were issued infrequently, and at all times there were thousands of Afghans in Iran without documents. Many found jobs in the construction industry, receiving wages far below the customary wage paid to Iranians. Being illegal, their children were denied the right to attend school. Among them were Zahra and her sister. On a regular basis, Zahra's father sent his family money from Afghanistan. Hoping to fulfill the desire of her husband, Zahra's mother hired a private instructor for the girls, and when their documents arrived, she registered them in a regular school. It was in that school that Zahra became curious about Islam and the *hijab,* or veil.

Growing up in Afghanistan, Zahra had seen some women who were covered, while others appeared in public like the women in Western movies. Those were different days in Afghanistan.

"*Hijab* was a choice. Some wore scarves and skirts. Some were covered."

Her mother wore a black *chador,* but she did not force the girls to follow suit. Her father encouraged Zahra to choose a *hijab* of some sort. Her sister had already adopted the head scarf. "I sometimes covered my head," she said, as if talking about one of her childhood games.

In the Islamic Republic of Iran, all women were forced to cover themselves, wearing a *manto,* a dark-colored baggy robe that covered all their body curves, making them look nonsexual. Girls were considered women at age nine. They aroused men, the religious leaders thought, and so at that age had to cover their hair and their not-yet-existing body curves.

"I didn't like the *hijab* in Iran. All the girls in school had to wear a black *manto* and a white *maghna-eh* [a mandatory long head scarf covering the head, most of the forehead, and the area under the chin]. I didn't like to wear white and black together. Anytime I went to see my religious studies teacher, I took off the *maghna-eh* and just wore a regular head scarf. She didn't mind. She was a good woman and talked to us anytime we were free."

The teacher was Zahra's principal guide to the world of *hijab.* Young and eager, Zahra inquired, discussed the matter with her teacher, and read books about the *hijab* and virtue. Through these conversations, to her surprise, she realized that "the *hijab* was not for all women, but only for Muslims after the age of nine." Zahra was a Muslim, and so she too decided to wear an Islamic *hijab,* even outside Iran. Her own choice was for a modest head scarf, long-sleeved shirt, and long pants. That was her personal construction of the *hijab.* "Islam does not say how you should cover yourself. All it says is that women's hair should not be shown. *Burqa* and the *hijab* in Iran have nothing to do with Islam," she told me.

☒

With the seizure of Kabul by the Taliban in 1996, Zahra's father lost his civil service job. There was no more money for the girls in Iran, and Zahra had to return to Kabul.

But in her home under the Taliban, Zahra's simple *hijab* was called non-Islamic, shameful, and a sin. She was asked to go under the *burqa* and cover her face, hands, feet, everything. Using her hands, Zahra demonstrated for me the *burqa*. Even there in New York City, away from Afghanistan and the Taliban, she looked petrified.

"At first, I refused to give in. I was too young for that." She tried everything to escape the Taliban's mandatory *hijab*.

"I will wear the *burqa* once I get married," she said to her parents.

That did not change anything. She had either to stay in the confines of her home or go out in public disguised under the *burqa*.

"I decided not to go out of my home in order to avoid the *burqa*. Father wanted me to cover myself and go out. I hated that. I could not breathe under the face cover. I cried a lot. Father insisted. He wanted to protect me from the Taliban." The pressure worked, and she finally gave in.

She recalled the first time she wore the *burqa*. "We were going to my aunt's house. I covered my whole body, my face, and everything. I could not breathe. I got sick when I got to my aunt's. They gave me medicine. It was so difficult. I did not want to return home that night. I begged to stay. I did not want to cover myself again. But I had to leave."

After that Zahra stayed home. With horror, she watched the changes in her country.

"They flogged a dead man for not having the Islamic beard. I first laughed. Later, I was sad," she said, shaking her head.

The Taliban soldiers forcibly took women out of their homes and married them. "They knew the number of girls and unmarried women in every house." The Taliban would visit the house with an equal number of men and a mullah. The mullah would read verses from the Qur'an and marry the men to the girls.

"They killed the parents on the spot if they resisted. The Taliban took many of my neighbors."

Many girls committed suicide to escape the possibility of being snatched by the Taliban. Young girls slit their wrists or jumped into deep wells. They preferred death to submitting to the Taliban. Thirty girls drowned themselves in a ditch outside Kabul. Two were Zahra's neighbors.

Zahra was fifteen, ripe for the Taliban. Girls younger than she were taken by them, raped, married by force, or killed. Zahra was saved because her father sent his wife and the girls to Bamiyan, an Afghan city west of Kabul. He stayed behind, promising to join them in two weeks, when they would all proceed to Pakistan.

The girls and their mother waited in Bamiyan. The two weeks came and went with no word from their father. Then a family friend arrived with news. Their father had been taken and killed by the Taliban for his earlier work in the government of Najibullah.

"He stayed behind to make things look normal, but he never came. He did not join us. We never saw his dead body," Zahra said.

A family friend tried to get the body from the Taliban, but they refused. The body would only be handed over to the immediate family members, the Taliban told him.

The girls were no longer safe in Afghanistan, the family friend told them. Once again, they had to leave behind their home. "We had to climb mountains again," Zahra said. They walked long hours and crossed the border, and took refuge in Peshawar in Pakistan.

Living in Pakistan could not ease the pain of the mother who had lost a husband and become displaced with her two daughters. She had to see the husband's body, bury him, say farewell, and go on with her life far away from home. "Mother was restless. She had to return to Afghanistan." Leaving the girls in Pakistan, she returned home with her husband's friend in search of her husband's body. "She couldn't travel alone in Afghanistan. Women had to be accompanied by a man, and it didn't matter who the man was."

The girls waited. Weeks passed. There was no news from their mother. Then Zahra's uncle appeared at their door in Peshawar to tell them their mother would not return. The Taliban had taken her. Now Zahra was orphaned. All she had left was a sister three years older.

"How did you feel when you heard the news?" I asked.

"I had no feelings. It was a few months later that I actually realized what had happened to me. I became ill. I had become weak from the inside. I was feeling lonely, the same feeling I have now.

"We left Peshawar after the death of my mother. My uncle took us to Quetta. We lived there in a house with my cousin. We didn't have any money. Finding work was not easy in Pakistan. Most Afghan women cleaned other people's homes. My sister knew how to sew. I knew sewing too, but I wasn't very good. I was learning. My sister worked for one of our neighbors. The woman brought her work at home. My sister sewed *chadors* for her, and she sold them to her customers. I don't remember how much she paid my sister."

With the encouragement of an older male cousin, Zahra and her sister left Quetta for Islamabad.

"My cousin and his wife and children already had a case with the UNHCR. He told us to apply for asylum. At first I thought there was no use doing that. We had heard from many Afghans that they had to wait many months before they got an answer.

"From outside, the building looked like a prison. There were three or four guards outside the door and barbed wire on the walls. There was always so many people waiting in front of the UNHCR. Every day, the UNHCR would only see a small number of people. You had to go there at four in the morning and wait on a line outside in order to get a chance to talk to someone and get an application. We went there once, but they stopped seeing people right before it got to us.

"A few weeks later, we returned at four in the morning. They called our names at ten and we went inside. We waited in the court-yard for another two hours. Then they called our names again. We went to a corridor and waited for another hour until they came to register us.

"My sister and I were interviewed four times. They would put us in different rooms and ask us about Afghanistan, our family, and what we did in Pakistan. One day, without having told us, three people came to our home. There was a Pakistani, an Afghan who spoke Persian, and an American—I don't actually know, he might have been European. He was blond and spoke English. They checked every room, and looked at everything we had. They had asked our neighbors about us."

Four months after the two sisters opened a case with the UNHCR, their application for asylum was accepted. They were given international protection and resettled in the United States. Zahra and her sister flew to Michigan in July 2001. Not long after, they went to New York City, where Zahra enrolled in a special high school for immigrants.

Zahra was saved from the Taliban, but her fears remained. Thousands of miles away from Afghanistan, she feared the men who had orphaned her and caused her to leave the land she loved so dearly.

"I get scared when I see bearded men in Islamic outfits. I think the Taliban is following me. I run to the other side of the street if I see them walk behind me."

There was a mosque near Zahra's home in Queens. She did not feel safe there either. The sight of the bearded men entering and leaving the mosque frightened her. She avoided walking by the mosque, hid from the men, and shared the fears of many non-Muslims in her neighborhood and her new home.

She was caught between two worlds: the world of the fundamentalists in her faith—those misrepresenting her beliefs—and the world of those not of her faith who misunderstood her beliefs. Zahra wished to show the world an accurate image of her faith. But she was seen as a fundamentalist by some, a deviant by others, and was subject to discrimination all around. Yet she did not remove her head scarf. After September 11 she stayed home for two weeks, missing school. "I was afraid of being beaten up."

Worried about her, Zahra's sister asked her to drop her *hijab*. She refused. Willing to pay the price for her beliefs, she remained loyal to her Islam and her own image of a Muslim woman.

Zahra fashioned her own model of the Islamic dress code. In New York City, both Muslims and non-Muslims stared at her. Her appearance was unusual. Some Muslims scorned her for not following a stricter *hijab*. Others were embarrassed to be seen with her in public.

The Pakistani boys in her school tormented her. To these Muslim boys, she was a disgrace to Islam and their image of a virtuous sister from Afghanistan.

"Don't say you are an Afghan," some would tell her.

"We like the Taliban. How about you?" others would ask her, intimidating her, harassing her for her views. And when Zahra told them of her horrifying experiences in Afghanistan, the experiences that had traumatized her and left deep scars in her soul, the boys would praise the Taliban.

The Pakistanis scorned her for her inadequate *hijab*. But others ridiculed her when they saw her with her *hijab*. "Why don't you wash your hair? Are you embarrassed about your dirty hair? Is this why you are covered?" three Chinese students told Zahra at her high school.

Psychologically assaulted by the Muslim boys, she was distrusted by others who saw in her their image of fundamentalism. Zahra represented an alien and hostile world. She was a misfit, an outcast.

She lived in Queens with her older sister and a cousin she rarely saw. She saw her sister only for a few short minutes a couple of times a week, she complained. Full-time work and schooling left no time for the affection and compassion Zahra so desperately longed for. The cousin returned home late in the evening only to leave for work in the early hours of the next morning. He and others "live to work," she said. Zahra felt trapped in a world without people. "This is unbearable."

Zahra hoped for a different life, the type of life she spent with her family in her childhood years. She longed for the simplicity of life she had once experienced.

"I feel lonely here," she said, calling her loneliness "an incurable illness." "Work and only work: that is all people do in the United States," she said. No one had any free time for anyone: "People only have phone relationships." This terrified Zahra. She longed for embracing, touching, and feeling the warmth of the actual presence of friends and loved ones. Despite the hardship and the traumas of her life in the past, she had felt alive then, loved and cared for.

"I like studying. But I hate my books sometimes," she said abruptly during our second conversation.

Shocked by her comment, I inquired about the reason. With eyes full of tears and her voice shaking, she said, "I hear my father's voice when I open my books. He always wanted my sister and me to get our education. That was what he cared about the most. But he did not live long enough to see my success."

In May 2004 Zahra finished her high school studies and enrolled at a community college in Manhattan. We met again in April 2005.

"In my college, students only talk to their own people. Polish students only talk to other Poles, Spanish students to the Spanish. Nobody associates with students in other groups.

"I came here looking for a better life. Things are not bad here, but I cannot connect with the people here. I don't feel a part of the society. I have a few friends from my high school. They call or come to visit only if they need something, if they want to know about the homework or want to borrow something.

"There is nothing to look forward to here. There is no joy. I would like to live around friends and family and at least once a week get together with them and do something. But that is not possible here. Everybody is very busy. I go to school until the afternoon, and then go to work right away until eight at night. I go home, eat, and go to sleep. Next day, I do the same thing. Every day is the same. Nothing ever changes. I am not the only one who lives this way. Everybody is like a machine. Sometimes I work on Saturdays, and on Sundays I do laundry, prepare lunch for the next few days, and do my homework. That is all I do. You cannot call this living. I miss the life I once had with my family.

"Father used to come home after work and we spent many hours together. We visited relatives and went to parties," she recalled.

"What is missing here?" I asked her.

"What is missing? Everything is missing. Family . . . friends . . . nobody has any free time. People stare at me. They are probably scared of me. That makes me feel very bad."

"Will you go back to Afghanistan despite what has happened?"

"Yes, because I need that mentally. The only thing that keeps me here is my studies."

Two weeks before our last meeting, Zahra had received her green card in the mail. She was planning a summer trip. Zahra's sister was to be married to an Afghan man in Pakistan. "I will go to Pakistan for the wedding, but really, the wedding is an excuse. I want to get out of here for a while. I need fresh air.

"My uncle and my cousins will be in Pakistan. I would like to go to Afghanistan, but my uncle won't let me. He thinks Afghanistan is not safe. It is not possible to go to Kabul directly. You have to go to Kandahar first, and Kandahar is not a safe place. There are many Taliban people there.

"I would like to visit my parents' graves just once. I know it will be very difficult to find them. There are thousands of graves in the cemetery, and the tombs do not have any name. But I will be close to them, at least. I will say a prayer for them even if I am not standing by their tomb.

"My soul is not in peace here. Going back may be very hard, but I may have more peace of mind. Maybe nobody will stare at me there."

"Will you wear the *burqa*?"

"If I have to, I will even wear the *burqa*. I will get used to it after a while, I am sure. It will be difficult for me at first. But I am not any different from other girls. They are doing it. Maybe it is not that difficult after all."

"What is it that pulls you there?"

"I would like to see it one more time."

Epilogue

By the time I returned to New York City in September 2004, most of the migrants I had met on the journey had moved forward. Some were deported to their places of birth, and others remained waiting.

Deported to Iran, Nima and Shadi returned to Sanandaj. One day in fall 2003, almost a year later, my phone rang.

"*Salam, dadash* Behzad."

I recognized Nima's voice, and we both laughed in delight.

"What happened? What do you do now?" I asked.

Deportation to Iran turned Nima's life around. He moved back to his grandfather's home and enrolled in a vocational high school, majoring in computers. When we spoke, he was a couple of months away from graduation. Nima was excited.

"Are you working at your grandfather's grocery store?"

The grandfather had sold the store two years after Nima left Iran, he told me. Nima was out of work, but the loving grandfather took care of him as he had before. Pocket money was ample.

"How about your military service? What happened when you returned to Kurdistan?"

The grandfather had taken care of Nima's military service too. Paying off a few low-level government employees, he bought his grandson an exemption. Nima laughed when he told me about the deal. His mischievousness had returned once again.

"I will never forget those days, *dadash* Behzad. Tell me about Istanbul. Do you go to Aksaray? How is the book?"

I told Nima about Aksaray and other places we had visited together, and of mutual friends. A feeling of melancholy overcame him. His voice changed. He missed Istanbul despite all the traumas he had experienced there.

"I will come to see you once I get my passport," he said.

At that point Shadi grabbed the telephone from Nima.

"I am very happy to be talking to you, Behzad."

"How is being back in your father's home? Are you happy?" I asked.

"Like before," she said. Silence followed. Then she said, "Everything is okay, Behzad. Don't worry about me. Life goes on."

Our conversation was brief. I said a word or two about my life. We said goodbye and promised to stay in touch. Weeks later, Nima called me again with the news of his graduation.

Shahrokh Khan remained in Istanbul clandestinely. Sometime in the winter of 2003, a ray of hope appeared in his life. A Canadian expatriate I had once introduced to him had become his advocate. Contacting people in Canada, she put together a group of Canadians willing to sponsor Shahrokh Khan for humanitarian asylum. An application for asylum was made, and the preliminary procedures were completed in Canada. The application was sent to Istanbul for further verification and completion. Shahrokh Khan thought he would soon be on his way to the West.

But his joy did not last long. Pressured by the Turkish government, the Canadians decided not to pursue sponsorship cases of those residing in Turkey illegally. The Turks accused the Canadians of encouraging trafficking in people by sponsoring and accepting illegal immigrants in Turkey. Shahrokh Khan's case was closed. Obtaining a legal status was the only condition under which the case could be reopened.

Shahrokh Khan had never registered with the police in Turkey. If he went to the police to register at this point, he risked deportation to Iran, the third country he had crossed to enter Turkey. In Iran, he faced the risk of imprisonment. Many deportees from Egypt, Palestine, and other countries had spent time in jail in Iran. Some reported physical abuse.

Once again, Shahrokh Khan was trapped, but two years of clandestine life in Istanbul had taught him the art of survival. He contacted friends, asking them to put pressure on the Canadians. Meeting lawyers and refugee advocates, he inquired about the possibilities of registering with the police without being deported. There was no chance.

In early 2004, Shahrokh Khan met and befriended a thirty-year-old Afghan-born American citizen. The two bonded. The Afghan friend was charmed and deeply touched by his story. Helping him leave Turkey became a priority for her. She too contacted lawyers and embassies. Championing Shahrokh Khan's case, she contacted the UNHCR office in Ankara. A near miracle happened. The UNHCR staff member in charge of Shahrokh Khan's case was persuaded to contact the Canadians, he told me. A call was made, and his case was reopened. Soon after, he was called in for the routine medical examination. "I passed the examination," he told me on the phone in October 2004, screaming in joy.

Months passed, and there was no word from the Canadians. "I am worried. Why is this taking so long?" he wrote in an e-mail. "I am still waiting. Nothing is happening here. I am tired of this long wait. . . . Life is very expensive here. . . . I have told them everything. Why can they not make a decision?" he wrote in his next e-mails.

In early 2005 he was once again called for an interview. "The interview went very well. They asked me about the article you had published about me. They will give me an answer in two months."

He continues to wait for a response.

After waiting in agony for more than half a year, Nur was reunited with her family in Athens. Yussuf and Nur began taking English and Greek classes. Yussuf worked odd jobs, and Nur remained home with the girls. "I will take a course in computers. I promise to be very good," she told me.

I last spoke to Roberto in Athens in the winter of 2003. He was toiling hard, six days a week, and saving money. "Will you ever stay here, Roberto?" I asked him. Giggling like a shy boy, he said, "Of course, if I find a woman and get married here. My legs are tired, Behzad. If I go somewhere next, I will be flying, not crossing the mountains. I'll be staying here now."

Babak found a job as a landscaper, working for a young Greek entrepreneur. As in Iran and Turkey, he quickly learned his new job and charmed his employer and others working with him.

"I am very good at this job. My boss loves me. He considers me family; he even introduced me to his wife," he told me on the phone.

"Will you stay in Greece?"

"I want to rent a room for myself and start a new life. I like the job. Maybe, soon, like my boss, I can start my own landscaping business here."

I lost contact with Purya. His number was out of service every time I called. In my last visit to Athens in the summer of 2003, I inquired about him from the men on the market on Athenas Street. He had left for Italy in May 2003 and called from Rome a few days after, they told me. That was the last time anyone had heard from him.

I tried reaching Azar and Uncle Suleiman without success. I do not know if Azar's boys ever reunited with their father, or if Uncle Suleiman returned to northern Iraq.

Arshan was granted asylum somewhere in Europe. "*Agha* Behzad, you are the first person I am calling to give the good news. I can now start a new life," he told me on the phone in November 2003. A few months later, Cyrus was granted asylum. And Kia moved to Athens, where we met for the last time in June 2003.

I showed Kia a flyer for a talk I gave in New York City. The flyer had his picture in the Eagle's Fort in the center. He stared at his picture for many long minutes, then looked away and gave me an ambiguous smile. "I am glad to be a part of the novel that is in the making," he said. "I am not an outsider, a reader. These are the moments that make me happy. I don't want to be a reader of this novel. I like my role in it. I don't ask God to change my position."

The last time I met Kia, walking to the bus station in Patras, he said, "We will never be normal." I asked him about feeling normal.

"Of course we are different from other people. We live a different life. Normal is the way the majority lives. We are not a part of that. We hope to be normal, have a family and live the life of normal people, but we cannot.

"I am young, only twenty-two years old. I see other young people in the rest of the world. I know how they live, how they look at the world. But I cannot be like them. I am not normal. I have been on a road with no return. The return to normal is not possible.

"See, some migrants die in the sea. Others die crossing the mountains. These are the fortunate ones. They die with no pain. The rest live to see their slow death. Dying takes different forms. Some shoot heroin. Some go with a *baba*. They are all the same, those who beg in Patras and those who go with a *baba* in Athens.

"Look them in the eye. You will see the same pain of not achieving the goal, not reaching the destination. You change when you go with men for money. You become a different person. You die."

Kia had tears in his eyes. Long silent minutes followed his last statements. He looked reflective.

"Many talk about the difficulties of crossing borders, the beatings by the Bulgarian border guards, the dogs, and all of that. These are not the real problems of the journey. The difficulty is finding a place to start a new life, a chance, and an opportunity to live.

"You fall in love with the first place, the first village, you enter. You don't want to leave the village. It does not matter where that is. You want a place that is yours, your home, and a place you can start a life with others, have contacts with the neighbors, and be normal. But that is not possible. Place after place, we look for that chance. Many of us never find it. That is the difficulty. We cannot start a normal life. We remain isolated, outsiders, strangers. That is the problem.

"I knew the difficulties of the journey when I left Iran. What I did not know was that the journey changes you. You can never be who you once were even if you return to the same conditions.

"The journey transforms you. The person you were when you picked up your bag for the road dies. You are a different person when you put your bag on the ground."

Kia remained in Athens and saved money. Months after our meeting, he left Greece for Italy.

Soon after our last meeting, Tufan submitted his appeal application. A hearing was held in February 2005, and a decision was made in March. Tufan's case for asylum was finally accepted, and he became a recognized refugee.

"I have never been so happy in my life. I can now get my own place and start a new life," he told me on the phone. Tufan's next plan was to file for his wife's papers and bring her to Paris.

Zia stayed in London, hoping to receive a permanent refugee status. In partnership with another Afghan refugee, he opened a pizzeria, but the business was a failure. Zia's fiancée still waits for him in Afghanistan.

Notes

[1]"Turkey/Greece: Confusion on dumped Africans," UNHCR Briefing Notes, July 27, 2001.

[2]"Turkey/Greece: Fear for safety, torture, ill-treatment," Amnesty International, July 25, 2001, http://web.amnesty.org/library/Index/ENGEUR 440452001?open&of=ENG-369.

[3]European Commission, Justice and Home Office Affairs, *Turkey—Adoption of the Community Acquis*, "Area of Freedom, Security, and Justice," February 7, 2002, http://europa.eu.int/scadplus/leg/en/lvb/e22113.htm.

[4]Presidency Conclusions: European Council, Laeken, 14 and 15 December 2001 (extract), http://www.europaworld.org/DEVPOLAWAR/Eng/Refugees/Refugees_DocB_ eng.htm.

[5]Embassy of Greece, Washington, DC, European Migration Observatory, March 12, 2005, http://www.greekembassy.org/Embassy/content/en/Article.aspx?office=1&folder=39&article=56.

[6]"Greece: UNHCR concerned at drop in recognition rate," UNHCR Briefing Notes, December 10, 2002.

[7]Sophia I. Wanche, "Assessment of the Iraqi Community in Greece," UNHCR Working Paper no. 101, January 2004.

[8]U.S. Committee for Refugees, "World Refugee Survey 2002 Country Report."

[9]European Council on Refugees and Exiles, "EU Asylum Facts."

[10]Council Regulation (EC) no. 2725/2000 of 11 December 2000 concerning the establishment of "Eurodoc" for the comparison of fingerprints for the effective application of the Dublin Convention, December 15, 2000, pp. 1–10, *Official Journal* L 316, http://europa.eu.int/smart api/cgi/sga_doc?smartapi!celexapi!prod!CELEXnumdoc&lg=EN&num doc=32000R2725&model=guichett.

[11]Steve James, "Sangatte camp exposes brutal French and British asylum

policy," World Socialist Web Site, August 31, 2001, http://www. WSWS.org/articles/2001/aug2001/ asyl-a31.shtm

[12]Paul Webster, "Sangatte Refugees Freeze on Paris Streets," *The Observer,* January 12, 2003.

[13]Tomas Van Houtryve, "Europe's Illegals Trapped in Catch," *Christian Science Monitor,* December 2, 2003, online edition.

[14]UNHCR statistics.

[15]Jitendra Joshi, "Britain Defends Proposal to Process Refugees Outside EU," Agence France-Presse via News Edge Corporation, March 27, 2003, http://www.eubusiness.com/imported/2003/03/106565.

[17]Quoted in "The backlash—human rights at risk throughout the world," Amnesty International press release, http://www.amnesty.org.il/11sep/ USA_back2.html.

[18]"Blunkett's 'go home' call sparks row," BBC News, September 19, 2002, http://news.bbc.co.uk/1/hi/uk_politics/2267312.stm.

[19]Refugee Report, *A News Service of Immigration and Refugee Services of America,* December 31, 2003, http://72.3.131.88/data/refugee_reports/ archives/2003/RRDec. pdf.

Acknowledgments

I am above all indebted to the migrants I encountered during my two-year journey. I am grateful for their hospitality and kindness, their humility, their trust in me, and their ability to remain hopeful in the most difficult times. It was their determination and positive approach to life that gave me the strength to pursue this project. They are the heroes of my book. I hope I have done justice to their stories. This book is dedicated to them.

Many people in different countries gave me invaluable assistance. They housed me, listened to my stories when I needed to tell others of my encounters and experiences, and supported my work. I am grateful to all of them. Writing this book would not have been possible without their support. I name only a few in this acknowledgment.

Professor Fikret Adaman of Boğaziçi University in Istanbul played an instrumental role. I am indebted to his friendship and his efforts to assist my work. I am grateful to Professor Kemal Kerişçi, the faculty of Boğaziçi University, and my students for supporting me and making me feel at home.

Helen Bartlett of the Helsinki Citizens Assembly Istanbul Refugee Legal Aid Program was my first contact in the world of migration in Istanbul. She became an invaluable friend and a source of inspiration for me. My work was greatly helped by cooperating with her. I am grateful to Ekin Oğutoğulları and the staff of the Istanbul office of the International Catholic Migration Commission for helping me during my research, and being my friends.

I would like to thank Louise Druke, the UNHCR representative in Sofia, for introducing me to the relevant NGOs and state organizations in Bulgaria. I am grateful to Jeff Crisp, the director of policy and research at the Global Commission on International Migration, Frosso Spentzou of the UNHCR in Athens, Elizabeth Frantz, Bahman Akhbari, Sou Abadi, and Olivier Kline for their support and friendship. I thank Wendy Kristianasen, editor of *Le Monde Diplomatique*

(English edition), for believing in this book and publishing earlier versions of two of its stories.

Ramapo College of New Jersey provided me with partial funding and release time for the project. I am grateful to my dean, Henry Vance Davis, and my colleagues for their support. Special thanks go to Diana Alspach of the School of Social Science and Human Services for her steady flow of e-mails during my absence, her sense of humor, and her friendship.

Rosalie Morales Kearns carefully and patiently read an earlier version of the manuscript and provided invaluable editorial suggestions. I am indebted to her insight and support.

Many thanks to my literary agent, Scott Mendel, who gave me his unending support and remained my advocate throughout the project. I could not have asked for a better agent.

I am greatly indebted to John Flicker, my editor at the Bantam Dell Publishing Group, for his thorough reading of my work and his insightful and constructive editorial instructions. I had the good fortune to work with an editor who understood and believed in my project.

Writing a book of this nature is a journey full of moments of sadness, anxiety, hopelessness, and happiness. Leyla Amzi accompanied me on this journey and on its emotional roller coaster. Her hospitality and compassion made our home a welcoming place to the migrants, a place they entered with trust. I am indebted to her patience, understanding, and support during very difficult times.

Index